21世纪专业英语系列丛书

人力资源管理专业英语

English in Human Resources Management

主　编　刘秀杰　王道理
副主编　岳文赫　吴会平　王倩玉
主　审　西　宝

哈尔滨工业大学出版社

内 容 提 要

本书为适应经济全球化的发展趋势,满足国内广大读者学习和借鉴国外先进的人力资源管理理论的需要而编写。本书主要包括专业学术阅读、案例、专业学术信息和专业词汇四部分。第一部分是主干内容,由人力资源管理概述、工作分析、人力资源规划、员工招聘与甄选、员工培训与开发、绩效考核与管理、薪酬设计、员工关系管理等章组成。第二部分是案例,由4个案例及其相应知识扩展组成。第三部分主要包括专业学术期刊、学术网站、学术组织及学会等内容。第四部分基本涵盖了人力资源管理领域的专业术语和常用词汇。本书可作为大专院校经济管理、人力资源管理等专业教材,也可作为相关管理人员的参考书。

图书在版编目(CIP)数据

人力资源管理专业英语/刘秀杰,王道理主编.—哈尔滨:哈尔滨工业大学出版社,2013.8
(21世纪专业英语系列丛书)
ISBN 978-7-5603-4177-4

Ⅰ.①人… Ⅱ.①刘…②王… Ⅲ.①人力资源管理-英语-高等学校-教材 Ⅳ.①H31

中国版本图书馆CIP数据核字(2013)第163518号

责任编辑	田新华
封面设计	卞秉利
出版发行	哈尔滨工业大学出版社
社　　址	哈尔滨市南岗区复华四道街10号 邮编150006
传　　真	0451-86414749
网　　址	http://hitpress.hit.edu.cn
印　　刷	哈尔滨工业大学印刷厂
开　　本	880mm×1230mm 1/32 印张11.75 字数338千字
版　　次	2013年8月第1版 2013年8月第1次印刷
书　　号	ISBN 978-7-5603-4177-4
定　　价	35.00元

(如因印装质量问题影响阅读,我社负责调换)

21世纪专业英语系列丛书

编委会

主　任　赵毓琴
副主任　闫纪红
编　委　（按姓氏笔画排序）
　　　　　于云玲　马玉红　王　洋　王　旸
　　　　　王　星　王倩玉　王艳薇　任　丽
　　　　　任　莉　任铭静　刘秀杰　李　莉
　　　　　李慧杰　杨　皓　吴　迪　陈　楠
　　　　　张凌岩　岳文赫　栾　岩　盖晓兰
　　　　　葛乃晟
总策划　田新华
总主编　赵毓琴　李慧杰

前　言

　　为适应经济全球化的发展趋势，满足国内广大学生和读者了解、学习和借鉴国外先进的人力资源管理理论，了解前沿动态的需求，使学生通过大量阅读英语文章来扩充词汇量，提高熟练获取信息和独立阅读原著的能力，我们编写了此书。

　　本书主要内容由专业阅读、案例、专业学术信息和专业词汇四部分组成。第一部分为主干内容，包括人力资源管理概述、工作分析、人力资源规划、员工招聘与选择、员工培训与开发、绩效考核与管理、薪酬设计、员工关系管理等九章，这也是人力资源管理的逻辑顺序。第二部分为案例，由4个案例及其相应知识扩展组成。第三部分的主要内容为人力资源管理专业的国内外相关学术信息，如专业学术期刊、学术网站、学术组织及学会等，可供读者了解最新人力资源管理专业学术动态。第四部分基本涵盖了人力资源领域的专业术语和常用词汇。

　　本书具有以下特点：第一，内容全面，时代感强。内容覆盖了人力资源管理的各个方面，所有文章均选自近年英美国家原版教材和期刊杂志。第二，内容实用，针对性强。专业学术信息篇提供了详尽的了解人力资源管理专业学术信息的渠道，能够有效促进学生的专业发展。第三，注释合理，可读性强。选文中的难点和重点词汇、句子都配有相应的中文解释和实用例句，能够激发学生进一步学习的积极性。

　　本书适用范围较广，可作为高校人力资源管理、工商管理专业教材，也可供人力资源管理专业人士阅读。

  在编写过程中，我们参考了部分作者的成果，在此一并表示谢意。由于编写时间仓促，且编者水平及经验有限，书中不妥和疏漏之处在所难免，恳请广大读者批评指正。

编 者
2013 年 7 月

CONTENTS

PART ONE　ACADEMIC READING
第一部分　专业阅读

1　Introduction to Human Resource Management
人力资源管理绪论 …………………………………………… 3
◆本章导读 …………………………………………………… 3
   1.1　Human Resource Management and Organizational Effectiveness
      人力资源管理和组织效能 ……………………………… 3
   1.2　Equal Employment Opportunity: the Legal Environment
      平等就业机会:法律环境 ……………………………… 11
   1.3　Spotlight on Human Resource Management
      人力资源管理热点 ……………………………………… 18

2　Job Analysis and Job Design
工作分析和工作设计 ………………………………………… 31
◆本章导读 …………………………………………………… 31
   2.1　Brief Introduction to Job Analysis and Job Design
      工作分析和工作设计简介 ……………………………… 31
   2.2　The Sociotechnical Approach to Job Design
      工作设计的社会技术方法 ……………………………… 40
   2.3　Barriers to Creating Healthier Workplaces
      创建健康工作场所的障碍 ……………………………… 47

3　Recruitment
招聘 ··· 56

◆本章导读 ··· 56

3.1　Brief Sketch of Recruitment
招聘概要 ··· 56

3.2　Methods of Recruiting
招聘方法 ··· 67

3.3　Employment Advertising and Organizational Self-presentation
招聘广告和组织的自我展示 ····················· 77

4　Employees Selection
员工甄选 ··· 86

◆本章导读 ··· 86

4.1　Generic Standards in Employees Selection
选择员工的一般标准 ····························· 86

4.2　Selection Methods
员工甄选的若干方法 ····························· 93

4.3　Implications of Selection Applications for MCGDS
多标准团体决议法在员工甄选中的应用 ········· 104

5　Training Employees
员工培训 ·· 114

◆本章导读 ·· 114

5.1　Brief Sketch of Training Employees
员工培训概要 ······································ 114

5.2　Methods of Training
培训方法 ·· 122

5.3　The Role of Employee Reactions in Predicting Training Effectiveness

员工在培训效果预评中的作用 ········· 129

6　Career Management
职业生涯管理 ································· 141
◆ 本章导读 ···································· 141
  6.1　Brief Sketch of Career Management
      职业生涯管理概要 ····················· 141
  6.2　Career Stages
      职业生涯阶段 ······························· 148
  6.3　The Impact on Career Development of Learning Opportunities and Learning Behavior at Work
      工作中的学习机会和学习行为对职业生涯的影响 ··· 158

7　Performance Appraisal
绩效考核 ····································· 165
◆ 本章导读 ···································· 165
  7.1　Brief Sketch of Performance Appraisal
      绩效考核概要 ······························· 165
  7.2　Appraisal Methods
      考核方法 ···································· 173
  7.3　Repertory Grid Procedure in Eliciting Personal Constructs of Appraisal Systems
      循环坐标法在人事评估系统构建中的应用 ········ 183

8　Payment
薪酬 ··· 192
◆ 本章导读 ···································· 192
  8.1　Developing Pay Levels
      不断改进的薪酬标准 ····················· 192
  8.2　Mandated Benefits Programs
      委托福利计划 ······························· 201

8.3 Gaps between What People Say and Do with Respect to Pay
人们关于薪酬问题的言行差异 ………………………… 210

9 Employee Relations
员工关系 …………………………………………… 218
◆ 本章导读 …………………………………………… 218

9.1 Discipline in Employee Relations
员工关系中的纪律 ………………………………… 218

9.2 The Organizing Campaign
工会运动 …………………………………………… 229

9.3 Exploring the Employment Relationship of Contracted Employees (background and results)
基于劳动合同的雇佣关系探讨 ………………… 240

PART TWO CASE
第二部分 案例

1 Daimler Has to Steer the Chrysler Merger
戴姆勒与克莱斯勒的并购之路 ………………… 251

2 What's Next for E-HRM?
电子化人力资源管理的未来之路 ……………… 256

3 Paul Anderson's BHP Experiment: Will It Work?
保罗安德森的必和必拓经验:这些经验可行吗? ………… 265

4 "Hello, Welcome to..."
"哈喽,欢迎拨打……" ………………………… 270

PART THREE ACADEMIC INFORMATION
第三部分 专业学术信息

1 Academic Journals
  专业学术期刊 ·· 277
2 Academic Conferences and Organizations
  专业学术会议与组织 ·· 297
3 Academic Websites
  专业学术网站 ·· 298

PART FOUR ACADEMIC GLOSSARY
第四部分 专业词汇

REFERENCES ··· 363

PART ONE
ACADEMIC READING

第一部分 专业阅读

1

Introduction to Human Resource Management
人力资源管理绪论

【本章导读】 本章是全书的引言部分,阐述人力资源管理的概念和重要性。1.1 介绍人力资源管理的四个特点和八个职能目标,如实现组织目标、有效利用劳动力技能、培养训练有素动力十足的员工、最大限度提高员工的工作满意度并达到自我实现等。1.2 介绍人力资源管理中要注意就业机会平等,遵守《平等薪酬法案》、《民权法案》第七条、《雇佣年龄歧视法案》等。1.3 阐释当今人力资源管理的一些热点问题,如人事变动和团队等。

1.1 Human Resource Management and Organizational Effectiveness
人力资源管理和组织效能

When an organization is really concerned about people, its total philosophy, culture, and tone will reflect this belief. In this book, human resource management (HRM) is used to describe the function that is concerned with people—the employees. Human resource management is the function performed in organizations that facilitates the most effective use of people (employees) to achieve organizational and individual goals[①].

The following four descriptions of HRM should be stressed at the outset:

- It is action-oriented. HRM emphasizes the solution of employment problems to help achieve organizational objectives and facilitate employees' development and satisfaction.
- It is individual-oriented. Whenever possible, HRM treats each employee as an individual and offers services and programs to meet the individual's needs, McDonald's, the fast-food chain, has gone so far as to give its chief personnel executive the title vice president of individuality.
- It is globally oriented. HRM is not only an American function or activity; it is being practiced efficiently and continuously in Mexico, Poland, and Hong Kong. Many organizations around the world treat people fairly, with respect, and with sensitivity.
- It is future-oriented. Effective HRM is concerned with helping an organization achieve its objectives in the future by providing for competent, well-motivated employees.

HRM activities play a major role in ensuring that an organization will survive and prosper. Organizational effectiveness or ineffectiveness is described in this book in terms of such criteria and components as performance, legal compliance, employee satisfaction, absenteeism, turnover, scrap rates, grievance rates, and accident rates[②]. Three crucial elements are needed for firms to be effective: (1) mission and strategy, (2) organizational structure, and (3) HRM. However, it is important to remember that people do the work and create the ideas that allow the organization to survive. Even the most capital-intensive, best-structured organizations need people to run them.

People limit or enhance the strengths and weaknesses of an organization. Current changes in the environment are often related to changes in human resources, such as shifts in the composition, education, and attitudes of employees. The HRM function should provide for or respond to these changes. The objectives of HRM function are as follows:

Helping the Organization Reach Its Goals

Bruce R. Elly, vice president of personnel at Pfizer, Inc., expresses the role of the HRM function this way:

The HR function is a very key portion of the organization today. That message is coming across consistently in surveys of CEOs. So far, the emphasis has been on doing things right. The real jump in effectiveness will come when the focus is first placed on doing the right things. I can't imagine how HR functions without thoroughly knowing the business issues of its organization. Every business issue has HR implications.

Efficiently Employing the Skills and Abilities of the Workforce

Clyde Benedict, the chief personnel officer for Integon Corporation, stated this purpose somewhat differently. He said the purpose is "to make people's strengths productive, and to benefit customers, stockholders, and employees. I believe this is the purpose Walt Disney had in mind when he said his greatest accomplishment was to build the Disney organization with its own people."

Providing Well-trained and Well-motivated Employees

This is a measure of effectiveness for HRM. David Babcock, chairman of the board and chief executive officer of the May Company, phrases this purpose as "building and protecting the most valuable asset of the enterprise: people." Mary Kay Ash is a master of motivation for her cosmetics sales force of over 300,000. Mary Kay believes that giving people recognition and not just cash is the key to motivation. She has become a master of employee recognition.

HRM's effectiveness measure—its chief effectiveness measure, anyway—is to provide the right people at the right phase of performing a job, at the right time for the organization.

Increasing to the Fullest Employees' Job Satisfaction and Self-actualization

Thus far, the emphasis has been on the organization's needs. But unlike computers or cash balances, employees have feelings. For employees to be productive, they must feel that the job is right for their abilities and that they are being treated equitably. For many employees, the job is a major source of personal identity. Most of us spend the majority of our waking hours at work and getting to and from work. Thus, our identity is tied closely to our job.

Achieving Quality of Work Life

This purpose is closely related to the previous one. Quality of work life is a somewhat general concept, referring to several aspects of the job experience. These include such factors as management and supervisory style, freedom and autonomy to make decisions on the job, satisfactory physical surroundings, job safety, satisfactory working hours, and meaningful tasks. Basically, a sound quality of work life (QWL) program assumes that a job and the work environment should be structured to meet as many of the worker's needs as possible[③].

Communicating HRM Policies to All Employees

Chuck Kelly, director of human resources of a small manufacturing firm, expressed this objective as follows: "We can't afford not to communicate our programs, policies, and procedures fully. There are effective, personal development and legal reasons why everyone in the firm has to be HRM-knowledgeable. Communicating HRM programs does not just happen; a manager has to work at it constantly." Closely related to communication within the organization is representation of the organization to those outside: trade unions and local, state, and federal government bodies that pass laws and issue regulations affecting HRM. The HRM department must also communicate effectively with other top-management people (e. g., marketing, production, and research and development) to illustrate what it can offer these areas in the form of support, counsel, and techniques, and to increase its contribution to the overall strategic mission and goals of the organization.

Maintaining Ethical Policies and Socially Responsible Behavior

The human resource manager plays an important role in showing by example that each employee is important and will be treated ethically. That is, any activity engaged in by the HRM area will be fair, truthful, and honorable; people will not be discriminated against, and all of their basic rights will be protected. These ethical principles should apply to all activities in the HRM area. The expected fairness and equitable treatment are spelled out in the code of ethics prepared by the Society for Human Resource Management.

Managing Change

In the past decade, there have been rapid, turbulent, and often strained developments in the relationship between employers and employees. New trends and changes have occurred in telecommuting, outsourcing HRM practices, family medical leave, child care, QWL programs, spouse-relocation assistance, pay for skills, benefit cost-sharing, union-management negotiations, testing, and many other HRM areas of interest[4]. Nearly all of these trends and changes can be traced to the emergence of new lifestyles and an aging population.

What these changes mean to HR managers is that new, flexible approaches must be initiated and used effectively without jeopardizing the survival of the organization. HR managers must cope with trends and changes while still contributing to the organization.

from: *Human Resource Management*: *Gaining a Competitive Advantage*, 1994

Words and Expressions

outset ['autset] *n.* 开始；开端
oriented ['ɔːrientid] *adj.* 以……为导向的
facilitate [fə'siliteit] *v.* 促进
individuality [ˌindiˌvidju'æliti] *n.* 个人；个性
sensitivity ['sensi'tiviti] *n.* 敏锐；敏感
competent ['kɔmpitənt] *adj.* 有能力的
motivated ['məutiveitid] *adj.* 有动机的
survive [sə'vaiv] *v.* 生存
prosper ['prɔspə] *v.* 发展
performance [pə'fɔːməns] *n.* 绩效
absenteeism [æbsən'tiːiz(ə)m] *n.* 罢工
turnover ['təːnˌəuvə] *n.* 人员周转率
implication [ˌimpli'keiʃən] *n.* 意义
stockholder ['stɔkhəuldə(r)] *n.* 股东
recognition [ˌrekəg'niʃən] *n.* 认可；赏识
balance ['bæləns] *n.* 余额
equitably ['ekwitəbli] *adv.* 公正地
identity [ai'dentiti] *n.* 身份
supervisory [ˌsjuːpə'vaizəri] *adj.* 管理的
knowledgeable ['nɔlidʒəbl] *adj.* 有……丰富知识的
turbulent ['təːbjulənt] *adj.* 剧烈的
jeopardize ['dʒepədaiz] *v.* 危害
outsource ['autˌsɔːs] *v.* 外部采购
legal compliance 守法

scrap rates 人事费用
grievance rates 抱怨补偿
accident rates 意外补偿
organizational structure 组织机构
capital-intensive 资本密集型的
sales force 销售人员
self-actualization 自我实现
quality of work life 工作环境质量理论
trade union 工会
government body 政府机构
to spell out 详细解释；详细阐释
an aging population 老龄化人口

Difficult Sentences

① Human resource management is the function performed in organizations that facilitates the most effective use of people (employees) to achieve organizational and individual goals.
人力资源管理是组织为实现公司和个人目标而促进雇员发挥最大效用的一种职能。

② Organizational effectiveness or ineffectiveness is described in this book in terms of such criteria and components as performance, legal compliance, employee satisfaction, absenteeism, turnover, scrap rates, grievance rates, and accident rates.
本书是按照组织的绩效、守法行为、雇员满意度、罢工情况、人事调整、人事费用、抱怨补偿和意外补偿等标准和要素来描述组织的有效性和无效性。

③ Basically, a sound quality of work life (QWL) program assumes that a job and the work environment should be structured to meet as many of the worker's needs as possible.
基本上，高质量工作环境规划认为工作安排及工作环境设计应该

要尽可能满足工人的需要。

④ New trends and changes have occurred in telecommuting, outsourcing HRM practices, family medical leave, child care, QWL programs, spouse-relocation assistance, pay for skills, benefit cost-sharing, union-management negotiations, testing, and many other HRM areas of interest.

在远程办公、人力资源管理实践、产假、照看子女、工作环境质量、配偶安置、技能酬金、收益成本分摊、协会管理、测试以及其他一些重要的人力资源管理领域都出现了新趋势和变化。

Phrases and Patterns

1. be concerned with 关于

   In this book, human resource management (HRM) is used to describe the function that is concerned with people—the employees.
   在本书中,人力资源管理是描述关于人——雇员的职能。

   Her latest documentary is concerned with youth unemployment.
   她最近的一部纪录片是关于青年人失业的。

2. strengths and weaknesses 优势与劣势

   People limit or enhance the strengths and weaknesses of an organization.
   人们弱化或强化组织的优点和缺点。

   For every strength we have, we have a lot of weaknesses.
   相对于我们所有的每个优点来说,我们有许多缺点。

3. provide for 为某事物可能发生做准备

   The HRM function should provide for or respond to these changes.
   人力资源管理职能应该有应对这些变化的措施或适应方案。

   The planners had not provided for a failure of the power system.
   计划制订者未对动力系统可能出现故障一事制定应变措施。

1.2 Equal Employment Opportunity: the Legal Environment
平等就业机会：法律环境

Introduction

Two of the most important external influences on human resource management are government legislation and regulations and court interpretations of the legislation and regulations. Numerous laws influence recruitment and selection of personnel, compensation, working conditions and hours, discharges, and labor relations. Whenever appropriate, this text describes government legislation and its court interpretations as they relate to the specific area of human resource management being discussed. This chapter describes the legal framework of equal employment opportunity.

The Equal Pay Act of 1963

The Equal Pay Act of 1963 prohibits sex-based discrimination in rates of pay paid to men and women working on the same or similar jobs. Specifically, the act states:

No employer having employees subject to the minimum wage provisions of the Fair Labor Standards Act shall discriminate, within any establishment..., between employees on the basis of sex by paying wages to employees in such establishment at a rate less than the rate at which he pays wages to employees of the opposite sex in such establishment for equal work on jobs the performance of which requires equal skill, effort, and responsibility, and which are performed under similar working conditions[①].

The act permits differences in wages if the payment is based on seniority, merit, quantity and quality of production, or a differential due to any factor other than sex②. The act also prohibits an employer from attaining compliance with the act by reducing the wage rate of any employee.

The Equal Pay Act is actually part of the minimum wave section of the Fair Labor Standards Act (FLSA). Thus, coverage of the Equal Pay Act is coextensive (covers the same groups) with the coverage of the minimum wage provisions of the FLSA. Generally, the act covers employers engaged in commerce or in the production of goods for commerce, employers that have two or more employees, and labor organizations. Responsibility for enforcing the Equal Pay Act was originally assigned to the secretary of labor but was transferred to the Equal Employment Opportunity Commission (EEOC) on July 1, 1979.

Title VII of the Civil Rights Act of 1964

Title VII of the Civil Rights Act of 1964 is the keystone federal legislation in equal employment opportunity. Several important provisions of Section 703 of the act state the following:

(a) It shall be an unlawful employment practice for an employer:

(1) to fail or refuse to hire or to discharge any individual, or otherwise to discriminate against any individual with respect to his compensation, terms, conditions, or privileges of employment, because of such individual's race, color, religion, sex, or national origin; or

(2) to limit, segregate, or classify his employees or applicants for employment in any way which would deprive or lend to deprive any individual, of employment opportunities or otherwise adversely affect his status as an employee, because of such individual's race, color, religion, sex, or national origin.

(b) It shall be an unlawful employment practice for an employment agency to fail or refuse to refer for employment, or otherwise to discriminate against, any individual because of his race, color, religion, sex, or national origin, or to classify or refer for employment any individual on the basis of his race, color, religion, sex, or national origin[3].

(c) It shall be an unlawful employment practice for a labor organization:

(1) to exclude or to expel from its membership, or otherwise to discriminate against any individual because of his race, color, religion, sex, or national origin;

(2) to limit, segregate, or classify its membership or applicants for membership or to classify or fail or refuse to refer for employment any individual, in any way which would deprive or tend to deprive any individual of employment opportunities, or would limit such employment opportunities or otherwise adversely affect his status as an employee or as an applicant for employment, because of such individual's race, color, religion, sex, or national origin; or

(3) to cause or attempt to cause an employer to discriminate against an individual in violation of this section.

(d) It shall be an unlawful employment practice for any employer, labor organization, or joint labor-management committee controlling apprenticeship or other training or retraining, including on-the-job training programs, to discriminate against any individual because of his race, color, religion, sex, or national origin in admission to, or employment in, any program established to provide apprenticeship or other training.

Section 703 covers two basic areas of discrimination: disparate treatment and disparate impact. Disparate treatment, Section 703 (a) (1), refers to intentional discrimination and involves treating one class of employees differently from other employees. Disparate impact, Section 703 (a) (2), refers to unintentional discrimination and involves employment practices that appear to be neutral but adversely affect a protected class of people.

Title VII, the name most frequently used to describe the Civil Rights Act, was amended by the Equal Employment Opportunity Act of 1972. Organizations covered by the provisions of Title VII include the following:

· All private employers of 15 or more people who are employed 20 or more weeks per year[④].

· All public and private educational institutions.

· State and local governments.

· Public and private employment agencies.

· Labor unions that maintain and operate a hiring hall or hiring office or have 15 or more members.

· Joint labor-management committees for apprenticeships and training.

Title VII also created the Equal Employment Opportunity Commission (EEOC) to administer the act and to prohibit covered organizations from engaging in any unlawful employment practices.

The Age Discrimination in Employment Act (ADEA)

The Age Discrimination in Employment Act (AREA), passed in 1967, prohibits discrimination in employment against individuals aged 40 through 69. An amendment to the ADEA that took effect on January 1, 1987, eliminates mandatory retirement at age 70 for employees of companies with 20 or more employees. The prohibited employment practices of ADEA include failure to hire, discharge, denial of employment, and discrimination with respect to terms or conditions of employment because of an individual's age within the protected age group[⑤].

from: *Human Resource Management*: *Gaining a Competitive*

Advantage, 1994

Words and Expressions

legislation [ˌledʒisˈleiʃən] *n.* 立法
regulation [regjuˈleiʃən] *n.* 法规
interpretation [inˌtəːpriˈteiʃən] *n.* 解释
recruitment [riˈkruːtmənt] *n.* 招募；招工
discharge [disˈtʃɑːdʒ] *v.* 解雇
discrimination [disˌkrimiˈneiʃən] *n.* 歧视
provision [prəˈviʒən] *n.* 规定
seniority [siːniˈɔriti] *n.* 资历
differential [ˌdifəˈrenʃəl] *n.* 工资级差
coverage [ˈkʌvəridʒ] *n.* 范围
coextensive [ˌkəuiksˈtensiv] *adj.* 同时包括的
enforce [inˈfɔːs] *v.* 执行
term [təːm] *n.* 期限；条款
segregate [ˈsegrigeit] *v.* 隔离
deprive [diˈpraiv] *v.* 剥夺
expel [iksˈpel] *v.* 开除
adversely [ˈædvəːsli] *adv.* 不利地；负面地
refer [riˈfəː] *v.* 指点到消息来源处寻求帮助
on-the-job [ˈɔnðəˈdʒɔb] *adj.* 在职的
apprenticeship [əˈprentisˌʃip] *n.* 学徒身份
amend [əˈmend] *v.* 修正
administer [ədˈministə] *v.* 执行
eliminate [iˈlimineit] *v.* 取消
mandatory [ˈmændətəri] *adj.* 强制性的；必须的
The Equal Pay Act 同酬法案
The Fair Labor Standards Act 合理劳动标准法案
the Equal Employment Opportunity Commission 平等就业机会委员会

The Civil Rights Act 民权法案
disparate treatment 异质对待
disparate impact 异质影响
labor unions 工会
Employment Act 雇佣法案
The Age Discrimination in Employment Act 雇佣法案中的年龄歧视

Difficult Sentences

① No employer having employees subject to the minimum wage provisions of the Fair Labor Standards Act shall discriminate, within any establishment..., between employees on the basis of sex by paying wages to employees in such establishment at a rate less than the rate at which he pays wages to employees of the opposite sex in such establishment for equal work on jobs the performance of which requires equal skill, effort, and responsibility, and which are performed under similar working conditions.
任何遵守合理劳动标准法案中最低工资法规的机构都不会对员工产生性别歧视，因为该机构支付给员工的薪水等级不会低于同一机构内从事相同工作的异性员工，完成这些工作需要员工具有同等技能、付出相同努力、承担同样责任，而且是在类似工作条件下完成。

② The act permits differences in wages if the payment is based on seniority, merit, quantity and quality of production, or a differential due to any factor other than sex.
（同酬）法案允许基于资历、优点和产品的数量和质量而产生的薪水差异或由于任何非性别因素而带来的工资级差。

③ It shall be an unlawful employment practice for an employment agency to fail or refuse to refer for employment, or otherwise to discriminate against, any individual because of his race, color, religion, sex, or national origin, or to classify or refer for employment any individual on the basis of his race, color, religion, sex, or national origin.

任何雇佣机构由于个体的种族、肤色、宗教、性别或国籍而没有或拒绝向个体提供就业机会,或者是在其他方面有所歧视,或者是根据个体的种族、肤色、宗教、性别或国籍把工作机会分类提供给他们,这些都是不合法的雇佣行为。

④ All private employers of 15 or more people who are employed 20 or more weeks per year.

雇佣 15 人或 15 人以上,并且人员雇佣周数每年达到 20 或 20 周以上的所有私有雇主。

⑤ The prohibited employment practices of ADEA include failure to hire, discharge, denial of employment, and discrimination with respect to terms or conditions of employment because of an individual's age within the protected age group.

雇佣法案中的年龄歧视法规禁止在受保护的年龄范围内(40~69 岁),由于个体的年龄原因而产生的诸如不雇佣、解聘、否认雇佣、针对雇佣条款或条件有所歧视等雇佣行为。

Phrases and Patterns

1. be transferred to 移交给

   Responsibility for enforcing the Equal Pay Act was originally assigned to the secretary of labor but was transferred to the Equal Employment Opportunity Commission(EEOC) on July 1,1979.

   实施同酬法案的职责最初由劳动部长承担,但是在 1979 年 7 月 1 日移交给平等就业机会委员会。

   The sovereignty of Hong Kong was transferred back to China on July 1, 1997.

   香港的主权在 1997 年 7 月 1 日移交回中国。

2. discriminate against 歧视;差别对待

   It shall be an unlawful employment practice for an employer to fail or refuse to hire or to discharge any individual, or otherwise to discriminate against any individual with respect to his compensation, terms, conditions, or privileges of employment, because of such individual's race, color, religion, sex, or national origin.

由于种族、肤色、宗教、性别或国籍的原因,不聘佣、解聘或是在薪金、工作期限、工作条件,或工作权限方面差别对待某些人,这些都是非法的雇佣行为。

The African people are still discriminated against because of their color in some countries,.

非洲人在一些国家由于其肤色的原因仍然受到歧视。

3. engage in 从事;忙于

Title VII also created the Equal Employment Opportunity Commission (EEOC) to administer the act and to prohibit covered organizations from engaging in any unlawful employment practices.

标题 7 规定建立平等就业机会委员会来执行该项法案,阻止公司暗地里从事非法雇佣行为。

An increasing number of people are engaged in picking stocks these days.

现在越来越多的人在从事炒股票的活动。

1.3 Spotlight on Human Resource Management
人力资源管理热点

Turnover

Employee turnover continues to be an issue of importance and study among researchers. Recent studies have examined turnover from a unit-level perspective to determine how units are affected, as well as the effect of turnover on interpersonal relationships. A study by Kacmar, Andrews, Van Rooy, Steilberg, and Cerrone was interested in determining whether turnover affects unit-level performance, and if so, whether there are any mediating mechanisms. The researchers were also interested in the value of a stable workforce. Data from a large "fast" food restaurant chain revealed that turnover does, in fact, affect unit-level performance, and that a stable workforce contributes significantly to efficiency, which in turn enhances performance. The researchers reasoned that the theoretical basis for their findings rests in social exchange, knowledge-based, and strategic choice theories. Testimonies from practitioners confirmed the value of having a stable, well-trained workforce and validated its contribution to performance. The researchers also explored the impact of turnover among crews as compared to managers and found a difference: crew turnover affected food waste, but management turnover affected how long customers waited for service. This finding led the researchers to suggest that, in organizations where fast service is important, a key role played by managers may be to create an environment for quickness.

Similar to the analysis of Kacmar et al. a study of a small (n = 38) chain of restaurants examined the impact on unit performance of losses of individuals in key network positions. The researchers found a negative relationship between turnover and store performance such that store performance was low across the board when turnover was high. The study also showed that a loss of key social capital was significantly related to lower performance. The researchers believe the results speak to the importance of understanding that turnover affects both efficiency and important interpersonal relationships.

The effect of turnover on relationships was also examined in a study of health care employees in a public medical center. Mossholder, Settoon, and Henagan found that network centrality and interpersonal citizenship behavior were predictors of turnover. The study demonstrated that employees who develop strong bonds with their co-workers are more likely to stay with the organization; similarly, employees who engage in helping behaviors where reciprocity is the norm are also more likely to stay. A withdrawal of citizenship behaviors, however, may signal a potential exit. If an employee is contemplating leaving, it is believed that he or she will likely not expend helping behaviors, knowing that his or her co-workers will not have an opportunity to later reciprocate.

Teams

Organizations continue to recognize the importance of, and rely upon, teams for conducting work. Accordingly, researchers persist in examining different aspects of team selection and composition, team environment and its effect on important organizational variables, and team training.

A group of researchers were curious as to whether traditional selection techniques (structured interviews, personality tests, and situational judgment tests) used to select individuals would also work for selecting team members. With the increasing prevalence of team-oriented work environments, the scholars noticed a paucity of research regarding team member selection. A study employing the three commonly used selection techniques was conducted in a highly team-oriented manufacturing environment to examine relationships between social skills, personality, situational judgment, and contextual performance. It was found that a relationship did, in fact, exist among the variables, and that most of the variables predicted contextual performance. The researchers concluded that the findings provide legitimacy to applying the commonly used selection techniques for team member selection.

Several studies have examined the effect of different types of diversity or team composition on outcomes. One study examined the influence of educational and national diversity on information use by the team. Small MBA teams were comprised of students from different disciplines (i.e., educational diversity) and national backgrounds (i.

e., national diversity). Interestingly, the results found that the difference in the type of diversity influenced the team's use of information in different ways. It was found that among the educationally diverse teams, the diversity was both a help and hindrance <u>such that</u> broader ranges and depths of information were used as the diversity increased, but only up to a point. Too much diversity resulted in teams resorting to lesser use of information that was similar to teams with little educational diversity. The finding regarding educational diversity was what the researchers predicted; however, the finding with national diversity was not as predicted. National diversity was shown to result in uses of narrower ranges of information as the diversity increased from low to moderate levels. However, the ranges of information increased as the diversity increased from moderate to high levels, but the depth and integration of information lessened. The researchers pointed out the complexity of the relationship between diversity and use of information, and attribute the complexity to the nature of team processes.

Boone, Van Olffen, and Van Witteloostuijn considered the effect of locus of control among team members and how the variable affects leadership structure, information acquisition, and financial performance. What is most interesting about the findings is that the results underscore the importance of going beyond the simple main effects of team composition variables and analyzing basic moderator variables. Based on the results, the researchers go as far as to suggest that lack of significance in many previous studies and mixed findings among some studies may have been due to a failure to examine important moderators.

In terms of locus of control, the study shows that internals process information better than externals at the group level[1]. The findings lead the researchers to suggest that internals are more likely to engage in superior performance without a leader, whereas groups comprised of externals are more productive with a designated leader to guide and direct them[②].

Gender diversity in teams continues to be an area of research interest. Hirschfeld, Jordan, Feild, Giles, and Armenakis examined the representation of females in male dominated teams. The study found that a high representation of women did not adversely affect the team's perceived potency, social cohesion, or assessments of the team's work. Additionally, the research was consistent with previous studies that reported greater problem solving and slightly poorer performance on physically demanding tasks with the increased representation of women. The researchers stress that an expected tradeoff of greater problem solving for lesser social-psychological factors, based on previous studies, is not necessarily a given. They suggest that contextual factors, such as cultures and policies promoting inclusion, may play a significant role.

An issue related to gender diversity in teams is sexual harassment. Raver and Gelfand conducted a study that provided data which shows that sexual harassment may affect team performance. While previous studies focused on individual outcomes, this study linked sexual harassment to team processes and team financial performance. It was found that, at the team level, ambient sexual harassment <u>was positively related to</u> relationship conflict and task conflict, and <u>negatively related to</u> team cohesion and team financial performance. The findings make clear the importance of examining the effects of sexual harassment on team-level outcomes, as well as the need for additional research and theory to better understand the phenomenon.

Many organizations have the need for action teams that are designed to handle a variety of complex, time sensitive, intensive tasks. Examples of action teams include surgical teams and military teams, which must be adaptable and able to handle a wide variety of situations (expected and unexpected) with speed and competence. It has been shown, however, that although team members might have a high level of functional expertise, their teamwork skills and knowledge are often lacking. This, in turn, may lead to unsuccessful outcomes. Ellis, Bell, Ployhart, Hollenbeck, and Ilgen examined whether providing generic teamwork skills training would boost action team effectiveness. The results of the study showed that team-generic training is beneficial for action team performance[3]. There was evidence that declarative knowledge increases and gains were made in the team's ability to plan, coordinate tasks, collaboratively problem solve, and communicate. The researchers suggest that their results also give some indication as to how the training has its effects.

Diversity

Diversity continues to be an area of significant interest among researchers, practitioners, and legislators at all levels of government. While many types of diversity are often examined, racial diversity is still a matter of concern that researchers have designed studies to explore. These studies range from an understanding of how racial conflicts in communities influence work relationships, to the continued examination of the impact of affirmative action policies.

Working from the perspective of realistic group conflict theory, two studies were conducted by a group of researchers to determine whether racial conflict within one's community affected racial relationships at work. Realistic group conflict theory holds that hostility may exist when groups compete for limited resources. Consequently, group members will cling to and favor their own groups rather than associate with the competing group. Out of this situation is borne factionalism, resentment, and conflict.

The first of the two aforementioned studies determined whether proximity of whites to blacks in communities would negatively affect hostility among groups in work settings. Results show that the relationship between the quality of work relationships and organizational diversity was moderated by the proximity of whites to blacks where they lived. The relationship became more negative as proximity increased. In the second study, the researchers assessed community intergroup conflict between whites and Latinos, and asked whites to indicate their attractiveness to an employer with a low or high representation of Latino employees. The results showed that increased perceptions of community conflict between the groups led to decreased attractiveness to ethnically diverse organizations. Altogether, the studies provide evidence that conflicts in racially diverse communities may lead to racial tensions in work settings[④]. The researchers offer implications for practice that may be useful for organizations grappling with issues related to racial diversity.

There is a considerable body of literature asserting that supportive relationships among co-workers reap performance benefits for individuals and organizations. Bacharach, Bamberger, and Vashdi set out to explore the antecedents of supportive relationships among racially dissimilar (black and white) co-workers. The results of the study revealed, interestingly, that individuals tend to look to their own racial group members for support when in work groups with employees who are racially dissimilar to themselves. The study did show, however, that this phenomenon existed until a representational balance of both groups was reached. Accordingly, as a practical implication of this finding, the researchers proffer that managers should strive for racially balanced work groups, as opposed to placing ethnic "tokens" in work groups.

Affirmative action has existed for over 40 years and continues to be controversial. Aquino, Stewart, and Reed conducted two experiments to examine judgments subjects made regarding an African American employee who was said to be or not be a beneficiary of affirmative action. The scholars wanted to determine whether social dominance orientation (SDO), beliefs favoring group-based inequality, was a predictor of how job performance and career success is evaluated for African American beneficiaries of affirmative action. The research found that high SDO individuals had more predictive evaluative judgments of a beneficiary of affirmative action compared to subjects with low SDO. The research provides additional evidence that SDO is a useful predictor of negative evaluations toward minority groups, and that its effect may be strengthened by social cues (e. g., affirmative action policy). As a practical implication, the researchers suggest that managers may be able to counter negative perceptions of high SDO employees by proactively promoting the competence and sociability of the affirmative action hire.

As part of the same study, the scholars also wanted to explore whether the type of job held by the employee influenced the evaluation. Their findings suggest that minorities in higher level positions were not stigmatized by affirmative action, even if an affirmative action policy was in place. For upper level positions, it is believed that role-based rather than race-based stereotypes affected perceptions about the employee.

Summary

As illustrated by this brief review of last year's research findings, human resource management continues to be an area of great interest. Based on the wealth of research generated during the past 12 months, next year's Spotlight will most likely have just as much (or more) to report regarding new insights in the field.

from: *Business Horizons*, 2006

Words and Expressions

spotlight ['spɔtlait] *n.* 聚焦;热点
mediate ['mi:diit] *v.* 调节
mechanism ['mekənizəm] *n.* 机制

testimony ['testiməni] n. 声明
validate ['vælideit] v. 证实
centrality [sen'træliti] n. 向心性
predictor [pri'diktə] n. 预报值
bond [bɔnd] v. 联结
reciprocity [ˌrisi'prɔsiti] n. 互惠
withdrawal [wið'drɔːəl] n. 取消
contemplate ['kɔntempleit] v. 思考
expend [iks'pend] v. 用尽
prevalence ['prevələns] n. 流行
legitimacy [li'dʒitiməsi] n. 合法性
hindrance ['hindrəns] n. 不利因素
moderate ['mɔdərit] adj. 中等的
integration [ˌinti'greiʃən] n. 整合
moderator ['mɔdəreitə] n. 缓和因素
internal [in'təːnl] n. 内控归因
external [eks'təːnl] n. 外控归因
representation [ˌreprizen'teiʃən] n. 比例
potency ['pəutənsi] n. 能力
tradeoff [treidəv] n. 折中
given ['givn] n. 已知事物
inclusion [in'kluːʒən] n. 归属；接纳；内化
ambient ['æmbiənt] adj. 周围的
surgical ['səːdʒikəl] adj. 手术的
generic [dʒi'nerik] adj. 通用的
expertise [ˌekspəˈtiːz] n. 专门技术
boost [buːst] v. 推进
declarative [di'klærətiv] adj. 便于公开的
affirmative [əˈfəːmətiv] adj. 肯定的
hold [həuld] v. 认为

factionalism ['fækʃənəlizəm] n. 党派纷争
aforementioned [ə'fɔːˌmenʃənd] adj. 上述的
proximity [prɔk'simiti] n. 接近
Latino [læ'tiːnəu] n. 拉丁美洲人
ethnically ['eθnikəli] adv. 从民族讲
reap [riːp] v. 收获
antecedent [ˌænti'siːdənt] n. 先例
proffer ['prɔfə] v. 提出
token ['təukən] n. 象征
beneficiary [beni'fiʃəri] n. 受益人
crew turnover 员工流动率
management turnover 管理层流动率
unit performance 单位绩效
citizenship behavior 公民行为
helping behavior 助人行为
structured interview 结构化面试
a paucity of 少量
contextual performance 关系绩效
to resort to 求助
locus of control 控制源理论
social cohesion 社会内聚力
physically demanding 体力要求高的
sexual harassment 性骚扰
action teams 行动队
time sensitive 时间敏感的
to cling to 依附
to grapple with 处理
social dominance orientation 社会支配取向

Difficult Sentences

① In terms of locus of control, the study shows that internals process information better than externals at the group level.
根据控制源理论,这项研究表明内控归因团队比外控归因团队信息处理得好。

② The findings lead the researchers to suggest that internals are more likely to engage in superior performance without a leader, whereas groups comprised of externals are more productive with a designated leader to guide and direct them.
这些研究发现是研究人员认为内控归因团队更有可能在没有团队领导人的情况下进行出色的表现,然而外控归因团队则会在有指定领导人的带领指挥下更加具有创造力。

③ The results of the study showed that team-generic training is beneficial for action team performance.
研究的结果表明适合于任何小组的培训对于行动队的绩效是有益的。

④ Altogether, the studies provide evidence that conflicts in racially diverse communities may lead to racial tensions in work settings.
总而言之,这些研究证明多种族团体内的冲突可以导致工作环境中的种族关系紧张。

Phrases and Patterns

1. the effect/influence/impact of A on B A 对 B 的影响
   Recent studies have examined turnover from a unit-level perspective to determine how units are affected, as well as the effect of turnover on interpersonal relationship.
   近期的一些研究从单位视角探讨人员流动率,以确定单位会受到怎样的影响以及人员周转率对人际关系的影响。
   One study examined the influence of educational and national

diversity on information use by the team.
一项研究探讨了教育和国籍的多样性对团队运用信息的影响。
2. such that 因而；所以
The researchers found a negative relationship between turnover and store performance such that store performance was low when turnover was high.
研究人员发现在员工流动率和店铺绩效之间存在着负相关，因而，员工流动率高的时候店铺绩效就低。
It was found that among the educationally diverse teams, the diversity was both a help and hindrance such that broader ranges and depths of information were used as the diversity increased.
有人认为在教育水平多样化的小队，多样性既是有利因素也是不利因素，因而，随着多样性的增强，所运用的信息的广度和深度就会增加。
3. A be positively related to B/A be negatively related to B A 与 B 正相关/A 与 B 负相关
It was found that, at the team level, ambient sexual harassment was positively related to relationship conflict and task conflict, and negatively related to team cohesion and team financial performance.
有人认为在小队内，性骚扰情况与关系冲突和任务冲突正相关，与小队内聚力和小队财务绩效负相关。
Within a certain limit of income, sense of happiness is positively related to the money available, but beyond the limit, they are negatively related to each other.
在一定收入范围内，幸福感和钱的多少成正比关系，超出这个范围，它们之间负相关。
4. There is a considerable body of literature asserting that... 有大量的文献认为……
There is a considerable body of literature asserting that supportive relationships among co-workers reap performance benefits for

individuals and organizations.

有大量的文献认为同事之间的互助关系可以给个人和组织带来绩效利益。

There is a considerable body of literature asserting that traditional incentives such as pay increases are now not as effective as they once were.

有大量的文献认为现在传统的激励机制,不如以前那样奏效了,例如加薪。

Questions

1. What is human resource management (HRM)?
2. How many goals of effective HRM? What are they?
3. What acts have been enforced in order to guarantee the equal employment?
4. In the third passage of 1.3, what spotlights have been discussed on HRM?

Job Analysis and Job Design
工作分析和工作设计

【本章导读】 本章介绍工作分析和工作设计的概念和主要方法。2.1 着重阐释工作分析和工作设计的定义，详细介绍工作分析的主要方法，如工作要素法、弗雷氏曼工作分析法、任务法等。2.2 介绍工作设计的社会技术方法的概念和要点，如工作物质环境、灵活的工作时间安排，包括弹性上班制、远程办公、工作共享、浓缩工作周等。2.3 讨论创建健康工作环境的主要障碍。

2.1 Brief Introduction to Job Analysis and Job Design
工作分析和工作设计简介

Introduction

The analysis and design of work is one of the most important components to developing and maintaining a competitive advantage. Strategy implementation is virtually impossible without thorough attention devoted work-flow analysis, job analysis, and job design[①]. Managers need to understand the entire work-flow process in their work unit to ensure that the process maximizes efficiency and effectiveness. To understand this, work-flow process, managers also must have clear, detailed information about the jobs that exist in the work unit, and the way to gain this information is through the job-analysis process. Equipped with an understanding of the work-flow process and the existing job, managers can redesign jobs to ensure that the work unit is able to achieve its goals while individuals within the unit benefit on the various work-outcome dimensions such as motivation, satisfaction, safety, health, and achievement②. This is one key to competitive advantage.

Job Analysis

Job analysis refers to the process of getting detailed information about jobs. Job analysis has deep historical roots. For example, in his description of the "just" state, Socrates argued that society needed to recognize three things. First, there are individual differences in aptitudes for works, meaning that individuals differ in their abilities. Second, unique aptitude requirements exist for different occupations. Third, to achieve high-quality performance, society must attempt to place people in occupations that best suit their aptitudes. In other words, for society (or an organization) to succeed, it must have detailed information about the requirements of jobs (through job analysis), and it must ensure that a match exists between the job requirements and individuals' aptitudes (through selection).

Whereas Socrates was concerned with the larger society, it is even more important for organizations to understand and match job requirements and people to achieve high-quality performance. This is particularly true in today's competitive marketplace. Thus, the information gained through job analysis is of utmost importance; it has great value to both human resource and line managers.

Job Analysis Methods

The different types of job analysis methods are the job Element Method, the Fleishman Job Analysis System, Task Analysis, and the Position Analysis Questionnaire.

Job Element Method

The Job Element Method entails asking subject-matter experts (SMEs) to generate a list of the knowledge, skills, abilities and personal traits (called job elements) that are required to perform a job. A group of SMEs then rates each job element on four scales. The "barely acceptable" scale is the percentage of barely acceptable employees who have a particular job element. The "superior" scale is the percentage of superior employees who have the job element. "Trouble likely" refers to the probability of trouble occurring in an employee who lacks the job element. The "practical" scale is concerned with the practicality of finding people with the job element.

As you can see, this method provides position-specific information about the characteristics a worker needs to succeed on the job. As previously discussed, this type of information is most relevant to developing selection, training, and some types of performance-appraisal systems. However, while the job element method may be appropriate for these human resource activities, it is not usually appropriate if the job-analysis information is to be used in human resource planning, career development or job evaluation.

Fleishman Job Analysis System

Another job-analysis technique that elicits information about the worker's characteristics is the Fleishman Job Analysis System (FJAS). This approach defines abilities as enduring attributes of individuals that account for differences in performance. The system is based on a taxonomy of abilities that adequately represent all the dimensions relevant to work. This taxonomy includes 52 cognitive, psychomotor, physical, and sensory abilities.

In using the job-analysis technique, SMEs are presented with each of the 52 scales. These experts indicate the point on the scale that best represents the level of that ability requirements of the job. Consistent with our matrix of job-analysis information, substantial research has shown the value of this general approach for human resource activities such as career development, selection, and training[3].

Gathering the Job Analysis Information

Having chosen the sources of job analysis information, it is important to plan the job-analysis meeting to elicit high-quality information. To do this, you can structure the job-analysis meeting in the following ways. These steps help people think through the job in a way that does not overwhelm them with information.

Identify the Major Job Dimensions

This can be done by drawing a big circle like a pie. Tell the job analysts to think about the job like a pie, where everything they do fits into that pie. Then ask them to cut the pie up into the four to eight major chunks of tasks that tend to be interrelated.

Identify the Tasks

Once the job is broken into the major dimension, it is easier to begin brainstorming the various tasks that are part of each dimension. For example, concerning teaching—and much to a student's dismay—a professor must (a) prepare lectures, (b) deliver lectures (c) hold office hours to answer student questions, (d) develop examinations, (e) grade examinations, and (f) compute final grades.

Identify the KSAs—having developed a list of tasks, it is now much easier to go back to each task and think about the KSAs that are necessary to perform those tasks effectively. For example, to deliver a lecture, a professor must possess (a) knowledge of the course material, (b) knowledge of effective teaching techniques, (c) good public-speaking skill, and, one would hope, (d) a good sense of humor.

Identify the Potential Factors that could Change Jobs

This entails having individuals who are part of the strategic planning process brainstorm the environmental, technological, and strategic factors that are likely to change in the next three to five years. For example, is the company planning to expand into international markets? Is it building plants with new and different technologies? These issues might have important implications for the type of work performed as well as the skills necessary for job incumbents to perform them.

Predict the Nature of the Changing Job

This requires job analysts to predict how the factors identified in step 4 might change the existing structure of jobs. For example, if the company plans to expand internationally, then managers will be required to change the way they do things. It also might require future managers to have international experience or foreign language skills.

Having completed this process, a manager now has a very accurate picture of the tasks performed in the job and the KSAs required of a jobholder to be effective in performing all the major tasks④. In addition, it should be clear what types of changes in the work unit are likely to affect the jobs in the future so that jobs can be strategically managed. This allows a manager process and the skills necessary to perform effectively. However, if the work load changes substantially, either positively or negatively, this may require redesigning the jobs. In the next section, we discuss the process of job design and job redesign.

Job Design

So far we have approached the issue of managing work in a passive way, focusing only on understanding what gets done, the way it gets done, and the skills required to get it done. While this is necessary, it is a very static view of jobs, in that jobs must already exist and that they are already assumed to be structured in the one best way. However, a manager may often be faced with a situation in which the work unit does not yet exist, requiring jobs within the work unit to be designed from scratch. Sometimes work loads within an existing work unit are increased, or work-group size is decreased while the same work load is required, a trend increasingly observed with the movement toward downsizing. Finally, sometimes the work is not being performed in the most efficient manner. In these cases, a manager may decide to change the way that work is done in order for the work unit to perform more effectively and efficiently. This requires redesigning the existing jobs.

Job design is the process of defining the way work will be performed and the tasks that will be required in a given job. Job redesign refers to changing the tasks or the way work is performed in an existing job. To effectively design jobs, one must thoroughly understand the job as it exists (through job analysis) and its place in the larger work unit's work-flow process (work-flow analysis). Having a detailed knowledge of the tasks performed in the work unit and in the job, a manager then has many alternative ways to design a job. This can be done most effectively through understanding the trade-offs between certain design approaches.

Recent research has identified four basic approaches that have been used among the various disciplines (e.g. psychology, management, engineering, and ergonomics) that have dealt with job-design issues. All jobs can be characterized in terms of how they fare according to each approach; thus, a manager needs to understand the trade-offs between emphasizing one approach over another⑤.

from: *Human Resource Management*: *Gaining a Competitive Advantage*, 1994

Words and Expressions

implementation [ˌimplimen'teiʃən] *n.* 实施

virtually ['və:tjuəli] adv. 事实上；实质上
dimension [di'menʃən] n. 方面；因素
just [dʒʌst] adj. 公正的
aptitude ['æptitju:d] n. 天资
entail [in'teil] v. 需要
practicality [,prækti'kæliti] n. 实用性
elicit [i'lisit] v. 得出
taxonomy [tæk'sɔnəmi] n. 分类
psychomotor [,saikəu'məutə] adj. 精神性运动的
matrix ['meitriks] n. 母体；发源地
substantial [səb'stænʃəl] adj. 实质的
overwhelm [,əuvə'welm] v. 过于大量地给予
analyst ['ænəlist] n. 分析家
brainstorm ['brein,stɔ:m] v. 脑力激荡
strategic [strə'ti:dʒik] adj. 战略上的
implication [,impli'keiʃən] n. 隐含的意义
incumbent [in'kʌmbənt] n. 任职者
approach [ə'prəutʃ] v. 着手处理
downsize ['daun,saiz] v. 缩减
effectively [i'fektivli] adv. 有效地
efficiently [i'fiʃəntli] adv. 有效率地
thoroughly ['θʌrəli] adv. 彻底地
alternative [ɔ:l'tə:nətiv] adj. 选择性的
discipline ['disiplin] n. 学科
fare [fɛə] v. 进展
competitive advantage 竞争优势
line manager 生产线管理人员
subject-matter experts (SMEs) 主题专家
personal traits 个性特征
job element 工作要素

position-specific 特定职位的
performance-appraisal 绩效评价
to account for 说明
work load 工作量
office hour 答疑时间
KSAs (Knowledge, Skills, Abilities and Other characteristics
job design) 工作设计
from scratch 从零开始

Difficult Sentences

① Strategy implementation is virtually impossible without thorough attention devoted work-flow analysis, job analysis, and job design.
如果不对工作流程分析、工作分析和工作设计投入充分的关注，实施策略实际上是不可能的。

② Equipped with an understanding of the work-flow process and the existing job, managers can redesign jobs to ensure that the work unit is able to achieve its goals while individuals within the unit benefit on the various work-outcome dimensions such as motivation, satisfaction, safety, health, and achievement.
由于对工作流程步骤和现有工作的了解，管理者能够重新设计工作来保证工作小组能够实现目标并且保证小组内的个体能够在各项工作成果，比如，动机、满意度、安全感、健康和成就等方面都能有所收益。

③ Consistent with our matrix of job-analysis information, substantial research has shown the value of this general approach for human resource activities such as career development, selection, and training.
和我们的工作分析信息的母体一致，真实性研究已经表明这种综合性方法对于事业发展、雇员甄选和培训等人力资源活动的价值。

④ Having completed this process, a manager now has a very accurate picture of the tasks performed in the job and the KSAs required of a jobholder to be effective in performing all the major tasks.
完成这个过程之后,现在管理者非常清楚工作中所要履行的任务和上岗者要有效完成所有主要任务应具备的知识、技能、态度等要素。

⑤ All jobs can be characterized in terms of how they fare according to each approach; thus, a manager needs to understand the trade-offs between emphasizing one approach over another.
任何工作的特征都可以根据他们在每一种方法下的进展情况来进行描述,因此,管理者需要知道平衡各种方法的重要性。

Phrases and Patterns

1. be of utmost importance... 是非常重要的……
   The information gained through job analysis is of utmost importance.
   通过作业分析获取的信息是非常重要的。
   This decision is of utmost political importance.
   这个决定具有重大政治意义。

2. rate... on... scales 按照……等级来评价……
   A group of SMEs rate each job element on four scales.
   一组主题专家按照四个等级来评价每一个作业要素。
   A group of test experts rate each grading criterion on five scales.
   一组测试专家按照五个等级来评定每一个评分标准。

3. much to one's dismay 令……沮丧的是
   Much to a student's dismay, a professor must (a) prepare lectures, (b) deliver lectures (c) hold office hours to answer student questions, (d) develop examinations, (e) grade examinations, and (f) compute final grades.
   令学生非常沮丧的是,教授必须要备课、讲课、安排答疑时间回答学生的问题、进行考试、评判试卷和录入期末成绩。

Much to his dismay, his application for the job in this small company was turned down.

令他非常沮丧的是,他申请到这家小公司工作都没有成功。

4. from scratch 从零开始

However, a manager may often be faced with a situation in which the work unit does not yet exist, requiring jobs within the work unit to be designed from scratch.

然而,管理者可能经常面临这样的情形:工作小组还没有成形,就要求从零开始进行工作设计。

There were so many spelling mistakes; I had to write the letter out again from scratch.

这封信的拼写错误太多,我必须重写。

2.2　The Sociotechnical Approach to Job Design
工作设计的社会技术方法

Introduction

The sociotechnical approach to job design was first introduced as an alternative to viewing job design strictly as a matter of specializing the job as much as possible. The thrust of the sociotechnical approach is that both the technical system and the accompanying social system should be considered when designing jobs. According to this concept, employers should design jobs by taking a holistic, or systems, view of the entire job situation, including its physical and social environment. The sociotechnical approach is situational because few jobs involve identical technical requirements and social surroundings: Specifically, the sociotechnical approach requires that the job designer carefully consider the role of the employees in the sociotechnical system, the nature of the tasks performed, and the autonomy of the work group. Ideally, the sociotechnical approach merges the technical needs of the organization with the social needs of the employees involved in decision making[1].

The Guidelines in Using the Sociotechnical Approach to Designing Jobs

A job needs to be reasonably demanding for the individual in terms other than sheer endurance, yet provide some variety (not necessarily novelty).

Employees need to be able to learn on the job and to continue learning.

Employees need some minimum area of decision making that they can call their own.

Employees need some minimal degree of social support and recognition in the workplace.

Employees need to be able to relate what they do and what they produce to their social lives.

Employees need to believe that the job leads to some sort of desirable future.

The sociotechnical approach to job design has been applied in many countries, often under the heading "autonomous work groups" or "individual democracy" projects. Modern-day job designs based on the concepts of self-managed work teams or groups productivity usually have their roots in the sociotechnical approach.

The Physical Work Environment

The physical work environment, which includes factors such as temperature, humidity, ventilation, noise, light, and color, can have an impact on the design of jobs. While studies clear show that adverse physical conditions have a negative effect on performance, the degree of influence varies from individual to individual.

The implementation of the Occupational Safety and Health Act (OSHA) in 1970 magnified the importance of safety considerations in the design process. Designed to reduce the incidence of job-related injuries and illnesses, the act outlines very specific federal safety guidelines that all organizations in the United States must follow.

In general, the work environment should allow for normal lighting, temperature, ventilation, and humidity. Baffles, acoustical wall materials, and sound absorbers should be used where necessary to reduce unpleasant noises. If employees must be exposed to less-than-ideal conditions, it is wise to limit these exposures to short periods of time to minimize the probability that the worker will suffer any permanent physical or psychological damage.

Alternative Work Schedule

Another factor that affects job design is the work schedule. In the last several years, organizations have increasingly <u>departed from</u> traditional work schedules <u>in an attempt to</u> increase productivity or decrease cost. While changes in the work schedule do not generally alter work to be done, they can affect how the work is allocated[2]. The most common alternative work schedules are flextime, telecommuting, job sharing, and the condensed workweek.

Flextime

Flextime, or flexible working hours, allows employees to choose, within certain limits, when they start and end their workday. Usually the organization defines a core period (such as 10 A.M. to 3 P.M.) when all employees will be at work. It is then left to each employee—to decide when to start and end the workday as long as the hours encompass the core period. Some flextime programs allow employees to vary the hours worked each day as long as they meet some specific total, which is usually 40 hours[3]. Flextime has the advantage of allowing different employees to accommodate different lifestyles and schedules. Other potential advantages include avoiding rush hours and having less absenteeism and tardiness. From the employer's viewpoint, flextime can have the advantage of providing an edge in recruiting new employees and also in retaining hard-to-find qualified employees. Organizations with flextime schedules may also see an increase in productivity. On the downside, flextime can create communication and coordination problems for supervisors and managers.

Telecommuting

Telecommuting is the practice of working at home or while traveling and being able to interact with the office. Today's information technology (PCs, the Internet, cellular phones, etc.) has made telecommuting a reality for many companies. According to the General Accounting Office, some 16.5 million Americans now telecommuted at least once a month, and nearly 9.3 million telecommute at least once a week. A large number of companies are now using telecommuting to recruit qualified employees; especially in tight labor markets.

Advantages of telecommuting include less travel time, avoiding rush hour, avoiding distractions at the office, and being able to work flexible hours. Potential disadvantages of telecommuting are insurance concerns relating to the health and safety of employees working at home. Another drawback is that some state and local laws restrict just what work can be done at home.

Job Sharing

Job sharing is a relatively new concept where by two or more part-time individuals perform job that would normally be held by one full-time person. Job sharing can be in the form of equally shared responsibilities or split duties, or a combination of both. Job sharing is especially attractive to people who want to work, but not full-time④. A critical factor relating to job sharing is how benefits are handled. Often benefits are prorated between the part-time employees. Some organizations allow job-sharing employees to purchase full health insurance by paying the difference between their prorated benefit and the premium for a full-time employee⑤.

Condensed Workweek

Under the condensed workweek, the number of hours worked per day is increased and the number of days in the workweek is decreased. Typically, this is done by having extra work 10 hours per day for four days per week (known as 4/40). Other variations of the condensed workweek include reducing the total hours worked to 36 or 38 hours. Advantages of the condensed workweek are lower absenteeism and tardiness, less start-up time, and time available for employees to take care of personal business. One potential disadvantage is the fatigue that often accompanies longer hours. A recent survey by the Society for Human Resource Management reported that 58 percent of employers offer flextime, 31 percent offer condensed workweeks, and 37 percent offer telecommuting.

from: *Human Resource Management*, 1994

Words and Expressions

thrust [θrʌst] *n.* 本质;要点
accompanying [əˈkʌmpəniŋ] *adj.* 附随的
holistic [həuˈlistik] *adj.* 强调整体的
situational [ˌsitjuˈeiʃənəl] *adj.* 视情况而定的
identical [aiˈdentikəl] *adj.* 同一的
specially [ˈspeʃəli] *adv.* 特别地
autonomy [ɔːˈtɔnəmi] *n.* 自主性
demanding [diˈmændiŋ] *adj.* 苛求的
sheer [ʃiə] *adj.* 完全的
endurance [inˈdjurəns] *n.* 耐久性
novelty [ˈnɔvəlti] *n.* 新颖
recognition [ˌrekəgˈniʃən] *n.* 公认

humidity [hju(:)'miditi] n. 湿度
ventilation [venti'leiʃən] n. 通风
magnify ['mægnifai] v. 夸大
incidence ['insidəns] n. 发生频率
baffle ['bæfl] n. 隔音板
telecommute [ˌtelikə'mju:t] v. 远程办公
flextime ['flekstaim] n. 弹性上班制
core [kɔ:] n. 核心
encompass [in'kʌmpəs] v. 包含
accommodate [ə'kɔmədeit] v. 考虑
absenteeism [æbsən'ti:z(ə)m] n. 旷工
tardiness ['tɑ:dinis] n. 缓慢
edge [edʒ] n. 优势
recruit [ri'kru:t] v. 招收
retain [ri'tein] v. 保留受雇状态
tight [tait] adj. 供不应求的
distraction [dis'trækʃən] n. 分心的事物
drawback ['drɔ:ˌbæk] n. 缺点
prorate [prəu'reit] v. 按比例分配
fatigue [fə'ti:g] n. 疲乏
sociotechnical approach 社会技术方法
autonomous work groups 自主工作组
individual democracy 个人民主
the physical work environment 工作物理环境
the occupational safety and health act 职业安全与健康法案
acoustical wall material 墙体消音材料
sound absorber 隔音材料
permanent physical or psychological damage 永久性身心伤害
work schedule 工作时间安排
to depart from 离开

rush hours 上班高峰时间

on the downside 从不利的方面来讲

to pay the difference 付差额金

Difficult Sentences

① Ideally, the sociotechnical approach merges the technical needs of the organization with the social needs of the employees involved in decision making.

理论上讲,这种社会技术方法把组织的技术需要和决策中所涉及的员工的社会需要结合起来。

② While changes in the work schedule do not generally alter work to be done, they can affect how the work is allocated.

虽然工作时间安排的变化一般不会改变需要完成的工作,但是却会影响工作的分配方式。

③ Some flextime programs allow employees to vary the hours worked each day as long as they meet some specific total, which is usually 40 hours.

一些弹性上班制组织允许员工改变每天用于工作的时间,只要他们的工作时间达到规定的总数即可,通常是40小时。

④ Job sharing can be in the form of equally shared responsibilities or split duties, or a combination of both. Job sharing is especially attractive to people who want to work, but not full-time.

工作共享可以是共同承担职责,或是平分职责,或是两者兼而有之。工作共享对于想要工作但是又无法全职工作的人特别有吸引力。

⑤ Some organizations allow job-sharing employees to purchase full health insurance by paying the difference between their prorated benefit and the premium for a full-time employee.

一些组织允许共享工作的员工通过支付他们按比例获得的利益额和全职员工的保险金之间的差额来购买全面的健康险。

Phrases and Patterns

1. vary from... to... 从……到……而不同
   The degree of influence varies from individual to individual.
   影响的程度因人而异。
   Corporate culture varies from company to company.
   企业文化因公司不同而不同。
2. depart from... in an attempt to... 背离……努力……
   In the last several years, organizations have increasingly departed from traditional work schedules in an attempt to increase productivity or decrease cost.
   在过去的几年里,组织越来越改变传统的工作时间安排来努力提高生产率、降低成本。
   Some innovative industrialists are departing from the old customs in an attempt to establish a new order in this field.
   一些具有创新精神的实业家在不断打破旧的习俗,努力建立这个领域的新秩序。

2.3 Barriers to Creating Healthier Workplaces
创建健康工作场所的障碍

Although many companies have WHP and OHS programs, the relation between organizational practices or the work itself and health and safety outcomes are rarely fully appreciated.

A major question is how to get genuine management commitment to improving workplace health and safety. Sometimes it results from catastrophes in the workplace such as a fatal accident. Some companies may respond to large increases in workers' compensation premiums, especially if they are based on experience rating. However, Hyatt and Thomason, while finding that firms respond to experience rating by attempting to reduce claim costs, acknowledge that they may do so by managing claims rather than safety—a notion supported by other qualitative research.

A systematic and detailed attempt to understand management commitment to OHS was compiled by Hopkins, based on his experience and research in Australia. He fist examined the "safety pays" argument that it is in the company's economic interest to improve safety. Hopkins pointed out that this does not always work. Indeed, if it really did, there would be little need for regulations since it would be in management's interest to deal well with safety.

Economic theory predicts that organizations will spend on health and safety up to the point where marginal benefits equal marginal costs[①]. However, the optimal degree of safety and health spending from the organization's viewpoint is likely not the same as from society's. This is because organizations often do not bear the full cost of injury and illness, especially where causal attribution is weak, i. e., where there are multiple causes and long latent periods between exposure and outcome[②]. Companies' reward structures tend to be based on production achievements (the primary purpose of the organization), not achievements in health and safety.

Hopkins found that managers can be motivated by a belief in their obligation to obey the law, fear of personal liability, a wish to be seen to be doing the proper thing, and real concern for the welfare of (or at least lack of harm to) workers. He believed that government intervention is the best way to focus management attention on safety. The consensus of his contacts was that the best government policy uses both punishment and persuasion, depending on local conditions. Some support for the effectiveness of inspections came from Mendeloff who reported that firms inspected showed a drop in injury rates, at least for one to two years, but was uncertain if the effect was long-lasting or how and why inspections worked.

While Hopkins' arguments, being based on direct interviews with many managers, are quite persuasive, they may depend on local circumstances, including, for example, whether CEOs and managers can be prosecuted as individuals over health and safety violations. Reason notes the difficulty under English law of successfully bringing charges against managers and corporations. While agreeing with Hopkins that the potential stigma of criminal conviction is a potent deterrent, Brown and Rankin and Ison note that the stigma is one reason why enforcement agencies may not use criminal prosecution. Instead, these authors favor administrative monetary penalties. It would be important to have data on the relative effectiveness of different approaches, although comparisons are difficult because of many other differences across jurisdictions.

A relationship between stress and the organization's effectiveness <u>is likely to</u> motivate management. Leiter et al., for example, found that the mean level of burnout in hospital nurses in different units was correlated with mean patient satisfaction levels on those units. What will likely not be effective are conditions that encourage managers "to go through the motions" of promoting OHS. Their commitment will need to be genuine to avoid their sending other signals that health and safety are not really important priorities.

<u>Another question is whether</u> decision makers believe a relationship between exposure and outcome exists, especially when the etiology of illness is multi-factorial. For example, the proposed ergonomics standard from the Occupational Safety and Health Administration (OSHA) in the US created a great deal of controversy, ostensibly focusing on the sufficiency of the scientific evidence.

Many senior managers believe that stress occurs only (or at least primarily) in higher grades of employment. They apparently fail to recognize that there is likely a more-than compensating increase in control. Meanwhile, despite the business texts which exhort executives to empower their workers, management seems unwilling to cede any real power (control) to lower level employees. There is also a tendency to believe that stress is fundamentally an individual's problem. Even though Rosner appreciated the impact of the workplace on health, he saw no solution other than initiatives taken by individuals on their own behalf.

When corporations do accept a broader view, it may still be limited. Thus, Sandroff et al. described an approach which "attempts to avoid the pitfalls of a univocal individual approach." However, while accepting the role of the physical work environment, they ignored the role that other aspects of work and the workplace can play in health, and hence possibilities of changing the workplace organization.

Israel et al. described several intervention studies. They found that to be successful, changes needed the participation and backing of not just the top management but also the top union leadership[3]. Yet unions may often feel the need to focus on wages and other issues. They point out that there can be resistance to using more comprehensive approaches to stress, and insufficient resources may be provided for a full evaluation of any intervention. After noting the challenges, they stated that it was "important to recognize that... efforts to affect legislation and policy are essential". Once again, there are substantial differences between North America and Europe. European Union directives have stimulated actions in risk assessment and monitoring, including stress risks. In North America, in contrast, approaches are less formal.

The perception held by employees that career advancement is impeded by taking family leave may limit the use of family-friendly policies. Among employees of private sector companies with 100 or more employees nationally, 40% agreed somewhat or strongly that using flexible schedules and taking time off for family reasons impedes job advancement[4]. Similarly, 24% of respondents in a Canadian survey felt that taking a leave of absence for family reasons will limit career advancement. Managers may be reluctant to implement policies because they feel that taking an employee's personal priorities into account will create either a sense of entitlement or feelings of resentment in other employees⑤.

Another barrier is that some managers feel that balancing work and life is a woman's issue and therefore not their problem. Eighty per cent of Canadian employers surveyed by the Conference Board of Canada felt that employees were primarily responsible for finding solutions to the problems that caregivers and working parents experience. Yet in Sweden and other Scandinavian countries, taking time off work to care for a terminally ill relative or compassionate leave with partial pay is a social right.

from: *American Journal of Industrial Medicine*, 2001

Words and Expressions

catastrophe [kə'tætrəfi] *n.* 大灾难
fatal ['feitl] *adj.* 致命的
compensation [kɔmpen'seiʃən] *n.* 赔偿
premium ['primjəm] *n.* 额外费用
claim [kleim] *v.* 索赔
marginal ['mɑːdʒinəl] *adj.* 边际效用的
causal ['kɔːzəl] *adj.* 因果关系的
attribution [ˌætri'bjuːʃən] *n.* 归因
latent ['leitənt] *adj.* 潜伏的
intervention [ˌintə(ː)'venʃən] *n.* 干涉
consensus [kən'sensəs] *n.* 一致同意
contact ['kɔntækt] *n.* 熟人
persuasive [pə'sweisiv] *adj.* 有说服力的
prosecute ['prɔsikjuːt] *v.* 起诉

stigma ['stigmə] n. 污名
potent ['pəutənt] adj. 有力的
deterrent [di'terənt] n. 威慑手段
administrative [əd'ministrətiv] adj. 行政的
monetary ['mʌnitəri] adj. 金钱的
penalty ['penlti] n. 处罚
jurisdiction [ˌdʒuəris'dikʃən] n. 权限
mean [miːn] adj. 平均的
burnout ['bəːnaut] n. 精疲力尽
priority [prai'ɔriti] n. 优先考虑的事
etiology [ˌiːti'ɔlədʒi] n. 病因
ergonomics [ˌəːgəu'nɔmiks] n. 工效因素
exhort [ig'zɔːt] v. 劝诫
cede [siːd] v. 让与
initiative [i'niʃiətiv] n. 开始
pitfall ['pitfɔːl] n. 缺陷
univocal [ˌjuːni'vəukəl] adj. 意义明确的
comprehensive [ˌkɔmpri'hensiv] adj. 全面的
legislation [ˌledʒis'leiʃən] n. 立法
directive [dai'rektiv] n. 命令或指示
assessment [ə'sesmənt] n. 估价
monitoring ['mɔnitəriŋ] n. 监测
impede [im'piːd] v. 妨碍
implement ['implimənt] v. 执行
WHP (workplace health promotion) 工作场所健康促进
OHS (occupational health and safety) 职业安全健康
experience ratings 资历等级
marginal benefits 边际收益
marginal costs 边际成本
occupational safety and health administration 职业安全健康局

working parents 双职工父母
Scandinavian countries 斯堪的纳维亚国家
family leave 产假
a terminally ill relative 临终亲属

Difficult Sentences

① Economic theory predicts that organizations will spend on health and safety up to the point where marginal benefits equal marginal costs.
经济学理论预测组织一定要在健康和安全上进行投入直至边际收益等同于边际成本。

② This is because organizations often do not bear the full cost of injury and illness, especially where causal attribution is weak, i. e., where there are multiple causes and long latent periods between exposure and outcome.
这是因为组织通常不会承担伤害和疾病的全部费用,特别是在诱发因素不是很清楚的情况下,也就是说,有很多原因会诱发疾病或带来伤害,并且从处于工作环境中到发病之间有很长的潜伏期。

③ They found that to be successful, changes needed the participation and backing of not just the top management but also the top union leadership.
他们认为要想变革成功,不仅需要高端管理层的参与和支持,还需要行会高层领导的参与和支持。

④ Among employees of private sector companies with 100 or more employees nationally, 40% agreed somewhat or strongly that using flexible schedules and taking time off for family reasons impedes job advancement.
全国拥有100名以上雇员的私营公司中,有40%的员工不同程度地认为采用弹性工作时间安排和由于家庭原因休假会妨碍工作进展。

⑤ Managers may be reluctant to implement policies because they feel that taking an employee's personal priorities into account will create either a sense of entitlement or feelings of resentment in other employees.

管理者不愿意执行这些政策因为他们认为考虑员工的个人重要事务会使员工产生特权感或使其他员工产生怨恨情绪。

Phrases and Patterns

1. be likely to 很可能会
   A relationship between stress and the organization's effectiveness is likely to motivate management.
   工作重点和公司效率之间的关系很可能会激发管理。
   This company is not likely to get involved in the upcoming bid.
   这家公司不可能参加即将举行的竞标活动。
2. Another... is whether/that... 另一个……是……
   Another question is whether decision makers believe a relationship between exposure and outcome exists.
   另一个问题是决策者是否相信处于工作环境中和发病之间存在着联系。
   Another barrier is that some managers feel that balancing work and life is a woman's issue and therefore not their problem.
   另一个障碍是有一些管理者认为平衡工作和生活是女人们考虑的问题而不是他们应该考虑的。
3. in contrast 相比之下
   In North America, in contrast, approaches are less formal.
   相比之下，在北美的方法就不那么正式了。
   In contrast with their system, our system seems to be old-fashioned.
   和他们的体制相比，我们的体制似乎是落伍了。

Questions

1. What are different job analysis methods? How are they different from each other?
2. What are job design and job redesign? What's the relationship between the two?
3. What do you think are the most common alternative work schedules?
4. What advantages and disadvantages does each alternative work schedule have?
5. What do you think about the bars to creating healthier working place?

3

Recruitment
招 聘

【**本章导读**】 本章介绍员工招聘过程中的一些主要问题。3.1 介绍影响招聘的主要因素,包括来自政府和工会的限制和受劳动力市场的影响等外部因素,以及雇主的各种要求和申请人的喜好等。3.2 介绍员工招聘的主要方法:对内招聘和对外招聘。对内招聘包括工作职位报告和内部兼职。对外招聘包括媒体广告、计算机数据库、职业介绍所、特殊情况聘用、暑期实习、招聘大学生等。3.3 通过两个案例论述招聘广告和组织的自我展示之间的关系。

3.1　Brief Sketch of Recruitment
招聘概要

Introduction

Before an organization can fill a job vacancy, it must find people who not only are qualified for the position but also want the job. This chapter describes the recruiting process as one of the ways that an organization can deal with shortages in its human resources needs. Recruitment refers to organizational activities that influence the number and types of applicants who apply for a job and whether the applicants accept jobs that are offered[①]. Thus, recruitment is directly related to both human resource planning and selection, as shown in Figure 3.1.

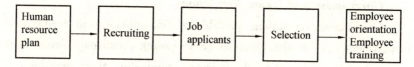

Figure 3.1   The Recruitment Process

Although recruitment can be quite expensive, organizations have not always treated it as systematically as other HR functions, such as selection. During the coming years, however, the importance of recruitment will probably increase for many organizations, for at least two reasons. First, experts are predicting labor shortages in many occupations because workers will not possess the skills needed for new technologies. Second, the downsizing and cost-saving measures undertaken by many companies in recent years have left human resource budgets much smaller than before. New and innovative approaches to recruiting qualified applicants will have to be found. Such approaches are highlighted later in this chapter.

A Diagnostic Approach to Recruitment

The recruiting process begins with an attempt to find employees with the abilities and attitudes desired by the organization and to match them with the tasks to be performed. Whether potential employees will respond to the recruiting effort depends on the attitudes they have developed toward those tasks and the organization on the basis of their past social and working experiences. Their perception of the task will also be affected by the work climate in the organization. How difficult the recruiting job is depends on a number of factors: external influences such as government and union restrictions and the labor market, plus the employer's requirements and candidates' preferences.

External Influences

Government and Union Restrictions

Government regulations prohibiting discrimination in hiring and employment have a direct impact on recruiting practices. Government agencies can and do review the following information about recruiting to see if an organization has violated the law:

· List of recruitment sources (such as employment agencies, civic organizations, schools) for each job category.

· Recruiting advertising.

· Estimates of the firm's employment needs for the coming year.

· Statistics on the number of applicants processed by demographic category (sex, race, and so on) and by job category or level.

· Checklists to show what evidence was used to verify the legal right to work.

The Immigration Reform and Control Act (IRCA) of 1986 has placed a major responsibility on employers for stopping the flow of illegal immigration to the United States. The employer—not the government—is the chief enforcer of the prohibition against the unauthorized recruitment and employment of foreign-born individuals. Under the law's "employer sanctions" arrangement, all employers are required to screen every applicant's eligibility for lawful employment and maintain records demonstrating employment authorization.

The IRCA is a complex piece of legislation, but its basic features fit into four broad categories:

· Employer's duty not to recruit, hires, or continue to employ "unauthorized aliens."

· Employer's duty not to verify the identity and work authorization of every new employee.

· Employer's duty not to discriminate on the basis of citizenship or national origin.

• Amnesty rights of certain illegal aliens who are eligible to achieve temporary or permanent resident status in the country.

The IRCA <u>went into effect</u> in May 1988, 18 months after the bill became to allow for a period of education among employers. Initial penalties for employers who violate the IRCA entail a cease and desist order along with a fine of between \$250 and \$2,000 for each unauthorized alien. Second violations result in a fine of between \$2,000 and \$5,000 per unauthorized alien. Third offenses lead to fines of \$3,000 to \$10,000 per unauthorized alien. A person or firm may be charged criminally for having a pattern of violations, with a maximum sentence per violation of six months' imprisonment or a \$3,000 fine, or both[2]. In addition, President Clinton signed an executive order in 1996 stipulating that contractors may be ineligible to receive new federal contracts for one year or longer if they are caught using undocumented workers[3].

Despite the difficulty that organizations have determining whether a worker is legally employable, the government is currently planning to step up its enforcement of the IRCA. Additional money will be spent on hiring more investigators, attorneys, and support staff, but some money will also be devoted to ensuring legal applicants are not discriminated against because of the stepped-up enforcement activities. At the same time, the government is also proposing to fund a system that will allow employers quicker and more accurate ways of determining if someone has the necessary documents to be legally hired, This system would include a telephone verification system that would allow employers to quickly determine if an applicant's work documentation is valid.

Labor Market Conditions

Another external environmental factor affecting recruiting is labor market conditions. If there is a surplus labor at recruiting time, even informal attempts at recruiting will probably attract more than enough applicants. However, when full employment has nearly reached an area, skillful and prolonged recruiting may be necessary to attract any applicants who fulfill the expectations of the organization④. Obviously, how many applicants are available also depends on whether the economy is growing. When companies are not creating new jobs, there is often an oversupply of qualified labor.

An employer can find out about the current employment picture in several ways. The federal Department of Labor issues employment reports, and state divisions of employment security and labor usually can provide information about specific types of employees. There are also sources of information on local employment conditions as they affect their members. Current college recruiting efforts are analyzed by the Conference Board, A. C. Nielsen, and the Endicott Report, which appears in the Journal of College Placement. Various personnel journals, the Monthly Labor Review, and The Wall Street Journal also regularly report on employment conditions.

Other sources provide summary data such as indexes of employment. One of the most interesting indexes is that of the Conference Board, which keeps track of help-wanted advertising in 52 major newspapers across the nation, using 1967 as the base year(100). Local conditions are more important than national conditions unless the employer is recruiting nationwide.

Composition of Labor Force and Location of Organization

As the number of legal requirements has increased, HRM law has become important for an organization to analyze the composition of its workforce. Such an analysis is done to determine whether the firm's employment practices are discriminatory.

The location of the organization and the relevant labor market will play a major role in the composition of the workforce. That is, the number of African-American, Hispanic, Asian or Pacific Islander, Native American, or Alaskan native employees in the workforce depends largely on the availability of these minority employees in the relevant labor market[5].

Therefore, government and union restrictions, labor market conditions, the makeup of the workforce, and the location of the organization are external forces that affect each other. None of these forces is necessarily more important than any other. Each of them must be considered in developing a sound recruitment plan that results in an effectively functioning organization.

Interaction of the Recruit and the Organization

After considering how external factors such as government, unions, labor market conditions, composition of the workforce, and location of the organization restrict recruiting options, the next step in understanding the recruiting process is to consider the interaction between the applicants and the organization in recruiting.

The diagnostic model shows that the nature of the organization and the goals of the managers are highlighted, as is the nature of the task. The techniques used and sources of recruits vary with the job. As far as the applicants are concerned, their abilities and past work experience affect how they go about seeking a job.

Recruiting Requirements

The recruiting process necessarily begins with a detailed job description and job specification. Without these, it is impossible for recruiters to determine how well any particular applicant fits the job. It should be made clear to the recruiter which requirements are absolutely essential and which are merely desirable. This can help the organization avoid unrealistic expectations for potential employees: An employer might expect applicants who stand first in their class, are presidents of extracurricular activities, have worked their way through school, are good-looking, have 10 years' experience (at age 21), and are willing to work long hours for almost no money. Contrasting with this unrealistic approach, the effective organization examines the specifications that are absolutely necessary for the job. Then it uses these as its beginning expectations for recruits.

Organizational Policies and Practices

In some organizations, HRM policies and practices affect recruiting and who is recruited. One of the most significant of these is promotion from within. For all practical purposes, this policy means that many organizations recruit from outside the organization only at the initial hiring level. Most employees favor this approach. They feel this is fair to present loyal employees and assures them of a secure future and a fair chance at promotion. Some employers also feel this practice helps protect trade secrets.

Is promotion from within a good policy? Not always. An organization may become so stable that it is set in its ways. The business does not compete effectively, or the government bureau will not adjust to legislative requirements. In such cases, promotion from within may be detrimental and new employees from outside might be helpful.

Other policies can also affect recruiting. Certain organizations have always hired more than their fair share of the disabled, veterans, or ex-convicts, for example, and they may look to these sources first. Others may be involved in nepotism to favor relatives. All these policies affect who is recruited.

Organizational Image

The image of the employer generally held by the public can also affect recruitment. All else being equal, it should be easier for an organization with a positive corporate image to attract and retain employees than an organization with a negative image. Thus, for organizations like Merck, 3M, Coca-Cola, and Johnson & Johnson that usually rank high on surveys such as those of Fortune magazine, the time and effort needed to recruit high-quality workers may be less than for their less fortunate competitors who rank poorly⑥. Recruitment should also be somewhat easier for companies that exude a strong community presence or positive name recognition.

How does this image affect recruiting? Job applicants seldom can have interviews with all the organizations that have job openings of interest to them. Because there are limits on the time and energy devoted to the job search, applicants do some preliminary screening. One of these screens is the image they have of the organization, which can attract or repel them.

In sum, the ideal job specifications preferred by an organization may have to be adjusted to meet the realities of the labor market, government, or union restrictions, the limitations of its policies and practices, and its image. If an inadequate number of high-quality people apply, the organization may have to adjust the job to fit the best applicant or increase its recruiting efforts.

from: *Human Resource Management*, 1998

Words and Expressions

vacancy ['veikənsi] *n.* 空缺
orientation [ˌɔ(ː)rien'teiʃən] *n.* 介绍
budget ['bʌdʒit] *n.* 预算
highlight ['hailait] *v.* 强调
diagnostic [ˌdaiəg'nɔstik] *adj.* 诊断的
recruiter [ri'kruːtə(r)] *n.* 招聘人员
discrimination [disˌkrimi'neiʃən] *n.* 歧视
civic ['sivik] *adj.* 公民的
demographic [deməˈgræfik] *adj.* 人口统计学的

verify ['verifai] v. 证实
eligibility [ə,lidʒə'biliti] n. 合格
citizenship ['sitizənʃip] n. 公民权
amnesty ['æmnest] n. 赦免
desist [di'zist] v. 终止
fine [fain] n. 罚款
attorney [ə'tə:ni] n. 律师
valid ['vælid] adj. 有效的
index ['indeks] n. 目录
discriminatory [di'skriminətɔ:ri] adj. 表现出歧视的
Hispanic [his'pænik] n. 美籍西班牙人
desirable [di'zaiərəbl] adj. 值得要的
detrimental [,detri'mentl] adj. 有害的
veteran ['vetərən] n. 退伍军人
ex-convict [,ekskən'vikt] n. 从前曾被判刑的人
nepotism ['nepətizəm] n. 重用亲信
exude [ig'zju:d] v. 洋溢
preliminary [pri'liminəri] n. 初步的
screening [skri:niŋ] n. 筛选
The Immigration Reform and Control Act (IRCA) 移民改革和管制法
employer sanction 雇主制裁
employment authorization 工作许可证
to fit into 适合
unauthorized aliens 没有公民权的外国人
a telephone verification 电话确认系统
work documentation 工作证件
The federal Department of Labor 联邦劳动部
State divisions of employment security and labor 州立就业安全与劳动部
to keep track of 跟踪
help-wanted ads 招聘广告

the base year 基年
promotion from within 内部提拔
Merck 默克集团有限公司
Johnson & Johnson 美国强生公司

Difficult Sentences

① Recruitment refers to organizational activities that influence the number and types of applicants who apply for a job and whether the applicants accept jobs that are offered.
招聘指的是影响申请获得工作职位人员数量和类型的组织活动，以及申请者是否接受工作职位。

② A person or firm may be charged criminally for having a pattern of violations, with a maximum sentence per violation of six months' imprisonment or a $3,000 fine, or both.
个人或公司可能会因为典型的违规行为受到刑事指控，每次违规最高处罚为6个月监禁或3,000美元罚款，或者两刑并用。

③ In addition, President Clinton signed an executive order in 1996 stipulating that contractors may be ineligible to receive new federal contracts for one year or longer if they are caught using undocumented workers.
此外，克林顿总统于1996年签署了一项行政法令，规定如果发现联邦合约的签署人使用没有身份证明的人做工，那么这些人将会在一年或更长的时间里不能接受新的联邦合约。

④ However, when full employment has nearly reached an area, skillful and prolonged recruiting may be necessary to attract any applicants who fulfill the expectations of the organization.
然而，在地区就业充分时，或许就需要技巧娴熟没有时间限制的招聘活动来吸引能够满足组织各项要求的申请人。

⑤ The number of African-American, Hispanic, Asian or Pacific Islander, Native American, or Alaskan native employees in the workforce depends largely on the availability of these minority employees in the relevant labor market.

组织中的员工总数中非裔美国人、拉丁美裔美国人、亚裔美国人或太平洋岛屿的居民、美国土著或阿拉斯加本土居民的数量在很大程度上取决于这些少数族裔雇员在相关劳动力市场的可获得情况。

⑥ Thus, for organizations like Merck, 3M, Coca-Cola, and Johnson & Johnson that usually rank high on surveys such as those of Fortune magazine, the time and effort needed to recruit high-quality workers may be less than for their less fortunate competitors who rank poorly.

因此，对于默克、3M、可口可乐和强生这样的经常荣登《财富》等杂志调查前列的公司来说，招聘到高素质的员工所花费的时间和力气可能会比排名靠后的竞争者所花费的要少。

Phrases and Patterns

1. Whether... depends on... 取决于
   Whether potential employees will respond to the recruiting effort depends on the attitudes they have developed toward those tasks.
   潜在的雇员是否会对这些招聘努力做出反应取决于他们对那些任务所采取的态度。
   How many applicants are available depends on whether the economy is growing.
   能有多少名申请者来应聘取决于经济水平是否在提高。

2. fit into 归为
   Its basic features fit into four broad categories.
   （移民改革和管制法）的基本特征归为四大类。
   This card just fits nicely into that envelope.
   这个卡片正好能装进那个信封里。

3. go into effect 生效
   The IRCA went into effect in May 1988.

移民改革和管制法在 1988 年 5 月生效。
The new seat-belt regulations went into effect last month.
新的安全带管理规则上月生效。
4. As far as... are concerned 就……而言

As far as the applicants are concerned, their abilities and past work experience affect how they go about seeking a job.
就申请者而言，他们的能力和以往的工作经历会影响他们着手寻找工作的方式。
The rise in interest rates will be disastrous as far as small firms are concerned.
利率增加对于小公司来说是大祸临头。
5. look to 指望；从……入手

They may look to these sources first.
他们会先从这些人员来源入手。
The organization can look to sources internal to the company.
组织可以从公司内部的人员来源入手。

3.2 Methods of Recruiting
招聘方法

Introduction

Once an organization has decided it needs additional or replacement employees, it is faced with the decision of how to generate the necessary applications. The organization can look to sources internal to the company and, if necessary, to sources external to the company. Most organizations have to use both internal and external sources to generate a sufficient number of applicants. Whenever there is an inadequate supply of labor and skills inside the organization, it must effectively "get its message across" to external candidates. It is here that the organization's choice of a particular method of recruitment can make all the difference in the success the recruiting efforts.

Internal Recruiting

Job Posting

Organizations can make effective use of skills inventories for identifying internal applicants for job vacancies. It is difficult, however, for HR managers to be aware of all current employees who might be interested in the vacancy. To help with this problem, they use an approach called job posting and bidding.

In the past, job posting was little more than the use of bulletin boards and company publications for advertising job openings. Today, however, job posting has become one of the more innovative recruiting techniques being used by organizations. Many companies now see job posting as an integrated component of an effective career management system.

A model job-posting program was implemented at National Semiconductor. Postings are computerized and easily accessible to employees. Computer software allows the employees to match an available job with their skills and experience. It then highlights where gaps exist so the employees know what is necessary if they wish to be competitive for a given job. Amoco's career management system includes a similar type of job posting program. Openings in this organization are posted on a worldwide electronic system. If an employee applies for a transfer to posted position and is turned down, then the person who posted the job is required to send the "applicant" specific feedback about why he or she was not selected[①].

Inside Moonlighting and Employees' Friends

If there is a short-term labor shortage, or if no great amount of additional work is necessary, the organization can use inside moonlighting. It could offer to pay bonuses of various types to people not on a time payroll. Overtime procedures are already developed for those on time payrolls.

External Recruiting

When an organization has exhausted its internal supply of applicants, it must turn to external sources to supplement its workforce. Research indicates that walk-ins provide an important external source of applicants. As the labor shortages of the 1990s increase, however, organizations are becoming more proactive in their recruitment efforts.

A number of methods are available for external recruiting. Media advertising, employment databases, employment agencies, executive search firms, special-events recruiting, and summer internships are discussed here. There is also a separate section on college recruitment of potential managers and professionals.

Media Advertisements

Organizations advertise to acquire recruits. Various media are used, the most common being help-wanted ads in daily newspapers. Organizations also advertise for people in trade and professional publications. Other media used are billboards, subway and bus cards, radio, telephone, and television. Some job seekers do a reverse twist; they advertise for a situation wanted and reward anyone who tips them off about a job[2].

In developing a recruitment advertisement, a good place to begin is with the corporate image. General Mills used its Trix cereal logo to create instant recognition among MBA graduates. The ad featured the Trix rabbit with the headline, "It's Not Kid Stuff Anymore." The copy continued, "Now you're an MBA who's looking for a dynamic growth-directed career environment···Look to General Mills, because it's not kid stuff anymore. It's your future."

Simply using a corporate logo is not enough, however. Effective recruiting advertising is consistent with the overall corporate image; that is, the advertisement is seen as an extension of the company. Therefore, it must be representative of the values that the corporation is seeking in its employees. Apple Computer's advertising campaign has been very successful, in large part because it has achieved this congruence.

Computer Databases

Resume databases are one of the most rapidly growing sources of potential applicants available to an organization. Just a few years ago, the only effective databases were those maintained by executive search firms. Now, hundreds of university alumni groups keep detailed records of their graduates. Even more dramatically, the Internet is becoming a primary source of recruiting information.

Organizations are beginning to understand the potential of the Internet as a recruiting tool and are also beginning to appreciate how cost-effective it can be. For example, using an executive search firm might cost an organization as much as 30 percent of a position's first-year salary as a commission. A large, multicolored advertisement in a professional journal can easily cost $10,000 or more. Compare these figures with membership fees of about $4,000 for an online employment site such as the Online Career Center (http://www.occ.com), which provides rapid access to literally thousands of prospective applicants.

Organizations are also beginning to see that having their own home page on the Internet can be an effective addition to their overall recruitment strategy. A typical organizational home page will provide background information about the company, its products and services, and employment opportunities and application procedures[③]. Many also include online resumes templates that can be completed and sent via the Internet.

Employment Agencies and Executive Search Firms

Although similar in purpose, employment agencies and executive search firms differ in many important ways. Executive search firms tend to concentrate their efforts on higher-level managerial positions with salaries in excess of $50,000, while agencies deal primarily with middle-level management or below. Most executive search firms are on retainer, which means that the organization pays them a fee whether or not their efforts are successful. In contrast, agencies are usually paid only when they have actually provided a new hire. Finally, executive search firms usually charge higher fees for their services, one of the reasons that organizations are willing to pay these higher fees is that executive search firms frequently engage in their recruiting efforts while maintaining the confidentiality of both the recruiting organization and the person being recruited.

Special-events Recruiting

When the supply of employees available is not large or when the organization is new or not well known, some organizations have successfully used special events to attract potential employees. They may stage open houses, schedule visits to headquarters, provide literature, and advertise these events in appropriate media[④]. To attract professionals, organizations may have hospitality suites at professional meetings. Executives also make speeches at association meetings or schools to get the organization's image across. Ford Motor Company has conducted symposia on college campuses and sponsored cultural events to attract attention to its qualifications as a good employer.

One of the most interesting approaches is to provide job fairs. A group of firms sponsors a meeting or exhibition at which each has a booth to publicize jobs available. Some experts claim that recruiting costs have been cut 80 percent using these methods. They may be scheduled on holidays to reach college students who are home at that time or to give people who are already employed a chance to look around. This technique is especially useful for smaller, less well known employers. It appeals to job seekers who wish to locate in a particular area and those wanting to minimize travel and interview time. For example, a recent job fair held in Virginia was able to generate 4,000 job candidates in a little under four hours of operation.

Summer Internships

Another approach to recruiting and getting specialized work done that has been tried by organizations is to hire students as interns during the summer or part time during the school year. The list of organizations using internships is extensive; it includes AT&T, General Motors, most major accounting firms, the life insurance industry, and so forth. The use of internships is, in fact, dramatically increasing. Some estimates suggest that nearly, one out of every three students at four-year universities will have one or more internship experiences before graduation. Internship programs have a number of purposes. They allow organizations to get specific projects done, expose themselves to talented potential employees who may become their "recruiters" at school, and provide trial-run employment to determine if they want to hire particular people full time.

A second new reason that organizations are using more internships is to improve the diversity of their recruitment efforts. Many companies claim that they want to be more aggressive in recruiting minorities but say that the competition for talented people is severe. To help, Inroads Inc. of Saint Louis locates and places high-performing minority students in internship programs. Inroads have working relationships with organizations in 33 different states. Its major supporters include NationsBank, GE Capital Services, and AT&T.

From the student's point of view, the summer internship means a job with pay; NCR, for example, provides students with approximately

600 paid internships each year. An internship can also mean real work experience for the student; a possible future job; a chance to use one's talents in a realistic environment; and in some cases, earning course credit hours. In a way, it is a short form of some co-op college work and study programs.

College Recruiting

There is a growing gap between the skills that organizations will need over the next several years and those currently possessed by potential employees. Also, although the number of jobs requiring a college degree is expected to increase rapidly, the Department of Labor predicts that there will be 18 million college graduates competing for the 14 million college-level jobs available in the year 2005[5]. College recruiting can be extremely difficult, time-consuming, and expensive for the organization. Nonetheless, recruiters generally believe that college recruiting is one of the most effective ways of identifying talented employees. All this suggests that college recruiting will continue to play an important role in organizations' overall recruitment strategies, but that organizations will be careful about controlling expenses.

Good recruiters are not going to guarantee success in filling positions, however. Although they can and do make a difference, applicants' decisions are affected more by characteristics of the job and the organization than they are by particular characteristics of recruiters. Other research also suggests that recruiters may have very little positive influence on an applicant's choice. Recruiters do make a difference when they do not present themselves well. In this case, they can have a negative effect on applicants even when the job and the organization are both appealing.

from: Human Resource Management, 1998

Words and Expressions

inventory ['invəntri] n. 清查；对能力的评估
transfer [træns'fə:] n. 调动
bonus ['bəunəs] n. 奖金
payroll ['peirəul] n. 薪金总额
exhaust [ig'zɔ:st] v. 使……枯竭
walk-in ['wɔ:k,in] n. 未经预约而来的人
proactive [,prəu'æktiv] adj. 抢先的
billboard ['bilbɔ:d] n. 广告牌
logo ['lɔgəu] n. 标识语
dynamic [dai'næmik] adj. 有活力的
extension [iks'tenʃən] n. 延伸
congruence ['kɔŋgruəns] n. 一致
alumni [ə'lʌmnai] [ə'lʌmnəs] n. 男校友(alumnus 的复数)
appreciate [ə'pri:ʃieit] v. 意识到
cost-effective ['kɔsti'fektiv] adj. 有成本效益的
commission [kə'miʃən] n. 佣金
template ['templit] n. 模板
managerial [,mænə'dʒiəriəl] adj. 管理的
confidentiality [kənfi,denʃi'æliti] n. 机密性
stage [steidʒ] v. 安排和进行
schedule ['skedʒjul] v. 制定计划
symposia [sim'pɔziə] n. 讨论会
booth [bu:θ] n. 售货亭
internship ['intə:nʃip] n. 实习期
intern ['in'tə:n] n. 实习生
extensive [iks'tensiv] adj. 大量的
working ['wə:kiŋ] adj. 运转的
job posting and bidding 工作职位与申请报告

inside moonlighting 内部兼职
General Mills 通用磨坊（大型跨国食品公司）
Trix 特里克斯（跨国公司生产系列硬盘录像机及矩阵系统）
MBA (Master of Business Administration) 工商管理硕士
employment agency 职业介绍所
executive search firms 猎头公司
in excess of 超过
hospitality suite 比较安静的度假酒店套房
professional meeting 就业供需洽谈会
to get cross 传达
job fairs 招聘会
General Motors 通用汽车公司
NationsBank 美国联机银行（位于得克萨斯州）
GE Capital Services 美国通用电气金融事业公司（通用公司的子公司）
At & T 美国电话电报公司
trial-run employment 模拟就业
NCR 全球领先的技术公司（总部设于美国俄亥俄州）
course credit hours 课程学分
co-op 合作（co-operation 的缩写）
to make a difference 要紧

Difficult Sentences

① If an employee applies for a transfer to posted position and is turned down, then the person who posted the job is required to send the "applicant" specific feedback about why he or she was not selected.
如果员工申请调动到公开招聘的岗位但是没有成功,那么公布招聘岗位的人需要给申请人发送具体的反馈信息说明没有被选择的原因。

② Some job seekers do a reverse twist; they advertise for a situation wanted and reward anyone who tips them off about a job.

有一些找工作的人采取相反的做法,他们刊登广告寻求招聘机会,出资酬谢给他们提供内部就业信息的人。

③ A typical organizational home page will provide background information about the company, its products and services, and employment opportunities and application procedures.

公司主页一般都会提供有关公司、公司产品和服务、就业机会和申请程序的背景信息。

④ They may stage open houses, schedule visits to headquarters, provide literature, and advertise these events in appropriate media.

他们会举行免费现场咨询,安排时间参观总部,提供文字资料,并且在相关媒体刊登广告进行宣传。

⑤ Also, although the number of jobs requiring a college degree is expected to increase rapidly, the Department of Labor predicts that there will be 18 million college graduates competing for the 14 million college-level jobs available in the year 2005.

而且,尽管要求大学学历的就业岗位数量有望迅速增加,但是劳动部预测在2005年将有1,800万大学毕业生竞聘1,400万个要求具有大学学历的就业岗位。

Phrases and Patterns

1. match... with... 匹配;相适合

   Computer software allows the employees to match an available job with their skills and experience.

   计算机软件可以使员工的工作技能和经验与可选择的工作匹配起来。

   It is considered to be very fortunate to be able to match one's career with his or her interest.

   能够从事自己感兴趣的事业是非常幸运的。

2. be representative of 体现出;代表

   Therefore, it must be representative of the values that the corporation is seeking in its employees.

因此,它(招聘广告)必须体现出公司在雇员身上所寻求的价值观念。

A questionnaire answered by 500 people is not truly representative of national opinion.

一份500人作答的调查问卷不能真正代表全国人民的意见。

3. access to 选取;访问;接近、进入、出去或使用的权力

The Online Career Center (http://www.occ.com) provides rapid access to literally thousands of prospective applicants.

通过事业中心在线可以访问成千上万的准申请人。

No one has access to the restricted area.

任何人都无权进入禁区。

3.3 Employment Advertising and Organizational Self-presentation
招聘广告和组织的自我展示

Available research on advertising has focused almost solely on consumer (product) ads, paying little or no attention to employment advertising. However, employment advertising has occupied organizational scholars, primarily in research on recruiting sources and surveys report that up to 90 per cent of organizations post-employment ads. The assumption in organizational research is that ads are vehicles for recruiting employees to fill job openings. Yet organizationally posted employment ads present more than a listing of available vacancies; this is suggested by the elaborate text of many ads, which provides more information than a notice about an employment opportunity would require[①]. Consider the following text taken from an ad posted by the Ernst & Young consulting firm, announcing an opening for an information technology consultant.

We empower the people who power the world. The power to move. The power to solve. The power to apply leading-edge technology and business expertise that keep top global Fortune 500 industries on target with aggressive goals and strategies. That's the power of a world leader—the power of Ernst & Young, the fastest growing professional services firm... There Isn't a Business We Can't Improve.

This text advertises aspects of the posting organization as an employer and an organization that far exceed the notice of a vacancy: that the organization is founded on power, that it is financially successful (one of the Fortune 500 group), that it is aggressive, fast-growing and professional, and that it is a services firm. A vacancy for a technology consultant could have been posted without this information. This ad makes available information about the way this employer views employment—in particular, information about the organizational culture that an employee is expected to embrace②.

This and similar texts in other ads are not uncommon, and may be viewed as organizational marketing of its cultural identity, perhaps in the face of institutional pressures. Other texts common in ads can be interpreted as displays of organizational compliance with the social order. Satisfying legal demands is clearly one incentive for posting employment ads, as evident in the US, for example, with text indicating compliance with equal employment opportunity requirements (e.g., "We are an equal opportunity employer" or "An EEO employer"). However, ads include far more than would be necessary to satisfy legal requirements, typically offering a rich set of information about the organization and its conceptions of employment③.

This is a critical foundation for the claim posited in Proposition 1— namely, that individuals use employment ads to make sense of employment. Proposition 1 suggests that people view the ads they read- which generally are placed in groups; it is rare to find an employment ad in isolation—as a survey of alternative conceptions of employment. Proposition 2, below, suggests that, at the organizational level, ads provide pertinent information about employment at a given time. Since ads are clearly planned rather than spontaneous, Proposition 2 refers to ads as presenting organizational conceptions of employment, rather than actual employment:

Proposition 2: Employment advertising offers organization-level self-presentation of how employment is conceived by the posting employer.

As with Proposition 1 and job-seeking, Proposition 2 does not try to argue that ads do not serve to attract candidates for employment with an organization. However, it does make the case that beyond this traditional purpose, employment ads serve as a forum for organizational self-presentation, with a particular focus on self-presentation of organizational conception of employment[4]. As such, multiple ads can provide information about alternative conceptions of employment by different employers.

For example, the employer cited above, which presented itself in an employment ad as powerful, aggressive, growing, and successful, suggests to readers that these organizational culture values can be integral to the employment experience. Alternately, an organization may present employment as involving non-traditional thinking and focusing on the future. For instance, ads by an Indianapolis manufacturer of electronic goods featured a work of modern art and the inscription "the future belongs to those who can go beyond the obvious." Likewise, a series of ads by Intel Corporation featured headings like "Does your life offer enough variety?" and "Is variety really the spice of life?" followed by the challenge "Answer the Question." Extrapolating from these ads, readers might presume that variety and challenge can be features of current employment. The organizational self-presentation in employment ads referred to in Proposition 2 is distinct from self-presentation of the organization as, for example, a producer of goods, as found in product advertising. Employment advertising may include elements related to the product, but would more likely focus on issues related to requirements from employees, intrinsic and extrinsic rewards from employment, psychological climate, and organizational culture⑤. Note that just as product ads do not necessarily describe the item being touted accurately and fully, employment ads may not accurately and fully represent the employment experience in the posting organization. But since ads are paid for and clearly associated with the organizations that post them, they can be viewed as organizational artifacts, similar to logos, brand names, uniforms, or office design. The involvement of advertising agencies in posting employment ads, and the use of corporate logos, slogans, and colors in employment ads, further suggests ads to be related to the posting employer's image and identity.

Several empirical observations could constitute support for Proposition 2. The proposition would be qualitatively supported if ads were shown to convey accepted components of the idea of employment. Most basically, ads should convey the idea that employment is an exchange between employers and employees, identifying possible rewards to be provided by the former for the skills and abilities of the latter. Additional support would be if ads convey differences between professions and societies in elements of the employment exchange. Mental models of employment are unlikely to be idiosyncratic but rather are likely to be shared by communities, and so elements of these shared assumptions, and of cultural variations between societies, should be evident in employment ads. For example, Proposition 2 would predict a heavy emphasis on equal opportunity in employment ads in North America, but not in other countries where equal opportunity is not a major value. Further support for Proposition 2 would be ads that include information about the context and culture of employment and organizations but do not specify a particular job vacancy.

In summary, Proposition 2—that ads are instances of organizational self-presentation of their conception of employment—is a foundation for Proposition 1, that the reading of employment ads facilitates individual sense-making of employment. The two propositions together <u>lay the ground for</u> a theory of the evolution of communal conceptions of employment. Individual participants in the job market, as they engage in sense-making toward continually refining their mental model of the idea of employment, turn to information about alternative employment arrangements. Such information is offered by organizational employment ads. Organizations therefore influence individual sense-making of the idea of employment through their self-presentation in employment ads. The two propositions suggest that the influence of employment ads follows the dramaturgical process described by Goffman and Brissett and Edgley: The reality depicted in advertising may become a reality assumed by people who read advertising. Employment advertising becomes a pivotal connection not only between new hires and vacant employment slots, but also between individual sense-making and organizational self-presentation.

Two studies, as described next, offer initial support for the two propositions. Study 1 maintains an individual level of analysis, reporting on when and why people read employment ads. Study 2 reports on an ad-level of analysis, interpreting the information about employment disseminated by employment advertising.

from: *Sense-making of employment*, *Journal of Organizational Behavior*, 2006

Words and Expressions

vehicle ['viːikl] *n.* 手段

aggressive [ə'ɡresiv] *adj.* 积极进取的

consultant [kən'sʌltənt] n. 顾问
compliance [kəm'plaiəns] n. 顺从
incentive [in'sentiv] n. 诱因
posit ['pɔzit] v. 提出以
proposition [ˌprɔpə'ziʃən] n. 命题
spontaneous [spɔn'teiniəs] adj. 自然产生的
forum ['fɔːrəm] n. 论坛
integral ['intigrəl] adj. 必须的
alternately [ɔːl'təːnitli] adv. 或者
Indianapolis ['indiə'næpəlis] n. 印第安纳波利斯[美国印第安纳州首府]
spice [spais] n. 调味品
extrapolate [eks'træpəleit] v. 推断
intrinsic [in'trinsik] adj. 本质的
extrinsic [eks'trinsik] adj. 非本质的
tout [taut] v. 吹捧
artifact ['ɑːtifækt] n. 典型产物
slogan ['sləugən] n. 口号
image ['imidʒ] n. 形象
identity [ai'dentiti] n. 身份
empirical [em'pirikəl] adj. 经验的
constitute ['kɔnstitjuːt] v. 构成
additional [ə'diʃənəl] adj. 另外的
convey [kən'vei] v. 传达
idiosyncratic [ˌidiəusin'krætik] adj. 特殊的
specify ['spesifai] v. 明确说明
facilitate [fə'siliteit] v. 使容易
pivotal ['pivətəl] adj. 关键的
slot [slɔt] n. 职位
disseminate [di'semineit] v. 散布

self-presentation 自我展现
in the face of 面对
to make sense of 弄懂……的意思
as such 同样地
to serve as 充当
Intel Corporation 英特尔公司
employment advertising 招聘广告
psychological climate 社会心理环境
mental models of employment 就业心智模式

Difficult Sentences

① Yet organizationally posted employment ads present more than a listing of available vacancies; this is suggested by the elaborate text of many ads, which provides more information than a notice about an employment opportunity would require.
然而,组织公布的招聘广告呈现的不仅仅是简单罗列的空缺职位;许多详细阐述的广告文本就表明这一点,这些广告提供的信息比就业机会通知所要求的信息要多。

② This ad makes available information about the way this employer views employment—in particular, information about the organizational culture that an employee is expected to embrace.
这条广告提供信息表明这家企业对雇用的看法,特别是雇员将要迎接的企业文化信息。

③ However, ads include far more than would be necessary to satisfy legal requirements, typically offering a rich set of information about the organization and its conceptions of employment.
然而,广告所包括的信息远远超过满足法律要求所必须的信息,一般来讲,这些广告都提供了大量的信息,让人能够了解这个组织,了解它的雇用观念。

④ However, it does make the case that beyond this traditional purpose, employment ads serve as a forum for organizational self-presentation, with a particular focus on self-presentation of organizational conception of employment.

然而,实际情况也确实是这样:除了这一传统的目的(吸引候选者到组织就业),招聘广告还可以是组织进行自我展示的论坛,展示的核心是组织的雇佣观念。

⑤ Employment advertising may include elements related to the product, but would more likely focus on issues related to requirements from employees, intrinsic and extrinsic rewards from employment, psychological climate, and organizational culture.

招聘广告可以包括有关产品的要素,但是更多的是着眼于有关对雇员的要求、内部和外部的工作激励、社会心理环境或氛围和组织文化等方面的问题。

Phrases and Patterns

1. in the face of 面临;不管
   This and similar texts in other ads may be viewed as organizational marketing of its cultural identity, perhaps in the face of institutional pressures.
   这个广告中的文字信息可以看做是公司对其文化身份的营销,或许置各种制度压力于不顾。
   A lot of middle-aged intellectuals devote all their time and energy to work, even in the face of physical pressures.
   很多中年知识分子把全部时间和精力都用来工作,不考虑身体情况。

2. refer to... as... 称……为……;认为……是……
   Proposition 2 refers to ads as presenting organizational conceptions of employment, rather than actual employment.
   命题 2 认为广告体现出公司对雇佣的理解,而不是实际雇佣行为。

They refer to mutual understanding as thinking from each other's perspective.

他们认为相互理解就是从对方的角度进行考虑。

3. lay the ground for 为……奠定基础

The two propositions together lay the ground for a theory of the evolution of communal conceptions of employment.

这两个命题一起给共有的雇佣观念的演化奠定了理论基础。

Early experiments with military rockets laid the ground for space travel.

早年对军用火箭进行的试验为发展航天技术奠定了基础。

Questions

1. What factors play a major role in the recruiting job?
2. What are the methods of internal recruiting?
3. What are the methods of external recruiting?

4

Employees Selection
员工甄选

【本章导读】 本章介绍甄选员工过程中的一些主要问题。4.1 介绍选择员工的主要标准,如信度、效度、普遍性、一致性、法律性等。4.2 介绍选择员工的主要方法,包括面试、推荐人和自我介绍材料、体能测试、智力测试、性格测试、实践操作、诚实测试和毒品测试等。4.3 论述应用多标准群体决议支持对于员工选择的意义。

4.1 Generic Standards in Employees Selection
选择员工的一般标准

Introduction

The competitive aspects of selection decisions become even more critical when firms hire from the same labor market. If one company systematically skims off the best applicants, the remaining companies must make do with what is left. For example, in the California labor market for security guards, 20 percent of the applicants have prior criminal convictions. If half of the companies in this market are systematically screening and half are not, it is only a matter of time until those who fail to screen experience one problem or another[1].

The purpose of this chapter is to familiarize you with ways to minimize errors in employee selection and placement and, in doing so, to increase your company's competitive position.

Selection Method Standards

Personnel selection is the process by which companies decide who will or will not be allowed into their organization. Several generic standards should be met in any selection process. We focus on five: (1) reliability, (2) validity, (3) generalizability, (4) utility, and (5) legality. The first four of these standards build off each other: The preceding standard is often necessary but not sufficient for the one that follows[2]. This is less the case with legal standards. However, a thorough understanding of the first four standards helps us understand the rationale underlying many of the legal standards.

Reliability

Much of the work in personnel selection involves measuring characteristics of people to determine who will be accepted for job openings. For example, we might be interested in applicants' physical characteristics (e. g., strength or endurance), their cognitive abilities (e. g., mathematics ability or verbal reasoning capacity), or aspects of their personality (e. g., their initiative or integrity). Whatever the specific focus, in the end we need to quantify people on these dimensions (i. e., assign numbers to them) so we can order them from high to low on the characteristic of interest. Once people are ordered in this way, we can then make decisions about whom to hire and whom to reject.

One of the key standards for any measuring device is its reliability. We <u>define</u> reliability <u>as</u> the degree to which a measure is free from random error. If a measure of some supposedly stable characteristic such as intelligence is reliable, then the score a person receives based on that measure will be consistent over time and over different contexts.

Validity

We <u>define</u> validity <u>as</u> the extent to which performance on the measure is associated with performance on the job. A measure must be reliable if it is to have any validity. On the other hand, we can reliably measure many characteristics (e. g. , height) that may have no relationship to whether someone can perform a job. For this reason, reliability is <u>a necessary but insufficient condition</u> for validity.

There are two primary methods for determining the validity of a selection method. One of these focuses on the relationship between scores on the selection measure and scores on some measure of job performance. The other focuses on the relationship between the content of the selection method (e. g. , the nature of the items) and the content of the job.

Generalizability

Generalizability is defined as the degree to which the validity of a selection method established in one context extends to other contexts. There are three primary "contexts" over which we might like to generalize: different situations (i. e. , jobs or organizations), different samples of people, and different time periods. Just as reliability is necessary but not sufficient for validity, validity <u>is necessary but not sufficient</u> for generalizability.

It was once believed, for example, that validity coefficients were <u>situationally</u> specific—that is, the level of correlation between test and performance varied as one went from one organization to another, even though the jobs studied seemed to be identical[3]. Subsequent research has indicated that this is largely false. Rather, tests tend to show similar levels of correlation even across jobs that are only somewhat similar (at least for tests of intelligence or cognitive ability). Correlations with these kinds of tests do change as one goes across widely different kinds of jobs, however. Specifically, the more complex the job, the higher the validity of many tests.

It was also believed that tests showed differential subgroup validity, which meant that the validity coefficient for any test-job performance pair was different for people of different races or sex. This belief was also refuted by subsequent research, and in general, one finds very similar levels of correlations across different groups of people.

Because the evidence suggests that test validity often extends across situations and subgroups, validity generalization stands as an alternative for validating selection methods for companies that cannot employ criterion-related or content validation. Validity generalization is a three-step process. First, the company provides evidence from previous criterion-related validity studies conducted in other situations that shows that a specific test (e.g., a test of emotional stability) is a valid predictor for a specific job (security guard in a large company)[4]. Second, the company provides evidence from job analysis to document that the specific job (security guard in a small company) is similar in all major respects to the job validated elsewhere (in the large company). Finally, if the company can show that it uses a test that is the same as or similar to that used in the validated setting (i.e., the large company), then one can "generalize" the validity from the first context (large company) to the new context (small company).

Although recent evidence supports the generalizability of many kinds of tests across situations and subgroups, it does not support the generalizability of tests across time. Indeed, it seems that the correlations tend to get smaller as the time interval lengthens. Although there is some controversy over the consistency of this downward pattern, the fact that the validities vary over time seems well accepted by researchers in this area[5].

Utility

Utility is the degree to which the information provided by selection methods enhances the effectiveness of selecting personnel in real organizations. In general, the more reliable, valid, and generalizable the selection method is, the more utility it will have. On the other hand, many characteristics of particular selection contexts enhance or detract from the usefulness of given selection methods, even when reliability, validity, and generalizability are held constant.

Legality

The final standard that any selection method should adhere to is legality. All selection methods should conform to existing laws and existing legal precedents. Many of the issues related to selecting employees safely under U.S. law were discussed generically in following passages.

from: *Human Resource Management*: *Gaining a Competitive Advantage*, 1994

Words and Expressions

criminal ['kriminl] *adj.* 刑事的
conviction [kən'vikʃən] *n.* 定罪
placement ['pleismənt] *n.* 工作安排
reliability [ri͵laiə'biliti] *n.* 信度
validity [və'liditi] *n.* 效度
coefficient [͵kəui'fiʃənt] *n.* 系数
generalizability ['dʒenərə͵laizə'biliti] *n.* 普遍性
utility [juː'tiliti] *n.* 效用性
legality [li(ː)'gæliti] *n.* 合法性
rationale ['ræʃə'nɑːli] *n.* 基本原理
personality [͵pəːsə'næliti] *n.* 个性
initiative [i'niʃiətiv] *n.* 进取心

integrity [in'teɡriti] *n.* 正直
quantify ['kwɔntifai] *v.* 量化
order ['ɔ:də] *v.* 排序
random ['rændəm] *adj.* 随机的
supposedly [sə'pəuzidli] *adv.* 按照推测
generalize ['dʒenərəlaiz] *v.* 归纳
subsequent ['sʌbsikwənt] *adj.* 后来的
refute [ri'fju:t] *v.* 驳倒
validate ['vælideit] *v.* 使有效
consistency [kən'sistənsi] *n.* 一致性
hold [həuld] *v.* 认为
precedent [pri'si:dənt] *n.* 先例
to skim off 提出精华
to make do with 设法应付
security guard 警卫
physical characteristics 身体特征
random errors 随机失误
verbal reasoning 语言推理
content validation 内容的正确性
downward pattern 自上而下的模式
to detract from 降低
to adhere to 坚持
to conform to 遵照

Difficult Sentences

① If half of the companies in this market are systematically screening and half are not, it is only a matter of time until those who fail to screen experience one problem or another.
如果这个市场上有一半的公司在进行系统的筛选(工作申请者)而另一半没有,那么没有进行系统筛选的公司迟早会遇到接踵而

来的问题。

② The first four of these standards build off each other: The preceding standard is often necessary but not sufficient for the one that follows.
前四个标准都是在彼此基础之上发展起来的:前一个标准是后一个标准的必要但不充分条件。

③ It was once believed, for example, that validity coefficients were situationally specific—that is, the level of correlation between test and performance varied as one went from one organization to another, even though the jobs studied seemed to be identical.
例如,曾经一度有这样的观点:效度系数是视情况而定的,也就是,测试和绩效之间的关联程度随着雇员在不同的组织工作变更而变化,即使所研究的工作岗位似乎是一样的。

④ First, the company provides evidence from previous criterion-related validity studies conducted in other situations that shows that a specific test (e.g., a test of emotional stability) is a valid predictor for a specific job (security guard in a large company).
首先,该公司用以前在其他情况下进行的关于标准的效度研究作为证据表明特定的测试(例如情感稳定性测试)可以有效地预测特定的工作岗位(大公司里的保安职位或岗位)。

⑤ Although there is some controversy over the consistency of this downward pattern, the fact that the validities vary over time seems well accepted by researchers in this area.
尽管这种自上而下的模式还存在着一些争论,但是该领域的研究者完全同意效度随时间变化而变化。

Phrases and Patterns

1. define... as... 把……定义为……
We define reliability as the degree to which a measure is free from random error.
我们把信度定义为量度标准没有随机失误的程度。

We define validity as the extent to which performance on the measure is associated with performance on the job.

我们把效度定义为测量出来的绩效和工作中要求的绩效的相关程度。

2. a necessary but insufficient condition 必要但不充分条件

For this reason, reliability is a necessary but insufficient condition for validity.

由于这个原因,信度是效度的必要但不充分条件。

Just as reliability is necessary but not sufficient for validity, validity is necessary but not sufficient for generalizability.

就像信度是效度的必要但不充分条件一样,效度也是普遍性的必要但不充分条件。

3. the more..., the more... 越……,越……

The more complex the job, the higher the validity of many tests.

工作难度越大,多次测试的效度就越高。

The greater the obstacle, the more glory in overcoming.

障碍越是巨大,逾越它也就越感自豪。

4.2 Selection Methods
员工甄选的若干方法

Introduction

The first half of this chapter laid out the five standards by which we can judge selection measures. In the second half of this chapter, we examine the common selection methods used in various organizations and discuss their advantages and disadvantages in terms of these standards.

Interviews

A selection interview has been defined as "a dialogue initiated by one or more persons to gather information and evaluate the qualifications of an applicant for employment"①. The selection interview is the most wide-spread selection method employed in organizations.

Unfortunately, the long history of research on the employment interview suggests that, without proper care, it can be unreliable and low invalidity. It is simply not reasonable to think that unstructured, rambling conversations between interviewers and applicants will provide much information useful in predicting the job candidate's future success. Moreover, interviews are relatively costly because they require at least one person to interview another person, and these persons have to be brought to the same geographic location.

Finally, in terms of legality, the subjectivity embodied in the process often makes applicants upset, particularly if they fail to get a job after being asked apparently irrelevant questions like, "If you were a car, what kind of car would you be?" This only increases the probability that the applicants will take legal action against the company.

References and Biographical Data

Just as few employers would think of hiring someone without an interview, nearly all employers also use some method for getting background information on applicants before an interview. This information can be solicited from the people who know the candidate through reference checks. It can also be solicited directly from the candidate through an application that asks for biographical data.

The evidence on the reliability and validity of reference checks suggests that these are, at best, weak predictors of future success on the job. The main reason for this low validity is that the evaluations supplied in most reference letters are so positive that it is hard to differentiate applicants. As Northwestern Bell's district manager of management employment notes, they all say, "This is the greatest individual the world has ever seen, the next president, at least."... It isn't always accurate.

This problem with reference letters has two causes. First, the applicant usually gets to choose who writes the letter and can thus choose only those writers who think the highest of his or her abilities. Second, since letter writers can never be sure who will read the letters, they may fear that supplying damaging information about someone could come back to haunt them. This fear is well placed. Singer Diana Ross once circulated a letter that read, "If I let an employee go, it's because either their work or their personal habits are not acceptable to me. I do not recommend these people." She then listed seven names. One of those on the list sued her for libel, and Ross avoided legal reproach only by arriving at a costly out-of-court settlement. This is hardly an isolated incident: Over 8,000 such suits have been filed since 1983. In 72 percent of these cases, the recipient of the bad reference prevail, and the average award is over $500,000 (the record is $1.9 million).

The evidence on the utility of biographical information collected directly from job applicants is much more positive, especially for certain occupational categories such as clerical and sales. The low cost of obtaining such information significantly enhances its utility especially when the information is used <u>in conjunction with</u> a well-designed follow-up interview.

<u>In terms of</u> legal concerns, it should be noted that asking certain questions is illegal regardless of its impact. There is substantial variation from state to state on what constitutes a legal versus an illegal inquiry, and the reader should consult the Fair Employment Practices Commission in his or her home state to find out more[②].

Physical Ability Tests

Although automation and other advances in technology have

eliminated or modified many physically demanding occupational tasks, a large number of jobs still require certain physical abilities[3]. In these cases, tests of physical abilities may not only be relevant to predicting performance but relevant to predicting occupational injuries and disabilities as well. There are seven classes of tests in this area, ones that evaluate (1) muscular tension, (2) muscular power, (3) muscular endurance, (4) cardiovascular endurance, (5) flexibility, (6) balance, and (7) coordination.

The criterion-related validities for these kinds of tests for certain jobs are quite strong. Unfortunately, these tests are likely to have an adverse impact on some disabled applicants and many female applicants, particularly the strength tests. For example, roughly two-thirds of all males score higher than the highest-scoring female on muscular tension tests.

There are two keys in deciding whether to use these kinds of tests. First, is the physical ability essential to performing the job and is this prominent in the job description? Neither the Civil Rights Act nor ADA requires employers to hire individuals who cannot perform essential job functions; and both accept a written job description as evidence of the essential functions of the job[4]. Second, is there a probability that failure to adequately perform the job would result in some risk to the safety or health of the applicant, coworkers, or clients? The "direct threat" clause of the ADA makes it clear that adverse impact against the disabled is warranted under such conditions.

Cognitive Ability Tests

Cognitive ability tests differentiate individuals on their mental rather than physical capacities. Cognitive ability has many different facets, although we will focus on three dominant ones. "Verbal comprehension" refers to a person's capacity to understand and use written and spoken language. "Quantitative ability" concerns the speed and accuracy with which one can solve arithmetic problems of all kinds. "Reasoning ability," a broader concept, refers to a person's capacity to invent solutions to many diverse problems.

Personality Inventories

While ability tests attempt to categorize individuals relative to what they can do, personality measures tend to categorize individuals by what they are like. Two recent reviews of the personality literature independently arrived at five common aspects of personality. We refer to these five major dimensions as (1) extroversion, (2) adjustment, (3) agreeableness, (4) conscientiousness, and (5) inquisitiveness.

Although it is possible to find reliable, commercially available measures of each of these traits, the evidence for their validity and generalizability is low. Only conscientiousness displays any validity across a number of different job categories, and here the correlations are in the .10s and low .20s. Extroversion is relevant to a few types of jobs such as sales and management, but here, too, the level of predictability is low. These tests sometimes perform better when used in conjunction with more traditional ability tests, but this is not always the case.

Work Samples

Work-sample tests and job-performance tests attempt to simulate the job miniaturized form—for example, a typing test for prospective clerical workers. An "in-basket test" is another example. In an in-basket test, job candidates are asked to respond to memos that typify the problems confronted by those who already hold the job. The key in this and other forms of work-sample tests is the behavioral consistency between the requirements of the job and the requirements of the test.

Work-sample tests tend to be job specific—that is, tailored

individually to each different job in each organization. On the positive side, this has resulted in tests that demonstrate a high degree of criterion-related validity. In addition, the obvious parallels between the test and the job make content validity high. In general, this reduces the likelihood that rejected applicants will challenge the procedure through litigation. What evidence is available also suggests that these tests are low in adverse impact.

With all these advantages come two drawbacks. First, by their very nature the tests are job specific, so generalizability is low. Second, partly because a new test has to be developed for each job, and partly because of their nonstandardized formats, these tests are relatively expensive to develop. It is much more cost-effective to purchase a commercially available cognitive ability test that can be used for a number of different job categories within the company than to develop a test for each job[5]. For this reason, some have rated the utility of cognitive ability tests higher than work-sample tests despite the latter's higher criterion-related validity.

Honesty Tests and Drug Tests

Many of the problems that confront society also exist within organizations, which have led to two new kinds of tests: theft tests and drug-use tests. Many companies used to employ polygraph tests, or lie detectors, to evaluate job applicants, but this changed with the passage of the Polygraph Act in 1988. This act banned the use of polygraphs in employment screening for all private companies except for pharmaceutical companies and companies that supplied security guards for operations involved in health and safety.

Although the 1988 act eliminated polygraph testing, it did not eliminate the problem of theft by employees. As a result, the paper-and-pencil honesty testing industry was born. A mere one year after the

Polygraph Act, 3.5 million such tests were administered to prospective American workers

Paper-and-pencil honesty tests typically ask applicants directly about their attitudes toward theft or their past experiences with theft. Given the recent development of these tests, there is not a great deal of independent evidence (i.e., evidence not generated by those who publish and sell the tests) on their reliability and validity. This problem is compounded by the fact that it is difficult to <u>come up with</u> a criterion to use in validation studies of employee theft.

Some have asked whether these kinds of tests should be held to higher standards than traditional tests. Accusing someone of being a thief is a stronger assertion than suggesting that he or she is low on quantitative ability. Even the most liberal estimates of validity for these tests are insufficient to pass the "reasonable doubt" standard applied by the judicial system. Moreover, when mistakes are made, these tend to falsely classify honest individuals as thieves rather than the other way around. Finally, any industry that grows as fast as the honesty test industry is subject to growing pains. One review of these tests noted the frequency of false or misleading claims found in the brochures published by many of the testing companies. Although it is always a good rule to locally evaluate the reliability and validity of any selection method, this may be even more critical with honesty tests.

from: *Human Resource Management: Gaining a Competitive Advantage*, 1994

Words and Expressions

rambling [ˈræmbliŋ] *adj.* 不连贯的
geographic [ˌdʒiəˈgræfik] *adj.* 地理的
subjectivity [ˌsʌbdʒekˈtivəti] *n.* 主观性
embody [imˈbɔdi] *v.* 包含

probability [ˌprɔbə'biliti] n. 可能性
biographical [baiəu'græfikəl] adj. 传记的
differentiate [ˌdifə'renʃieit] v. 区分
haunt [hɔ:nt] v. 使困窘
circulate ['sə:kjuleit] v. 使散布
recommend [rekə'mend] v. 推荐
sue [su:] v. 提出诉讼
libel ['laibəl] n. 诽谤罪
reproach [ri'prəutʃ] v. 责备
clerical ['klerikəl] n. 牧师
automation [ɔ:tə'meiʃən] n. 自动化
eliminate [i'limineit] v. 淘汰
modify ['mɔdifai] v. 更改
endurance [in'djurəns] n. 忍耐(力)
cardiovascular [ˌkɑ:diəu'væskjulə] adj. 心脏血管的
flexibility [ˌfleksə'biliti] n. 弹性
balance ['bæləns] n. 平衡性
coordination [kəuˌɔ:di'neiʃən] n. 协调性
warrant ['wɔrənt] v. 辩解
arithmetic [ə'riθmətik] n. 算术
invent [in'vent] v. 发现
categorize ['kætigəraiz] v. 加以类别
extroversion [ˌekstrəu'və:ʃən] n. 外向
adjustment [ə'dʒʌstmənt] n. 调节适应
agreeableness [əˌgri:'eiblnis] n. 令人愉悦
conscientiousness [kɔnˌsaiən'tiəusnis] n. 谨慎
inquisitiveness [inkwi'zaitivnis] n. 好奇
simulate ['simjuleit] v. 模拟
miniaturize ['miniətʃəraiz] v. 使微型化
prospective [prəs'pektiv] adj. 未来的

memo ['meməu] *n.* 备忘录
tailor ['teilə] *v.* 调整
parallel ['pærəlel] *n.* 相似
litigation [,liti'geiʃən] *n.* 诉讼
polygraph ['pɔligrɑ:f] *n.* 测谎仪
pharmaceutical [,fɑ:mə'sju:tikəl] *adj.* 制药的
compound ['kɔmpaund] *v.* 使增加
reference check 背景调查
reference letter 推荐信
to think the highest of 对……的看法最高
to arrive at 努力达到
out-of-court settlement 庭外和解
an isolated incident 孤例
in conjunction with 与……协力
regardless of 不管
occupational injuries and disabilities 因工伤残
muscular tension 肌肉紧张
relative to 相对于
in-basket test 公文筐测验
polygraph test 测谎测试
lie detector 测谎器
Polygraph Act (Employee Polygraph Protection Act of 1988)
  《雇员测谎保护法案》
growing pains 个人、企业等发展初期所遇的困难

Difficult Sentences

① A selection interview has been defined as "a dialogue initiated by one or more persons to gather information and evaluate the qualifications of an applicant for employment".
选拔面试被定义为"由一个或多个人引发,目的在于收集工作申

请人的信息、评价其资格的对话"。

② There is substantial variation from state to state on what constitutes a legal versus an illegal inquiry, and the reader should consult the Fair Employment Practices Commission in his or her home state to find out more.
每个州规定的合法询问和非法询问的构成要素大不相同,因此读者应该咨询自己家乡所在州的公平就业管理委员会来获取更多信息。

③ Although automation and other advances in technology have eliminated or modified many physically demanding occupational tasks, a large number of jobs still require certain physical abilities.
尽管自动化等其他先进的技术已经取消了许多对体力要求很高的工作岗位或对这些岗位进行了改进,但是还有许多工作岗位对体能有一定的要求。

④ Neither the Civil Rights Act nor ADA requires employers to hire individuals who cannot perform essential job functions; and both accept a written job description as evidence of the essential functions of the job.
《民权法案》和《美国残疾人士法案》都没有规定雇主招聘不能履行基本工作职责的人;而且这两个法案都认定书面职位描述为规定工作岗位基本职责的证据。

⑤ It is much more cost-effective to purchase a commercially available cognitive ability test that can be used for a number of different job categories within the company than to develop a test for each job.
购买一个可以用来测试公司内部不同类别工作岗位的商业认知能力测试系统比给每个工作岗位开发一个测试系统要划算得多。

Phrases and Patterns

1. in terms of 根据;按照;用……的话,在……方面
   In terms of legality, the subjectivity embodied in the process often

makes applicants upset, particularly if they fail to get a job after being asked apparently irrelevant questions like, "If you were a car, what kind of car would you be?"
从法律义务上来讲,这一过程中体现出来的主观性经常让申请人很沮丧,如果申请人被问道了一些明显无关的问题,如:"假设你是一辆车,你愿意成为什么样的车?"他们在得知没有被聘用时会特别沮丧。
These are the facilities planned and programmed in terms of their interrelationships, instead of evolving haphazardly.
按照其内在的关系来营造设施以防止其产生灾难性的进展。

2. in conjunction with 结合;一起
The low cost of obtaining such information significantly enhances its utility especially when the information is used in conjunction with a well-designed follow-up interview.
以低成本获取这样的信息大大地提高了它的效用,特别是当这种信息和设计充分的后续面试结合在一起的时候。
The moon is in conjunction with the sun.
月亮与太阳处在合点。

3. come up with 提出;制定
This problem is compounded by the fact that it is difficult to come up with a criterion to use in validation studies of employee theft.
制定确认雇员偷窃的标准是很难的,这一点增加该问题的复杂性。
More often than not, it is more difficult to come up with regulations than to enforce them.
很多时候,执行规则要比制定规则难。

4.3 Implications of Selection Applications for MCGDS
多标准团体决议法在员工甄选中的应用

Introduction

In summary, a proactive, non-discriminatory hiring practice should be fair, consistently applied, and well documented. Further, it should use job-related criteria and reduce the impact of illegal personal biases. The use of MCGDS (Multi-Criteria Group Decision Support) in this type of process requires careful consideration of the basic elements of MCDA (structuring and weighting criteria; evaluating alternatives on each criterion; synthesizing the evaluations across the criteria) as well as the type of group process used[①]. We use the term, weight, generically to describe some measures of the relative importance for a criterion. We will also use synthesis method to discuss the synthesis of evaluations across criteria. Belton and Pictet provide a useful framework for our discussion of MCDA and the group process. They categorize the three elementary procedures typically found in MCGDS for handling group input relative to the basic elements of MCDA.

Sharing: obtain a common element through consensus.

Aggregating: obtain a common element through compromise by voting or the calculation of a representative group value.

Comparing: compare individual elements without necessarily attempting to reduce differences to a common element.

These procedures may occur in conjunction with any or all of the MCDA basic elements.

We discussed our observations on the issues raised for MCGDS in conjunction with a description of the decision process used in our search. Our search committee consisted of five faculties with teaching responsibilities in statistics, management science and/or operations management. The first author coordinated this curriculum group and served as the search committee chair. Our tasks consisted of the following.

Set minimum requirements and determine which applicants meet them.

Select a short list of candidates for campus visits from a pool of applicants (exceeding 50). Share this short list with the Dean, who must approve all visits.

Evaluate the candidates who visit. Make recommendations to the remaining departmental faculty prior to a departmental vote.

Present our recommendations, along with departmental vote results, to the Dean, who makes the final decision on job offers.

As is often the case, the committee conducted two selection phases. The first phase involved the selection of a subset of candidates from the larger pool to invite for campus interviews. The second phase included a post-visit hiring recommendation for the department and Dean from the short list of candidates who visited.

Issues in Criterion Determination, Criterion Weighting and Constraint Setting

The first and, perhaps foremost, issue relates to whose values should be captured in the decision process[2]. In this case, it is clearly not the committee members' individual, possibly discriminatory, values. The decision makers in this case are agents for their organization. The values reflected in the criteria and their relative importance should be organizational values. We are, of course, assuming that the organizational values are non-discriminatory. One characteristic of a good set of criteria is that it be exhaustible in that all relevant considerations are included. In the case of selection decisions, however, it is clear that exhaustiveness should not extend beyond organizational criteria to personal ones. While we acknowledge the difficulty in separating personal from organizational views, the effort to do so helps the committee reduce potential bias in the selection process[③].

In selection decisions, we recommend that both the determination of the relevant criteria and their relative importance be shared activities. This corresponds to the MCGDS process with agreed upon criteria and weights described by Hwang and Lin. In accordance with good selection practices, the criteria should be clearly job-related. While common criteria are typical in MCGDS, common weights are not as widely used. Many MCGDS systems allow decision makers the freedom to determine and use individual weights (Iz and Gardiner, 1993). It would not be advisable for selection decision processes to allow individual decision makers to develop and use their own criteria and weights since this would increase the potential for inconsistent treatment of applicants, which could be determined to be either disparate treatment or disparate impact[④].

In the typical case of disparate treatment, the court's goal will be to determine whether similarly situated individuals are treated the same. In other words, were men and women applicants treated consistently at every point in the decision-making process and, thereby, provided equal opportunity to obtain the job? A case of disparate impact is found where a facially neutral process eliminates members of a protected class (e.g. people age 40 or over) at a significantly higher rate than nonmembers (e.g. people under 40). Even if the group establishes common criteria, the ability for individuals to adjust their own weights would introduce the possibility of the weight adjustments being manipulations to achieve biased results. As an example, suppose a minority candidate emerged as the top contender using one set of weights but not with another. The choice of the second weights in lieu of the first might be viewed as evidence of discrimination.

Constraints may be used to reduce the number of alternatives considered. An approach similar to that discussed for criteria should be taken for constraint setting. Constraint definition should be a shared activity and not individually imposed. Constraints should be job-related and care should be taken that constraints do not eliminate protected classes from further consideration.

When our committee met to discuss the desired characteristics for our job candidates, we used the faculty handbook as a guide for organizational values. We determined that good teaching experience in the relevant fields (statistics, management science and operations management), strong research potential, industrial experience and collegiality were the most important criteria. Teaching, research and collegiality are three main considerations in granting tenure at our university. We teach in a business school and have a large number of students at the MBA level with extensive industrial experience. We viewed a faculty member with good industrial experience as bringing a richer background to both teaching and research than one without it. For this reason, we added the quality of a candidate's industrial experience as an additional criterion. While collegiality is an important criterion, we agreed that we could only evaluate collegiality for those candidates making campus visits. For the remaining three criteria, the group expressed a strong consensus for equal weights. For this reason, we did not use a formal procedure for shared weight assessment. Our initial constraint took the form of a minimal job requirement. We would not hire any candidate who did not have a completed PhD in one of the relevant fields prior to our start date. The group further felt that we would need to establish a minimum acceptable lower bound on our measure of research potential due to long-term tenurability considerations.

Concluding Remarks

Employee selection decisions, whether by individuals or committees, are an indispensable aspect of functioning organizations. Countless resources are spent, however, in hiring discrimination litigation that results from either intentional discrimination, ignorance of the law or poor managerial judgment[5]. Yet the lack of cross-fertilization between the MCDA and human resources management selection literature becomes evident when one looks for an intersection of the two. Our investigation of academic journals for the application of MCDA or MCGDS to employee selection revealed the three faculty selection articles described in the Introduction, all written by academics about 'close to home' decisions. We found no applications of MCDA to other employee selection decisions. The human resources literature led us to Roth and Bobko, who describe how multi-attribute utility analysis can be used to choose between alternative types of selection plans, but not as part of the selection process itself.

As demonstrated above, non-discriminatory hiring decisions present unique design requirements for MCGDS. Research such as that of Moshkovich et al. sheds light on the comparative performance of different multi-criteria approaches in an employee selection decision. Belton and Hodgkin raise interesting possibilities in their discussion of intelligent decision support system features for MCGDS. They suggest intelligent support to remind decision makers of the appropriate procedures to follow. They also describe intelligent support for facilitators in determining when a decision maker is 'out of line' with the rest of the group. From time to time, MCDA researchers decry the lack of real applications of their methodology. The application of MCGDS to real employee selection decisions offers rich potential benefit to organizations and merits further exploration and research.

from: *Journal of Multi-Criteria Decision Analysis*, 2000

Words and Expressions

consistently [kən'sistəntli] adv. 始终如一地
apply [ə'plai] v. 应用
bias ['baiəs] n. 偏见
structure ['strʌktʃə] v. 设计
weight [weit] n. 权数
synthesize ['sinθisaiz] v. 合成
generically [dʒinə'rikəli] adv. 一般地
handle ['hændl] v. 处理
input ['input] n. 输入
consensus [kən'sensəs] n. 一致同意
aggregate ['æɡriɡeit] v. 合计
statistics [stə'tistiks] n. 统计学
operations [ˌɔpə'reiʃəns] n. 运营
coordinate [kəu'ɔːdinit] v. 协调
curriculum [kə'rikjuləm] n. 课程
minimum ['miniməm] adj. 最低的
pool [puːl] n. 资源的集合
subset ['sʌbset] n. 子集
value ['vælju] n. 价值标准
capture ['kæptʃə] v. 给与重视
discriminatory [di'skriminətɔːri] adj. 差别对待的
exhaustible [iɡ'zɔːstəbl] adj. 可穷尽的
acknowledge [ək'nɔlidʒ] v. 承认
potential [pə'tenʃ(ə)l] adj. 可能的
disparate ['dispərit] adj. 完全不同的
impact ['impækt] n. 影响
facially ['feiʃəli] adv. 表面上
eliminate [i'limineit] v. 排除

contender [kən'tendə(r)] n. 竞争者
lieu ['lju:] n. 替代
constraint [kən'streint] n. 约束措施
collegiality [kəˌli:dʒi'æliti] n. 共同掌权
tenure ['tenjuə] n. 终身职位
initial [i'niʃəl] adj. 最初的
bound [baund] n. 范围
tenurability [ˌtenjərə'biliti] n. 可成为终身职位
indispensable [ˌindis'pensəbl] adj. 不可缺少的
intentional [in'tenʃənəl] adj. 故意的
intersection [ˌintə(:)'sekʃən] n. 交叉点
multi-attribute ['mʌltə'tribju(:)t] n. 多种属性
intelligent [in'telidʒənt] adj. 显示出可靠的判断和推理的
decry [di'krai] v. 谴责
methodology [meθə'dɔlədʒi] n. 方法
MCGDS (Multi-Criteria Group Decision Support) 多标准团体决议支持
MCDA (Multi-Criteria Decision Analysis) 多目标决策分析
prior to 在前
to relate to 涉及
in lieu of 替代
to shed light on 使某事清楚明白地显示出来
out of line 不一致

Difficult Sentences

① The use of MCGDS (Multi-Criteria Group Decision Support) in this type of process requires careful consideration of the basic elements of MCDA (structuring and weighting criteria; evaluating alternatives on each criterion; synthesizing the evaluations across the criteria) as well as the type of group process used.

在这种过程中运用多标准团体决议支持甄选方法要充分考虑到

多目标决策分析(建构和加权选择标准;按照每项标准评估申请人的资格;综合所有标准下的评估意见)的基本要素以及所运用的团体决议过程的类型。

② The first and, perhaps foremost, issue relates to whose values should be captured in the decision process.
首要的问题就是关于在决议过程中应该以谁的价值标准为主。

③ While we acknowledge the difficulty in separating personal from organizational views, the effort to do so helps the committee reduce potential bias in the selection process.
尽管我们承认区分个人见解和组织见解存在着一定的困难,但是这种行为本身有助于评委会在甄选过程中降低可能存在的偏见。

④ It would not be advisable for selection decision processes to allow individual decision makers to develop and use their own criteria and weights since this would increase the potential for inconsistent treatment of applicants, which could be determined to be either disparate treatment or disparate impact.
既然在甄选决议过程中允许个体决议制定者确立并使用他们自己的标准和权数将会增加对待申请人有别的可能性,很可能会造成异质对待和异质影响,所以这么做是不明智的。

⑤ Countless resources are spent, however, in hiring discrimination litigation that results from either intentional discrimination, ignorance of the law or poor managerial judgment.
然而,大量的资源花费在雇请律师接手或是由于故意歧视、不懂法或是管理决策失误而导致的歧视诉讼案。

Phrases and Patterns

1. provide a useful framework for 给……提供了有用的框架
Belton and Pictet provide a useful framework for our discussion of MCDA and the group process.

Belton 和 Pictet 给我们讨论多目标决策分析和团体决议过程提供了有用的框架。

2. in conjunction with 连同；一起

These procedures may occur in conjunction with any or all of the MCDA basic elements.

这些程序可以连同多目标决策分析的任何一个或所有基本要素一起出现。

We discussed our observations on the issues raised for MCGDS in conjunction with a description of the decision process used in our search.

我们讨论了多标准团体决议支持甄选方法问题观察报告，还连同地讨论了甄选决议过程说明。

3. As is often the case 按照惯例

As is often the case, the committee conducted two selection phases.

按照惯例，委员会进行了两个阶段的甄选。

As is often the case, the employee of gross misconduct was dismissed from the company.

按照惯例，这个严重失职的雇员被公司解雇了。

4. Care should be taken that... 应该注意的是……

Care should be taken that constraints do not eliminate protected classes from further consideration.

应该注意的是约束措施不要把受保护的群体排出在进一步考虑的范畴之外。

Care should be taken that employers must go beyond the traditional incentives to motivate people.

应该注意的是雇主必须要采取一些非传统的激励机制来推动大家。

5. view... as... 认为……；视为……

We viewed a faculty member with good industrial experience as bringing a richer background to both teaching and research than one without it.

我们认为拥有丰富行业经验的教员比那些没有经验的教员能给教学和科研带来更丰富的背景知识。

The refusal of a pregnant woman to be head of the department was viewed as an act of sexual discrimination.

拒绝任命怀孕的女性为该部门的主管被视为性别歧视行为。

Questions

1. What are the five standards by which selection measures can be judged?
2. Can you name some commonly used selection methods?
3. What advantages and disadvantages do they have in terms of the five standards mentioned in Question 1?

5

Training Employees
员工培训

【本章导读】 本章介绍员工培训过程中的一些主要问题。5.1 介绍员工培训过程中的主要注意事项,如需求评估、建立培训目的、选择培训方式、学习原则和培训评价等。5.2 介绍四个培训方式,即在职培训与工作轮换、学徒、课堂培训和网络培训。5.3 说明员工的反应在预评培训效果中的作用,指出区别员工反映的有效性和认知性有助于对培训活动效果的预评。

5.1 Brief Sketch of Training Employees
员工培训概要

Introduction

Training is a learning process that involves the acquisition of skills, concepts, rules, or attitudes to enhance the performance of employees[①]. Generally, the new employee's manager has primary responsibility for job training. Sometimes this training is delegated to a senior employee in the department. Regardless, the quality of this initial training can have a significant influence on the employee's productivity and attitude toward the job.

Economic, social, technological, and governmental changes significantly influence the objectives and strategies of all organizations. Changes in these areas can make the skills learned today obsolete in the future. Also, planned organizational changes and expansions can make it necessary for employees to update their skills or acquire new ones.

Needs Assessment

Training must be directed toward accomplishment of some organizational objective, such as more efficient production methods, improved quality of products or services, or reduced operating costs[2]. This means an organization should commit its resources only to those training activities that can best help in achieving its objectives. Needs assessment is a systematic analysis of the specific training activities the organization requires to achieve its objectives[3]. In general, five methods can be used to gather needs assessment information: interviews, surveys/questionnaires, observations, focus groups, and document examination.

Interviews with employees can be conducted by specialists in the human resource department or by outside experts. Basic questions that should usually be asked are as follows:

· What problems is the employee having in his or her job?

· What additional skills and/or knowledge does the employee need to better perform the job?

· What training does the employee believe is needed?

Of course, in conducting interviews, every organization would have several additional questions about specific issues. In addition, if interviews are to provide useful information, employees must believe their input will be valued and not be used against them.

Surveys and/or questionnaires are also frequently used in needs assessment. Normally this involves developing a list of skills required to perform particular jobs effectively and asking employees to check those skills in which they believe they need training[④]. Employee attitude surveys can also be used to uncover training needs. Usually most organizations bring in an outside party or organization to conduct and analyze employee attitude surveys. Customer surveys can also indicate problem areas that may not be obvious to employees of the organization. Responses to a customer survey may indicate areas of training for the organization as a whole or particular functional unit.

To be effective, observations for determining training needs must be conducted by individuals trained in observing employee behavior and translating observed behavior into specific training needs[⑤]. Specialists in the human resource department who have been trained in performing job analyses should be particularly <u>adept at</u> observing to identify training needs.

Focus groups are composed of employees from various departments and various levels within the organization. A specialist in the human resource department or an outside expert can conduct the focus group sessions. Focus group topics should address issues such as the following:

• What skills/knowledge will our employees need for our organization to stay competitive over the next five years?

• What problems does our organization have that can be solved through training?

Document examination involves examining organizational records on absenteeism, turnover, and accident rates to determine if problems exist and whether any problems identified can be addressed through training. Another useful source to examine is performance appraisal information gathered through the organization's performance appraisal system. Performance problems common to many employees are likely areas to address through training. <u>Regardless of</u> the method employed, a systematic and accurate needs assessment should be undertaken before any training is conducted.

Establishing Training Objectives

After training needs have been determined, objectives must be established for meeting those needs. Unfortunately, many organizational training programs have no objectives. "Training for training's sake" appears to be the maxim. This philosophy makes it virtually impossible to evaluate the strengths and weaknesses of a training program.

Effective training objectives should state what will result for the organization, department, or individual when the training is completed. The outcomes should be described in writing.

Training objectives can be categorized as follows:
- Instructional objectives.
- Organizational and departmental objectives.
- Individual performance and growth objectives.

When clearly defined objectives are lacking, it is impossible to evaluate a program efficiently. Furthermore, there is no basis for selecting appropriate materials, content, or instructional methods.

Selecting the Methods of Training

Several methods can be used to satisfy an organization's training needs and accomplish its objectives. Some of the more commonly used methods include on-the-job training, job rotation, apprenticeship training, classroom training and Web-based training.

Principles of Learning

Previous sections of part discussed not only how training needs are determined but also how they can be met. To make use of sound learning principles during the development and implementation of these programs helps to ensure that the programs will succeed. The following sections present several principles of learning:

- Motivation to achieve personal goals.
- Knowledge of results.
- Reinforcement.
- Flow of the training program.
- Practice and repetition.
- Spacing of sessions.
- Whole or part training.

Evaluating Training

When the results of a training program are evaluated, a number of benefits accrue. Less effective programs can be withdrawn to save time and effort. Weaknesses with established programs can be identified and remedied:

- Reaction: How much did the trainees like the program?
- Learning: What principles, facts, and concepts were learned in the training program?
- Behavior: Did the job behavior of the trainees change because of the program?
- Results: What were the results of the program in terms of factors such as reduced costs or reduction in turnover?

from: *Human Resource Management*, 7th Edition, 2007

Words and Expressions

delegate ['deligit] *v.* 委派……为代表

regardless [ri'gɑːdlis] *adj.* 不管

obsolete ['ɔbsəliːt] *adj.* 荒废的；陈旧的

update [ʌp'deit] *v.* 使现代化；更新

survey [səː'vei] *n.* 测量；调查

questionnaire [ˌkwestiə'nɛə] n. 调查表;问卷
observation [ˌɔbzəː'veiʃən] n. 观察
conduct ['kɔndəkt] n. 引导;管理
adept ['ædept] adj. 熟练的
competitive [kəm'petitiv] adj. 竞争的
address [ə'dres] v. 把注意力集中于
absenteeism [ˌæbsən'tiːiz(ə)m] n. 旷工
turnover ['təːnˌəuvə] n. 营业额;周转;轮换
appraisal [ə'preizəl] n. 评价
undertake [ˌʌndə'teik] v. 采取;承担……工作
maxim ['mæksim] n. 格言;座右铭
content [kən'tent] n. 内容
rotation [rəu'teiʃən] n. 旋转;轮换
apprenticeship [ə'prentisˌʃip] n. 学徒的身份;学徒的年限
implementation [ˌimplimen'teiʃən] n. 执行
accrue [ə'kruː] v. 自然增加;产生
withdraw [wið'drɔː] v. 收回;撤消
remedy ['remidi] v. 补救;矫正
reaction [ri(ː)'ækʃən] n. 反应
trainee [trei'niː] n. 练习生

focus group 核心小组
document examination 记录审查
performance appraisal 成绩评价
flow of the training program 训练流程
on-the-job training 在职培训
job rotation 工作轮换
apprenticeship training 学徒式培训
web-based training 网上培训
spacing of sessions 培训间隔安排

Difficult Sentences

① Training is a learning process that involves the acquisition of skills, concepts, rules, or attitudes to enhance the performance of employees.
培训是一个涉及掌握技能、概念、规则或态度的学习过程,以提高职员的成绩。

② Training must be directed toward accomplishment of some organizational objective, such as more efficient production methods, improved quality of products or services, or reduced operating costs.
培训的方向必须是实现组织的目标,如更有效的生产方式、改善产品或服务质量或是降低运作成本。

③ Needs assessment is a systematic analysis of the specific training activities the organization requires to achieve its objectives.
需求评估是指对组织为实现其目标所需要的专业培训活动所进行的系统分析。

④ Normally this involves developing a list of skills required to perform particular jobs effectively and asking employees to check those skills in which they believe they need training.
通常情况下,这需要出具有效完成特定工作所必备的各项技能,同时要求雇员们核查这些他们相信应该进行培训的技能。

⑤ To be effective, observations for determining training needs must be conducted by individuals trained in observing employee behavior and translating observed behavior into specific training needs.
为有效起见,确定培训需求的观察必须由接受过职员行为观察培训的人员来完成,并且将行为观察转化为特定的培训需求。

Phrases and Patterns

1. commit... to... 把……托交给……;答应负责

This means an organization should commit its resources only to those training activities that can best help in achieving its objectives.

这就意味着一个组织应该把它的资源只用于那些能为其实现目标提供最好帮助的培训活动。

The specialists committed themselves to conducting a systematic and accurate needs assessment.

专家们答应进行一次系统而精确的需求评估活动。

2. be adept at... 擅长……

Specialists in the human resource department who have been trained in performing job analyses should be particularly adept at observing to identify training needs.

人力资源部的专家,接受过分析工作表现的训练,应该尤其擅长识别培训需求的观察活动。

We needs experts who are adept at translating career intentions into action.

我们需要擅长化事业意图为行动的专家。

3. Regardless of... 不管……;不顾……

Regardless of the method employed, a systematic and accurate needs assessment should be undertaken before any training is conducted.

不管采取何种方式,任何培训活动进行之前都应进行系统而精确的评估。

The needs assessment should not be conducted regardless of achieving an organization's objectives.

需求评估的进行不应不顾及组织目标的实现。

5.2 Methods of Training
培训方法

Introduction

Several methods can be used to satisfy an organization's training needs and accomplish its objectives. Some of the more commonly used methods include on-the-job training, job rotation, apprenticeship training, and classroom training.

On-the-job Training and Job Rotation

On-the-job training (OJT) is normally given by a senior employee or a manager. The employee is shown how to perform the job and allowed to do it under the trainer's supervision.

One form of on-the-job training is job rotation, sometimes called cross training. In job rotation, an individual learns several different jobs within a work unit or department and performs each job for a specified time period. One main advantage of job rotation is that it makes flexibility possible in the department. For example, when one member of a work unit is absent, another can perform that job.

The advantages of on-the-job training are that no special facilities are required and the new employee does productive work during the learning process. Its major disadvantage is that the pressures of the workplace can cause instruction of the employee to be haphazard or neglected.

In training an employee on the job, the trainer can use several steps to ensure that the training is effective.

Preparation of the Trainee for Learning the Job

An employee almost always desires to learn a new job. Showing an interest in the person, explaining the importance of the job, and explaining why it must be done correctly enhance the employee's desire to learn. Determining the employee's previous work experience in similar jobs enables the trainer to use that experience in explaining the present job or to eliminate unnecessary explanations[1].

Breakdown of Work into Components and Identification of Key Points

This breakdown <u>consists of</u> determining the segments that make up the total job. In each segment, something is accomplished to advance the work toward completion. Such a breakdown can be viewed as a detailed road map that guides the employee through the entire work cycle in a rational, easy-to-understand manner, without injury to the person or damage to the equipment[2].

A key point is any directive or information that helps the employee perform a work component correctly, easily, and safely[3]. Key points are the "tricks of the trade" and are given to the employee to help reduce learning time. Observing and mastering the key points help the employee acquire needed skills and perform the work more effectively.

Presentation of the Operations and Knowledge

Simply telling an employee how to perform the job is usually not sufficient. An employee must not only be told but also shown how to do the job. Each component of the job must be demonstrated. While each is being demonstrated, the key points for the component should be explained. Employees should be encouraged to ask questions about each component.

Performance Tryout

An employee should perform the job under the guidance of the trainer. Generally, an employee should be required to explain what he or she is going to do at each component of the job. If the explanation is correct, the employee is then allowed to perform the component. If the explanation is incorrect, the mistake should be corrected before the employee is allowed to actually perform the component. Praise and encouragement are essential in this phase.

Follow-up when the trainer is reasonably sure an employee can do the job without monitoring, the employee should be encouraged to work at his or her own pace while developing skills in performing the job and should be left alone[④]. The trainer should return periodically to answer any questions and see that all is going well. Employees should not be turned loose and forgotten. They will have questions and will make better progress if the trainer is around to answer questions and help with problems.

Apprenticeship Training

Apprenticeship training provides beginning workers with comprehensive training in the practical and theoretical aspects of work required in a highly skilled occupation. Apprenticeship programs combine on-the-job and classroom training to prepare workers for more than 800 skilled occupations such as bricklayer, machinist worker, computer operator, and laboratory technician. About two-thirds of apprenticeable occupations are in the construction and manufacturing trades, but apprentices also work in such diverse fields as electronics, the service industries, public administration, and medical and health care. The length of an apprenticeship <u>varies by</u> occupation and is determined by standards adopted by the industry.

A skilled and experienced employee conducts on-the-job training during the apprenticeship period. The purpose of this training is to learn the practical skills of the job. Apprentices learn the theoretical side of their jobs in classes they attend. Some of the subjects that might be covered in the classroom training include mathematics, blueprint reading, and technical courses required for specific occupations.

Wages paid apprentices usually begin at half those paid fully trained employees. However, the wages are generally advanced rapidly at six-month intervals.

The U. S. Department of Labor's Office of Apprenticeship Training, Employer and Labor Services (OATELS) is responsible for providing services to existing apprenticeship programs and technical assistance to organizations that wish to establish programs[5]. The bureau has established the following minimum standards for apprenticeship programs:

· Full and fair opportunity to apply for apprenticeship

· A schedule of work processes in which an apprentice is to receive training and experience on the job

· Organized instruction designed to provide apprentices with knowledge in technical subjects related to their trade (e. g. , a minimum of 144 hours per year is normally considered necessary)

· A progressively increasing schedule of wages

· Proper supervision of on-the-job training, with adequate facilities to train apprentices

· Periodic evaluation of the apprentice's progress, both in job performances and related instruction, with appropriate records maintained

· No discrimination in any phase of selection, employment, or training

Classroom Training

Classroom training is conducted off the job and is probably the most familiar training method. It is an effective means of imparting information quickly to large groups with limited or no knowledge of the subject being presented. It is useful for teaching factual material, concepts, principles, and theories. Portions of orientation programs, some aspects of apprenticeship training, and safety programs are usually presented utilizing some form of classroom instruction. More frequently, however, classroom instruction is used for technical, professional, and managerial employees

Web-based Training

In some companies, employee training has moved from the classroom to the Internet. "Virtual" classrooms offer training in either self-paced courses, real-time courses through intranets, or even real-time videoconferencing.

from: *Human Resource Management*, 7th Edition, 2007

Words and Expressions

senior ['siːnjə] *adj.* 资格较老的;高级的
haphazard ['hæp'hæzəd] *adj.* 偶然的;随便的
eliminate [i'limineit] *v.* 除去
segment ['segmənt] *n.* 段;节;片断
cycle ['saikl] *n.* 周期;循环
rational ['ræʃənl] *adj.* 理性的;合理的
directive [di'rektiv] *n.* 指示
component [kəm'pəunənt] *n.* 成分
tryout ['trai‚aut] *n.* 试验;试用;尝试
phase [feiz] *n.* 阶段
pace [peis] *n.* 一步;速度;步调
monitor ['mɔnitə] *v.* 监控
periodically [‚piəri'ɔdikəli] *adv.* 周期性地
comprehensive [‚kɔmpri'hensiv] *adj.* 全面的
practical ['præktikəl] *adj.* 实际的
bricklayer ['brikleiə(r)] *n.* 砖匠
machinist [mə'ʃiːnist] *n.* 机械师
blueprint ['bluː‚print] *n.* 蓝图;计划

interval ['intəvəl] n. 间隔
bureau ['bjuərəu] n. 办公署
facility [fə'siliti] n. 设备
discrimination [dis,krimi'neiʃən] n. 歧视
impart [im'pɑːt] v. 传授；告知
factual ['fæktjuəl] adj. 事实的
portion ['pɔːʃən] n. 一部分
orientation [ˌɔ(ː)rien'teiʃən] n. 方向；定位
intranet [intrə'net] n. 企业内部互联网
utilize ['juːtilaiz] v. 利用
senior employee 高级职员
cross training 交叉培训
tricks of the trade 行业窍门
comprehensive training 综合培训
service industries 服务业
public administration 公共管理
medical and health care 医疗保健
OATELS 学徒培训、雇主及劳工服务办
"virtual" classroom 虚拟课堂
videoconferencing 视频会议

Difficult Sentences

① Determining the employee's previous work experience in similar jobs enables the trainer to use that experience in explaining the present job or to eliminate unnecessary explanations.
找出职员先前在类似工作中积累的经验，培训者可以用以说明当前的工作或排除不必要的解释。

② Such a breakdown can be viewed as a detailed road map that guides the employee through the entire work cycle in a rational, easy-to-understand manner, without injury to the person or damage to the equipment.

如此的细化可以看做是一个详尽的线路图,指导职员在整个工作周期中都持理性、易于理解的态度,避免造成个人伤害以及设备毁损。

③ A key point is any directive or information that helps the employee perform a work component correctly, easily, and safely.

有助于职员正确、轻松、安全地工作的指示或信息是关键。

④ When the trainer is reasonably sure an employee can do the job without monitoring, the employee should be encouraged to work at his or her own pace while developing skills in performing the job and should be left alone。

当培训人有理由确信职员能不受督导而工作时,应鼓励他在开发技能的同时按自己的步调工作,并且不横加干涉。

⑤ The U. S. Department of Labor's Office of Apprenticeship Training, Employer and Labor Services (OATELS) is responsible for providing services to existing apprenticeship programs and technical assistance to organizations that wish to establish programs.

学徒培训、雇主及劳工服务办有责任为在职学员计划提供服务、为希望制定计划的组织提供技术援助。

Phrases and Patterns

1. consist of... 由……组成

    This breakdown consists of determining the segments that make up the total job.

    该细化由确定组成整体工作的各个环节组成。

    The sample consisted of 283 automotive technicians from a large Midwest company who were eligible and volunteered for an internally developed program on brakes training.

    此次抽样调查包含来自中西部的一家大公司的283名汽车技师,他们有资格并自愿参加了一个内部的刹车培训计划。

2. vary by... 随……变化
The length of an apprenticeship varies by occupation and is determined by standards adopted by the industry.
学徒期的长度随职业的不同而有所改变,且决定于行业采用的标准。
The length of performance tryout varies by occupation, too.
试用期的长短也随职业的不同而有所改变。

5.3　The Role of Employee Reactions in Predicting Training Effectiveness
员工在培训效果预评中的作用

Introduction

Reactions to training programs tend to be poor predictors of training success, yet most training programs are evaluated based solely on trainee reactions[①]. In this study, we proposed that distinguishing between affective and cognitive employee reactions may improve the prediction of trainee learning. Our results indicated that cognitive employee reactions are related to both employee learning and employee behavior. Moreover, contrary to popular notion, negative affective reactions best predicted employee learning. Implications and future research directions of the results are discussed.

As the workplace undergoes sweeping changes, such as the pressure of more global competition, the need for strategies to keep up with these changes is increasingly important. Organizational training is a method used to enhance individual productivity as well as a company's success. An organization's investment in human capital through the education and training of its members is therefore a central component of competitive strategy.

Organizations often evaluate training effectiveness using one or more of Kirkpatrick's criteria. Although other approaches to training evaluation have been proposed, training success has most often been evaluated using paper-and-pencil measures. Research investigating the effect of various training design and workplace environment factors on workplace learning and transfer has been covered elsewhere. In this article, we address issues concerning the relation of paper-and-pencil measures of employee reactions to training with the actual learning imparted by the training program.

Training Evaluation Criteria

Training evaluation is a system for measuring changes due to training interventions-most important, whether trainees have achieved learning outcomes[2]. Few, if any, single measures can actually capture the complexity of training programs and transfer performance. Although the issue of conceptually based models to guide researchers in evaluating training effectiveness is still in its infancy, some advances have been made in this area recently. Russ-Eft and Preskill presented alternative methods of evaluation (for example, developmental evaluation). More recently, Preskill and Russ-Eft proposed a model based on the philosophies, theories, and practices in various fields such as evaluation, organizational learning, and systems thinking.

Despite these advances in training evaluation theory, the most developed and used of these models in the human resource literature focuses on defining different training effectiveness criteria and their organizational implications[3]. Common to these models is the use of multiple criteria to gather data on training effectiveness. As such, training evaluators need to view criteria as multidimensional in nature. For example, Kraiger et al. argued that learning outcomes can be divided into three types: cognitive (which reflect knowledge and cognitive strategies), skill based (reflecting constructs such as automaticity and compilation), and affective (reflecting constructs such as attitudes and motivation). These outcomes can be seen as analogous to Kirkpatrick's learning, behavior, and reactions criteria, respectively.

Varieties of Evaluation Criteria

Kirkpatrick outlined four steps or levels of measures of the effectiveness of training outcomes.

Level 1, reaction, is trainees' feelings for and liking of a training program. Reaction measures may indicate the trainee's motivation to learn; although positive reactions may not ensure learning, negative reactions probably reduce the possibility that learning occurs. A focus of this article is suggested improvements in the construction, expected relations, and interpretations of reactions measures.

Level 2, learning, was defined as the "principles, facts, and techniques understood and absorbed by the trainees". No change in behavior can be expected unless one or more of these learning objectives have been accomplished. Learning is most often assessed by giving the trainees tests that tap declarative knowledge.

Level 3, behavior, defined as transferring knowledge, skills, and attitudes learned during the training to the job, is typically measured on the job after a particular amount of time has passed. This is most often assessed through performance appraisal.

Level 4, results, was defined as the final results that occurred because the participants attended the program. These could include increased production, improved quality, decreased costs, reduced frequency and severity of accidents, increased sales, reduced turnover, and higher profits and return on investments.

Relations among Different Types of Criteria

Kirkpatrick's model has been misunderstood by researchers and practitioners to be hierarchical. Specifically, the following assumptions arose: (1) each succeeding level of evaluation criteria is more informative (or "better" in terms of information obtained for the organization; Russ-Eft & Preskill, 2001) than the last, (2) each level is caused by the preceding level, and (3) each succeeding level is correlated with the previous level. Using meta-analysis, Alliger and Janak (1989) clarified these misconceptions and found that reactions had a very weak correlation with learning ($r=.07$) and behavior ($r=.05$). They also found a correlation of .48 between reactions and results; however, this coefficient is based on only a single effect estimate. They found stronger relations between learning and behavior ($r=.13$), learning and results ($r=.40$), and behavior and results ($r=.19$).

More recently, Alliger and Tannenbaum decomposed the reaction criteria into three subcategories: affective, utility, and a combination of the two. Alliger, Tannenbaum, Bennet, Traver, and Shotland further subdivided Kirkpatrick's learning criteria into three components: immediate post training knowledge, knowledge retention, and behavior and skill demonstration. Alliger et al. found that affective and utility reactions were more strongly correlated with each other ($r=.34$) than with other measures and that immediate and retained learning measures were more strongly correlated with each other ($r=.35$) than with other measures. Alliger et al. also indicated that reaction measures are easy to collect and that this type of measure could be an ideal substitute for learning and transfer measures.

Echoing Alliger et al., Morgan and Casper argued that participant reactions can be used as predictors of more costly training effectiveness criteria: learning, behavior, and results. However, Morgan and Casper argued that constructs assessed by reaction measures may not be adequately captured by Alliger et al.'s affective and utility dimensions. In fact, previous research on training evaluation has called for the use of multidimensional criteria in assessing training effectiveness.

Transfer of Training and Criticisms of Kirkpatrick's Model

Despite the fact that organizations routinely use Kirkpatrick's criteria to evaluate training success, this model has been criticized in the literature. For example, Holton argued that Kirkpatrick's system is nothing more than a taxonomy of outcomes. Researchers have consequently proposed evaluation models that expand the predictor space by incorporating the effects of individual difference variables such as motivation to learn, trainability, job attitudes, personal characteristics, self-efficacy, and transfer of training conditions[4].

The inclusion of individual difference variables in models assessing training effectiveness has had mixed results. Dixon found that trainee perceptions of job relevance, amount learned, enjoyment, and instructor's skill were not significantly correlated with participants' posttest scores. Colquitt et al. found that trainee motivation to learn was significantly related to both declarative knowledge and skill acquisition. Furthermore, Tan found that learning goal orientation was significantly related with post-training behavior. An individual difference variable that is promising in a training context is the construct of intentions in the Theory of Planned Behavior[5]. Intentions are assumed to capture the joint effects of motivational factors that have an impact on a particular behavior. Intentions, in other words, indicate how hard people are willing to try or how much of an effort they are planning to exert in order to perform the behavior. These intentions remain as behavioral predispositions until an appropriate time and opportunity presents itself, at which point the individual attempts to translate intention into action[6].

In a recent study, for example, Tan found that trainee intentions were strongly correlated with their post training behaviors. Thus, intentions may be especially relevant to the issue of understanding transfer of training.

Hypotheses and Overview of the Study

In this article, we suggest that reactions criteria can be usefully grouped into two categories. The first is an affective category, <u>analogous to</u> the recommendations of Alliger and Tannenbaum and Alliger et al. . This is <u>in line with</u> more traditional measures of reactions, often obtained immediately after the training program, that ask for the trainee's liking or disliking of the training program.

The second category that we propose, however, differs from previous work. We suggest that it might be useful to distinguish reaction items that specifically tap instrumentality cognitions and behavioral intentions. Extensive work by Ajzen and his colleagues suggests that while beliefs and intentions influence a person's likelihood of performing a given behavior, these remain as behavioral predispositions until an appropriate time and opportunity presents itself on the job, after which the intention may then be translated into action. This model implies that items on a reaction measure that tap the intention factor should have a stronger relation with learning and behavior than will items that tap only the affective factor.

We propose to investigate the usefulness of the affective versus intention distinction for reactions criteria, as well as the relations among different types of training criteria. We collected measures of reaction, learning, and behavior in order to determine if the training program was effective and examine the pattern of relations among the three different types of criteria.

Specifically, we tested the following primary hypothesis:

HYPOTHESIS 1: Reaction items categorized as cognitive/intention will have a stronger relation with learning and behavior scores than will affective items.

Also, we tested the following hypotheses to demonstrate that the training program was indeed a successful one, as well as to replicate the results of previous training research.

HYPOTHESIS 2: There will be a statistically significant increase in the scores on the learning and behavior measures from pre-to posttest training, after controlling for relevant covariates (that is, previous experience).

HYPOTHESIS 3: Reactions will be positively correlated with learning and behavior. However, we expect that correlations of reactions with learning and with behavior will be of lower magnitude than the correlation between learning and behavior.

Results

We conducted a principal components analysis with oblimin rotation on the twenty affective and intention/cognition items. Results showed that items loaded on five factors.

Hypothesis 1 stated that cognitive/intention reaction items would have a stronger relation with learning and behavior scores than would affective reaction items. An examination of the correlation matrix presented revealed that both the Negative Evaluation ($r = .62$) and Improves ($r = .28$) dimensions positively correlated with post training learning. The Positive Evaluation, Improves, and Hands-on measures were also all positively correlated with the post-training self-ratings of behavior.

from: *Human Resource Development Quarterly*, vol. 14, no. 4, 2003

Words and Expressions

cognitive ['kɔgnitiv] *adj.* 认知的;认识的
notion ['nəuʃən] *n.* 概念;观念
enhance [in'hɑːns] *v.* 提高;增强
criteria [krai'tiəriə] *n.* (复数)标准
interventions [ˌintə(ː)'venʃən] *n.* 干涉
infancy ['infənsi] *n.* 幼年
alternative [ɔːl'təːnətiv] *adj.* 选择性的;二中择一的
compilation [ˌkɔmpi'leiʃən] *n.* 编辑
analogous [ə'næləgəs] *adj.* 类似的
absorb [əb'sɔːb] *v.* 吸收
accomplish [ə'kɔmpliʃ] *v.* 完成;实现
participant [pɑː'tisipənt] *n.* 参与者
severity [si'veriti] *n.* 严肃;严重
hierarchical [ˌhaiə'rɑːkikəl] *adj.* 分等级的
precede [pri(ː)'siːd] *v.* 先于
coefficient [kəui'fiʃənt] *n.* (数)系数
decompose [ˌdiːkəm'pəuz] *v.* 分解
utility [juː'tiliti] *n.* 效用
retention [ri'tenʃən] *n.* 保持力
taxonomy [tæk'sɔnəmi] *n.* 分类法;分类学
declarative [di'klærətiv] *adj.* 陈述的
predisposition [priːˌdispə'ziʃən] *n.* 易患病的体质
versus ['vəːsəs] *prep.* 与……相对
replicate ['replikit] *v.* 复制
covariate [kə'vɛəriit] *n.* 协方差
magnitude ['mægnitjuːd] *n.* 大小;数量
matrix ['meitriks] *n.* 矩阵
cognitive employee reaction 职员的认知反应

human capital 人力资本
declarative knowledge 已习得知识
to return on investment 投资回报
meta-analysis 隐含分析法
immediate post training knowledge 训后知识
multidimensional criteria 多边标准
self-efficacy 自我效能
behavioral predispositions 行为的本质特征
relevant covariates 相关的协方差
oblimin rotation 贡献循环比较法
hands-on 实习
self-ratings 自我评估

Difficult Sentences

① Reactions to training programs tend to be poor predictors of training success, yet most training programs are evaluated based solely on trainee reactions.
虽然对于培训计划的反应常常并不能很好地预测成功,但评估培训计划的唯一基础仍然是职员的反应。

② Training evaluation is a system for measuring changes due to training interventions—most important, whether trainees have achieved learning outcomes.
培训评估是检测源于培训干预所产生的变化的体系——最重要的是学员是否已经取得了一定的学习成果。

③ Despite these advances in training evaluation theory, the most developed and used of these models in the human resource literature focuses on defining different training effectiveness criteria and their organizational implications.
除了培训评估理论的这些进步,人力资源文献最为发达和广为利用的模式重点是定义不同培训效应标准及其组织内涵。

④ Researchers have consequently proposed evaluation models that expand the predictor space by incorporating the effects of individual difference variables such as motivation to learn, trainability, job attitudes, personal characteristics, self-efficacy, and transfer of training conditions.
所以研究者们提倡通过融合个人区别变量的效果以扩展预测空间的评估模式。个人区别变量主要有学习动机、可培训性、工作态度、个性、个人效能以及培训条件的改变。

⑤ An individual difference variable that is promising in a training context is the construct of intentions in the Theory of Planned Behavior.
受训环境下具有生命力的个人区别变量是"计划行为理论"中的意图构建。

⑥ These intentions remain as behavioral predispositions until an appropriate time and opportunity presents itself, at which point the individual attempts to translate intention into action
这些意图一直只是行为倾向,直到适当的时机出现,行为个体才会尝试化意图为行动。

Phrases and Patterns

1. contrary to... 与……相反
   Moreover, contrary to popular notion, negative affective reactions best predicted employee learning.
   此外,与流行观念相反,反面的情感反应却最好地预示了雇员的学习状况。
   Contrary to what we know, the trainees' reaction can't be a good predicator of the success of a definite training program.
   与我们所知相反,受训学员的反应并不能很好地预示某个特定培训计划的成功。

2. due to... 由于;应归于

Training evaluation is a system for measuring changes due to training interventions。
培训评估是检测源于培训干预所产生的变化的体系。
Due to the success of training program, the employees can now do their jobs by themselves without being monitored.
由于培训计划的成功,雇员们现在已能不受督导独立工作了。

3. as such... 同样地
As such, training evaluators need to view criteria as multidimensional in nature.
同样,培训评委们需要把标准看成其实质是多维的。
As such, this kind of needs assessment should also be done by specialists.
同样,此类需求评估也应由专家完成。

4. is correlated with... 使……与……发生关系;把……与……联系起来
Each succeeding level is correlated with the previous level.
每个下一级都与上一级相关。
They are not significantly correlated with the trainees' posttest scores.
它们与学员的试后得分没有太大的关系。

5. analogous to... 与……类似的、相似的
The first is an affective category, analogous to the recommendations of some specialists.
首先是情感类别,类似一些专家的推荐。
These outcomes can be seen as analogous to Kirkpatrick's learning behavior, and reactions criteria, respectively.
这些结果分别与 Kirkpatrick 的学问行为、反应标准类似。

6. in line with... 符合
This is in line with more traditional measures of reactions, often obtained immediately after the training program。
这与较为传统的衡量反应标准相符,培训后立刻可知。

It will be excellent if their employees' career plans are in line with those of the company.

如果雇员的事业计划与公司的一致就太好了。

Questions

1. As an employee, what kind of training you expect to have?
2. If you were the manager in charge of training the staff in a company, what factors would your detailed training plan involve?
3. If the effect of a training program isn't good enough, what would be possible problems? Where would you start to find them and how to solve them?

6

Career Management
职业生涯管理

【本章导读】 本章介绍职业生涯管理中的一些主要问题。6.1 在定义了职业生涯的概念后,介绍职业生涯的计划过程的主要环节,如自我评估、核实、建立目标、行动计划。6.2 则进一步详细区分职业生涯的各个主要阶段、特点、以及员工在不同职业阶段的不同需求。指出职业生涯阶段性的概念是理解和管理职业生涯发展的基础。6.3 关注的是员工个人职业生涯发展中的学习机会与学习行为的关系问题。

6.1 Brief Sketch of Career Management
职业生涯管理概要

Introduction

The trend toward flatter organizational structures means that career success can no longer be defined in terms of promotions because few will be available[①]. Companies have to help employees understand that other types of development activities, such as job rotation and lateral moves, are signs of career success, not failure. Flatter organizational structures also increase the likelihood that many employees will plateau. To combat plateauing (Sophia's career concern) companies have to take actions to ensure that employees receive challenging assignments with increased responsibilities. To succeed in a volatile and competitive business environment, companies have reduced their commitment to remain in specific businesses②. As a result, employees need to ensure that their skills are current in case they should lose their jobs.

Rapid changes in technology and a trend toward giving employees more responsibility has made work both more rewarding and more demanding. Because of the need to meet customers' needs, both employees and companies may neglect career-planning issues (Toran's career concerns). The failure to engage in career planning has negative results for both the company and its employees. From the company's perspective, the failure to help employees plan their careers can result in a shortage of employees to fill open positions. From the employee's perspective, the lack of career planning can result in frustration and feelings of not being valued by the company. As we will see in this chapter, companies, managers, and employees need to take actions to ensure that career planning occurs.

Companies need to help employees manage their careers to maximize their career motivation. Career motivation has three aspects: career resilience, career insight, and career identity. Career resilience is the extent to which employees are able to cope with problems that affect their work③. Career insight is how much employees know about their interests, their skill strengths and weaknesses, and the ways these perceptions relate to their career goals. Career identity is the degree to which employees define their personal value according to their work.④

Companies can only be innovative and adaptable to the degree that their employees have career motivation. Employees who have high career resilience are able to respond to obstacles in the work environment and adapt to unexpected events (such as changes in work processes or customer demands). They are willing to develop new ways to use their skills to cope with obstacles and unexpected events. Employees with high career insight set career goals and participate in development activities that help them reach those goals. They tend to take actions that keep their skills from becoming obsolete. Employees with high career identity are committed to the company; they are willing to do whatever it takes (e. g. , work long hours) to complete projects and meet customer demands. They also take pride in working for the company and are active in professional and trade organizations.

What Is a Career?

We consider a career to be "the pattern of work-related experiences that span the course of a person's life. " Work experiences include positions, job experiences, and tasks. Work experiences are influenced by employees' values, needs, and feelings. Employees' career needs vary depending on their stage of career development and their biological age[5]. As a result, it is important for managers to understand the career development process and the differences in employees' needs and interests at each stage of development.

Components of Career-planning Systems

Companies' career-planning systems vary in the level of sophistication and the emphasis they place on the different components of the process. However, all career-planning systems include the components shown in Figure 6. 1.

Self-assessment

Self-assessment helps employees determine their career interests, values, aptitudes, and behavioral tendencies. It often involves the use of psychological tests such as the Strong-Campbell Interest Inventory and

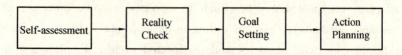

Figure 6.1 The Career-planning Process

the Self-Directed Search. The former helps employees identify their occupational and job interests; the latter identifies employees' preferences for working in different type of environments (e. g. , sales, counseling, landscaping). Tests may also help employees identify the relative value they place on work and leisure activities. Career counselors are often used to assist employees in the self-assessment process and interpret the results of psychological tests.

For example, a man who had served as a branch manager at Wells Fargo Bank for 14 years enjoyed both working with computers and researching program-development issues. He was experiencing difficulty in choosing whether to pursue further work experiences with computers or enter a new career in developing software applications. Psychological tests he completed as part of the company's career-assessment program confirmed that he had strong interests in research and development. As a result, he began his own software design company

Reality Check

Employees receive information about how the company evaluates their skills and knowledge and where they fit into the company's plans (e. g. , potential promotion opportunities, lateral moves). Usually, this information is provided by the employee's manager as part of the performance-appraisal process. It is not uncommon in well-developed career-planning systems for the manager to hold separate performance appraisals and career development discussions.[6] For example, in Coca-Cola U. S. A's career-planning system, employees and managers have a separate meeting after the annual performance review to discuss the employee's career interests, strengths, and possible development activities.

Goal Setting

Employees determine their short-and long-term career goals during this phase of the career-planning process. These goals usually relate to desired positions (e. g. , to become sales manager within three years), level of skill application(e. g. , to use one's budgeting skills to improve the unit's cash-flow problems), work setting (e. g. , to move to corporate marketing within two years), or skill acquisition (e. g. , to learn how to use the company's human resource information system). These goals are usually discussed with the manager and written into a development plan.

Action Planning

During this phase, employees determine how they will achieve their short-and long-term career goals. Action plans may involve enrolling in training courses and seminars, conducting informational interviews, or applying for job openings within the company.

from: *Human Resource Management: Gaining a Competitive Advantage* ,1994

Words and Expressions

flat [flæt] *adj.* 平坦的;扁平的
rotation [rəu'teiʃən] *n.* 旋转
lateral ['lætərəl] *adj.* 横向的
plateau ['plætəu] *v.* 趋于稳定;停滞
combat ['kɔmbət] *v.* 战斗;搏斗;抗击
volatile ['vɔlətail] *adj.* 可变的;不稳定的
ensure [in'ʃuə] *v.* 保证;保证得到
rewarding [ri'wɔːdiŋ] *adj.* 值得的
demanding [di'mændiŋ] *adj.* 苛求的
perspective [pə'spektiv] *n.* 观点;看法
frustration [frʌs'treiʃən] *n.* 挫败;挫折

identity [ai'dentiti] n. 同一性；一致
resilience [ri'ziliəns] n. 有弹力；恢复力
innovative ['inəuveitiv] adj. 创新的
obstacle ['ɔbstəkl] n. 障碍；妨害物
adapt [ə'dæpt] v. 使适应；改编
obsolete ['ɔbsəli:t] adj. 荒废的；陈旧的
span [spæn] v. 横越
vary ['vɛəri] v. 变化
sophistication [sə͵fisti'keiʃən] n. 复杂性；复杂
aptitude ['æptitju:d] n. 智能
counselor ['kaunsələ] n. 顾问
pursue [pə'sju:] v. 继续；从事
confirm [kən'fə:m] v. 确定
acquisition [͵ækwi'ziʃən] n. 获得
seminars ['seminɑ:] n. 研究会
career management 职业生涯管理
flatter organizational structures 扁平化组织结构
career plateau 职业发展停滞
career resilience 职业张力
career insight 职业洞察力
career identity 职业一致性
self-assessment 自我评估
the Strong-Campbell Interest Inventory 兴趣拓展训练营
the Self-Directed Search 自我调查
career counselor 职业顾问

Difficult Sentences

① The trend toward flatter organizational structures means that career success can no longer be defined in terms of promotions because few will be available.
组织结构扁平化的趋势意味着由于晋升的机会有限，事业的成功

与否不会再由它来定义。

② To succeed in a volatile and competitive business environment, companies have reduced their commitment to remain in specific businesses.
为了在动荡激烈的竞争环境中取得成功,公司减少了员工在特殊事务中所承担的义务。

③ Career resilience is the extent to which employees are able to cope with problems that affect their work.
事业张力指的是职员能够控制影响其工作问题的程度。

④ Career identity is the degree to which employees define their personal value according to their work.
事业身份指的是职员依照其工作定义个人价值。

⑤ Employees' career needs vary depending on their stage of career development and their biological age.
职员事业需求的变化取决于其事业发展阶段以及生理年龄。

⑥ It is not uncommon in well-developed career-planning systems for the manager to hold separate performance appraisals and career development discussions.
在高度发达的事业计划体系中,由经理们主持的独立的成绩考核以及事业发展讨论也不是不常见的。

Phrases and Patterns

1. take actions... 采取行动

   To combat plateauing (Sophia's career concern) companies have to take actions to ensure that employees receive challenging assignments with increased responsibilities.
   为了抗击事业停滞不前(Sophia 对事业的关心),公司必须采取行动以确保雇员们得到挑战性的工作和更多的责任。
   They tend to take actions that keep their skills from becoming obsolete.
   他们倾向于采取防止其技能过时的行动。

2. in case... 以防……

As a result, employees need to ensure that their skills are current in case they should lose their jobs.

其结果是雇员需要确保其技能不落伍以防失业。

The company may not neglect career-planning in case that there would be a shortage of employees to fill open positions.

公司不可忽视事业计划以防一些开放性的职位人员短缺。

3. relate to... 与……相关;涉及……

These goals usually relate to desired positions, level of skill application, work setting, or skill acquisition.

这些目标通常与理想职位、技能运用水平、工作环境和掌握技巧有关。

Action plans relate to enrolling in training course and seminars, conducting informational interviews.

行动计划涉及报名参加培训课程和研讨会、开办信息见面会。

4. enroll in... 报名参加……

Action plans may involve enrolling in training courses and seminars, conducting informational interviews, or applying for job openings within the company.

行动计划可能包括报名参加培训课程和研究会、展开信息会晤或申请公司内部的空岗。

The psychological test he enrolled in was part of the company's career-assessment program.

他报名参加的心理测试是公司评估计划的一部分。

6.2　Career Stages

职业生涯阶段

Introduction

Most working people prepare for their occupation by undergoing some form of organized education in high school, trade school, vocational school, or college. They then take a first job, but the chances are that they will move to other jobs in the same organization or in other organizations. Eventually, <u>over the course of</u> their career, they settle into a position in which they remain until retirement. The duration of each stage varies among individuals, but most working people go through all of these stages.

Studies of career stages have found that needs and expectations change as the individual moves through the stages. Figure 6.2 summarizes the relationship between career stages and individuals' needs.

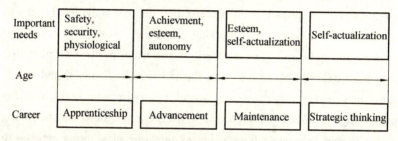

Figure 6.2 Career Stages and Important Needs

Managers at American Telephone and Telegraph (AT&T), for example, expressed considerable concern for safety needs during the initial years on their jobs. This phase, termed the establishment phase, ordinarily lasted during the first five years of employment.

Following the establishment phase is the advancement phase, which lasts approximately from age 30 to age 45. During this period, the AT&T managers expressed considerably less concern for safety and more concern for achievement, esteem, and autonomy.

The maintenance phase follows the advancement phase. This period is marked by efforts to stabilize the gains of the past. Although no new gains may be made, the maintenance phase can be a period of creativity, since the individual has satisfied many of the psychological and financial needs associated with earlier phases. Although each individual and each career will be different, it is reasonable to assume that esteem and self-actualization would be the most important needs in the maintenance phase. But, as we will see, many people experience what is called a mid career crisis during the maintenance phase. Such people are not achieving satisfaction from their work, and consequently they may experience psychological discomfort.

The maintenance phase is followed by the retirement phase. The individual has, in effect, completed one career, and he or she may move on to another one. During this phase, the individual may have opportunities to experience self-actualization through activities that it was impossible to pursue while working. Painting, gardening, volunteer service, and quiet reflection are some of the many positive avenues that have been followed by retirees. But the individual's financial and health status may make it necessary to spend the retirement years worrying about satisfying needs. Preretirement planning programs are becoming more common in organizations today as one way of allowing retirees to focus on other, more fulfilling needs.

The fact that individuals pass through different stages during their careers is evident. It is also understandable that individual needs and motives are different from one stage to the next. But managing careers requires a more complete description of what happens to individuals during these stages. One group of individuals whose careers are of special significance to the performance of modern organizations are the professionals. "Knowledge workers"—such as professional accountants, scientists, and engineers—are one of the fastest-growing segments of the workforce. This segment constitutes 32 percent of the workforce at present (blue-collar workers make up 33 percent). Many professionals spend their careers in large, complex organizations after having spent several years obtaining advanced training and degrees. The organizations that employ them expect them to provide the innovativeness and creativity for organizational survival in dynamic, competitive environments[1]. Obviously, the performance levels of professional employees must be of the utmost concern for the organization's leaders.

Stage I

Young professionals enter an organization with technical knowledge but often without an understanding of the organization's demands and expectations. Consequently, they must work fairly closely with more experienced people. The relationship that develops between the young professionals and their supervisors is an apprenticeship. The central activities in which apprentices are expected to show competence include learning and following directions. To move successfully and effectively through stage I, one must be able to accept the psychological state of dependence. Some professionals cannot cope with being placed in a situation similar to that which they experienced in school[2]. They find that they are still being directed by an authority figure, just as they were in school, whereas they had anticipated that their first job would provide considerably more freedom.

Stage II

Once through the dependent relationship of stage I, the professional employee moves into stage II, which calls for working independently. Passage to this stage depends on the employee's having demonstrated competence in some specific technical area. The technical expertise may be in a content area, such as taxation, product testing, or quality assurance, or it may be in a skill area, such as computer applications. The professional's primary activity in stage II is to be an independent contributor of ideas in the chosen area. The professional is expected to rely much less on direction from others. The psychological state of independence may pose some problems because it is in such stark contrast to the state of dependence required in stage I.③ Stage II is extremely important for the professional's future career growth. Those who fail at this stage typically do so because they do not have the necessary self-confidence.

In the Career Challenge at the beginning of this chapter, there is an indication that Jim Lucio is at stage II in his career development. Jim values his independence. He wants to be his own boss and run his own business. Independence is a high priority for him, as it is for most professionals at stage II.

Stage III

Professionals who enter stage III are expected to become the mentors of those in stage I. They also tend to broaden their interests and to deal more and more with people outside the organization. Thus, the central activities of professionals at this stage are training and interaction with others. Stage III professionals assume responsibility for the work of others, and this characteristic of the stage can cause considerable psychological stress. In previous stages, the professional was responsible only for his or her own work. But now it is the work of others that is of primary concern. Individuals who cannot cope with this new requirement may decide to shift back to stage II. Individuals who <u>derive satisfaction from</u> seeing other people move on to bigger and better jobs will be content to remain in stage III until retirement.

A mentoring relationship has been defined as the relationship between an experienced employee and a junior employee, in which the experienced person helps the junior person with effective socialization by sharing information gained through experience with the organization. This kind of relationship is expected to <u>contribute to</u> the junior employee's instruction, job performance, and retention. In a successful mentoring relationship, the junior person's career is enhanced by a range of activities (coaching, exposure and visibility, and protection) that the senior person facilitates. Also, the mentoring relationship provides the junior person with support that helps him or her acquire a sense of personal identity. The person in stage III serving as a mentor can derive tremendous satisfaction from the growth, development, and advancement of a protégé. In some organizations, such as JCPenney, Sears, and IBM, stage III professionals will not be promoted until they can demonstrate an ability to prepare junior subordinates for promotion and more job responsibilities.

In the past, it has been difficult for women and minorities to establish mentoring relationships. Research has suggested that some men hesitate to act as mentors for female protégés because of the sexual innuendoes that often accompany such relationships[④]. In addition, some research indicates that senior women are also somewhat reluctant to mentor junior women because they perceive significant organizational risks in doing so. As the number of women and minorities reaching senior levels of management increases, however, it is hoped that the opportunity for them to mentor junior colleagues will also increase.

Stage IV

Some professional employees remain in stage III; for these professionals, stage III is the career maintenance phase. Other professionals progress to yet another stage. Not all professionals experience stage IV, because its fundamental characteristic involves shaping the direction of the organization itself. Although we usually think of such activity as being undertaken by only one individual in an organization—its chief executive—in fact, it may be undertaken by many others. For example, key personnel in product development, process manufacturing, or technological research may be in stage IV. As a consequence of their performance in stage III of their careers, stage IV professionals direct their attention to long-range strategic planning. In doing so, they play the roles of manager, entrepreneur, and idea generator. Their primary job relationships are to identify and sponsor the careers of their successors and to interact with key people outside the organization. The most significant shift for a person in Stage IV is to accept the decisions of subordinates without second guessing them. Stage IV professionals must learn to influence—that is, practice leadership through such indirect means as idea planting, personnel selection, and organizational design. These shifts can be difficult for an individual who has relied on direct supervision in the past.

The concept of career stages is fundamental for understanding and managing career development. It is necessary to comprehend life stages as well. Individuals go through career stages as they go through life stages, but the interaction between career stages and life stages is not easy to understand.

from: *Human Resource Management*, 1994

Words and Expressions

eventually [i'ventjuəli] *adv.* 最后;终于
esteem [is'ti:m] *n.* 尊敬;尊重
autonomy [ɔ:'tɔnəmi] *n.* 自治
actualization [ˌæktjuəlai'zeiʃən] *n.* 实现
maintenance ['meintinəns] *n.* 维护;保持
stabilize ['steibilaiz] *v.* 稳定
consequently ['kɔnsikwəntli] *adv.* 从而;因此
pursue [pə'sju:] *v.* 追赶;继续
avenue ['ævinju:] *n.* 方法;途径
evident ['evidənt] *adj.* 明显的;显然的
segment ['segmənt] *n.* 段;节;片断

dynamic [dai'næmik] *adj.* 动态的
competence ['kɔmpətəns] *n.* 能力
anticipate [æn'tisipeit] *v.* 预期；期望
demonstrate ['demənstreit] *v.* 示范；证明；论证
expertise [ˌekspə'tiːz] *n.* 专家的意见；专门技术
assurance [ə'ʃuərəns] *n.* 断言；保证
pose [pəuz] *v.* 引起；造成
stark [stɑːk] *adj.* 十足的
interaction [ˌintər'ækʃən] *n.* 交互作用
mentor ['mentɔː] *n.* 贤明的顾问；指导者
derive [di'raiv] *v.* 源于
retention [ri'tenʃən] *n.* 保持力；张力
exposure [iks'pəuʒə] *n.* 揭露
facilitate [fə'siliteit] *v.* 推动；帮助；促进
subordinate [sə'bɔːdinit] *n.* 下属
minority [mai'nɔriti] *n.* 少数；少数民族
innuendo [ˌinju'endəu] *n.* 暗讽的话；影射的话
reluctant [ri'lʌktənt] *adj.* 勉强的
entrepreneur [ˌɔntrəprə'nəː] *n.* 企业家；主办人
sponsor ['spɔnsə] *v.* 发起；主办
shift [ʃift] *n.* 移动；轮班；移位
self-actualization 自我实现
American Telephone and Telegraph 美国电信
self-actualization 自我实现
a mid-career crisis 职业中期危机
preretirement planning programs 提前退休计划
dependent relationship 依赖型关系
a high priority 高优先性
psychological stress 心理压力
protégé（法语）受保护者

junior employee 初级雇员

chief executive 首席执行官

Difficult Sentences

① The organizations that employ them expect them to provide the innovativeness and creativity for organizational survival in dynamic, competitive environments.

雇佣他们的组织希望其能在动态的竞争环境中为组织的存活提供创新与创造力。

② Some professionals cannot cope with being placed in a situation similar to that which they experienced in school.

一些专业人士被置于类似于他们上学时的环境里,感到无所适从。

③ The psychological state of independence may pose some problems because it is in such stark contrast to the state of dependence required in stage I.

独立的心态也许会引发问题,因为这与阶段 I 中的依赖状态完全相反。

④ Research has suggested that some men hesitate to act as mentors for female protégés because of the sexual innuendoes that often accompany such relationships.

研究表明,由于性暗示常与此类关系相伴,一些男士不愿担当女学员的指导者。

Phrases and Patterns

1. associate... with... 联系……

Although no new gains may be made, the maintenance phase can be a period of creativity, since the individual has satisfied many of the psychological and financial needs associated with earlier phases.

尽管没有新的收获,由于个人已经满足了与早期相关的多种心理及经济需求,维持期仍可以是一个充满创造的阶段。
You normally wouldn't associate them with each other, their styles are completely different.
你通常不会把他们联系起来,他们的风格截然不同。
2. derive... from... 从……中得到
Individuals who derive satisfaction from seeing other people move on to bigger and better jobs will be content to remain in stage III until retirement.
从他人的升职和另谋高就中获得满足的人将满足于处在阶段III直到退休。
The person in stage III serving as a mentor can derive tremendous satisfaction from the growth, development, and advancement of a protégé.
处于阶段III的人员担任督导可以从学员的成长、发展和进步获取极大的满足。
3. contribute to... 有助于……
This kind of relationship is expected to contribute to the junior employee's instruction, job performance, and retention.
期望这种关系有助于对年轻职员的指导,有助于年轻职员的工作表现和工作张力。
What they learned in stage I has contributed a lot to their later career development.
他们在第I阶段的学习对于以后事业的发展大有益处。
4. as a consequence of... 因而;结果
As a consequence of their performance in stage III of their careers, stage IV professionals direct their attention to long-range strategic planning.
职业阶段III的结果是,身处阶段IV的职业人员把注意力投向长期战略筹划。
As a consequence of the intervention of training, most of the trainees

will accomplish positive learning effect.

由于培训的干预,大多数学员都将获取积极的学习效果。

6.3 The Impact on Career Development of Learning Opportunities and Learning Behavior at Work
工作中的学习机会和学习行为对职业生涯的影响

Introduction

Individual career development is becoming more important at a time when traditional lifetime employment is increasingly under attack. As Walton (1999) observes: "Individuals... need to take greater responsibility for their own career development.... The boundaries between what constitutes career development and what constitutes employee development are becoming blurred. Every development activity can be seen as a career experience". As a result, organizations have to make sure they attract people with proactive learning behavior, while offering ample learning opportunities in order to retain the best people. HRD professionals can make an important strategic contribution to their organizations if they succeed in offering the right learning opportunities to the right people.

Theoretical Framework

In order to study the effect of learning opportunities and individual learning behavior on career development. The interactive nature of career development is shown to be determined by the mutual relationships between the learning opportunities provided by the environment and the individual's learning behavior. Furthermore, several empirical studies have suggested that the personal development process on the job is a result of the interaction of personal and organizational characteristics[①].

The concept of career development and the two factors defined as its success factors, learning opportunities and learning behavior in the workplace, are explained below, followed by an overview of earlier studies into the impact of learning opportunities and learning behavior on career development.

Hypotheses

The study focused particularly on the relationships of learning opportunities and learning behavior with individual career development[②]. We wanted to test the impact of these factors on career development over time. Based on the literature review presented above, we first developed hypotheses about the effect of learning opportunities on career development. After that, we developed hypotheses about relationships between learning behavior and career development. The following hypotheses were investigated:

· Hypothesis 1a. More learning opportunities will result in higher income.

· Hypothesis 1b. A work environment with more learning opportunities has a positive effect on the perception of career development.

· Hypothesis 2a. Learning behavior affects income.

· Hypothesis 2b. Learning behavior affects the perception of career development.

Conclusions and Discussion

To test the influence of both learning behavior and learning opportunities as determinants of career development, we conducted a quantitative field study. Then we make conclusions below:

Two specific kinds of learning opportunities were found to be relevant: supervisory support and obstacles. Supervisory support has a positive effect on perceived career development, whereas obstacles—that is, lack of managerial and collegial support—affect this negatively. This illustrates the link between a stimulating, supportive job environment and an individual's career satisfaction. Apparently, current professionals have a desire for feedback on their performance, more or less related to an awareness of their own responsibility for their learning and development③.

Our results are consistent with this perspective, in that respondents who engage in tacit learning behavior with a deliberate focus on learning goals and developmental targets had higher perceptions of their personal career development. In other words, people are more satisfied with their own career development if goals and targets are set beforehand. This could be a result of creating a more realistic view of their learning and development. Besides, this planned learning behavior relates positively with the level of income. Apparently, defining clear goals and targets for one's career helps to generate more income. This could be the result of a personal development plan linked to a career path, which is reflected in the level of income.

This study indicates that both learning opportunities and learning behavior are success factors for career development of M. B. A. s. Their relative influence, however, depends on the outcome measure. More specifically, from related studies it followed that learning behavior is more important in predicting objective measures of career development (income and objective job performance), while learning opportunities explain more of the variance in subjective measures of career development (subjective job performance and perceived career development)④. These results indicate that personal but also organizational variables should be taken into account in order to predict career development of high-level professionals in the early career stage.

from: *Human Resource Development Quarterly*, vol. 14, no. 2, Summer 2003

Words and Expressions

impact ['impækt] n. 影响;效果
constitute ['kɔnstitju:t] v. 组成
blur [blə:] v. 涂污;污损(名誉)等
proactive [ˌprəu'æktiv] adj. (心理)前摄的
ample ['æmpl] adj. 充足的;丰富的
mutual ['mju:tjuəl] adj. 相互的;共有的
empirical [em'pirikəl] adj. 完全根据经验的
career [kə'riə] n. 事业
present [pri'zent] v. 提出
determinant [di'tə:minənt] adj. 决定性的
quantitative ['kwɔntitətiv] adj. 数量的;定量的
supervisory [ˌsju:pə'vaizəri] adj. 管理的;监督的
perceive [pə'si:v] v. 察觉
collegial [kə'li:dʒiəl] adj. 大学之组织的
apparently [ə'pærəntli] adv. 显然地
consistent [kən'sistənt] adj. 一致的;调和的
tacit ['tæsit] adj. 默许的
deliberate [di'libəreit] adj. 深思熟虑的
generate ['dʒenəˌreit] v. 产生;发生
variance ['vɛəriəns] n. 不一致;变化
predicate ['predikit] v. 断言
lifetime employment 终生雇佣
proactive learning behavior 前摄学习行为
perceived career development 事业发展感知
tacit learning behavior 默学行为
organizational variable 组织变量

Difficult Sentences

① Furthermore, several empirical studies have suggested that the personal development process on the job is a result of the interaction of personal and organizational characteristics.
此外,几项经验性研究表明个人的工作发展过程是个人性格与组织性格交互作用的结果。

② The study focused particularly on the relationships of learning opportunities and learning behavior with individual career development.
该项研究尤其重视学习机遇、行为与个人事业发展的关系。

③ Apparently, current professionals have a desire for feedback on their performance, more or less related to an awareness of their own responsibility for their learning and development.
显然,当今的职业人士渴望得到对其工作表现的反馈意见,这或多或少地与其意识到身负学习与发展的责任有关。

④ More specifically, from related studies it followed that learning behavior is more important in predicting objective measures of career development (income and objective job performance), while learning opportunities explain more of the variance in subjective measures of career development (subjective job performance and perceived career development).
更具体地说,相关研究表明,学习行为在预测事业发展(收入及客观工作表现)的客观标准中更为重要,而学习机遇却对事业发展的主观标准(主观工作表现及感知事业发展)的变化更具解释力。

Phrases and Patterns

1. take responsibility for... 对……负责
   Individuals need to take greater responsibility for their own career

development.

个人需要为自己职业的发展负更大的责任。

It means that the company should also take some responsibilities for their employees' career development.

亦即公司亦应对其雇员的事业发展负些责任。

2. make contribution to... 贡献

   HRD professionals can make an important strategic contribution to their organizations if they succeed in offering the right learning opportunities to the right people.

   如果人力资源开发人士能成功地为合适的人提供恰当的学习机会,他们就能为其组织做出重要的战略贡献。

   Right and enough learning opportunities will make great contribution to increase the income of both the company and its employees.

   恰当而足够的学习机会有助于增加公司及雇员两者的收入。

3. be consistent with... 与……一致

   Our results are consistent with this perspective, in that respondents who engage in tacit learning behavior with a deliberate focus on learning goals and developmental targets had higher perceptions of their personal career development.

   我们的研究成果与这一观点一致,即:在无声的学习行为中刻意注重学习目标,发展目标的受试人员对个人的事业发展更加敏感。

   Whatever the needs assessment are like, they should first be consistent with the development of both the company and the employees' personal careers.

   无论需求评估怎样,都应首先与公司和雇员个人职业发展一致。

4. take... into account 考虑……

   These results indicate that personal but also organizational variables should be taken into account in order to predict career development of high-level professionals in the early career stage.

结果显示,要预测高层职业人士事业早期的发展状况,不仅个人变量,组织变量也应予以考虑。

When it comes to career motivation, we should first take into account the following three aspects, career resilience, career insight and career identity.

谈及职业动机,我们首先应该考虑的是职业张力、职业洞察力和职业身份。

Questions

1. Explain from your own experience the relationship between career planning and success.
2. Learning opportunities and learning behavior have great impact on career development. What kind of role do they play in each of the following career stage: apprenticeship, advancement, maintenance, and strategic thinking?
3. How would you like to manage your own career development?

7

Performance Appraisal
绩效考核

【本章导读】 本章介绍成绩考核的内容及其主要方法。7.1 定义成绩考核的内容,主要介绍其决定性因素、阻碍绩效的环境因素、考核方法以及考核中易犯的错误。7.2 介绍目标法、多角度评价法、工作标准法和文字叙述评价法等九种考核方式。7.3 阐释人事评估系统循环坐标法中的九个评估因素,如参加考核培训、进行年度会见、阅读考核指南等。

7.1 Brief Sketch of Performance Appraisal
绩效考核概要

Definition and Uses

Performance refers to the degree of accomplishment of the tasks that make up an employee's job[①]. It reflects how well an employee is fulfilling the requirements of a job. Often confused with effort, which refers to energy expended, performance is measured in terms of results. For example, a student may exert a great deal of effort in preparing for an examination and still make a poor grade. In such a case the effort expended was high, yet the performance was low.

Performance appraisal is the process of determining and communicating to an employee how he or she is performing on the job and, ideally, establishing a plan of improvement. When properly conducted, performance appraisals not only let employees know how well they are performing but also influence their future level of effort and task direction. Effort should be enhanced if the employee is properly reinforced. The task perception of the employee should be clarified through the establishment of a plan for improvement.

One of the most common uses of performance appraisals is for making administrative decisions relating to promotions, firings, layoffs, and merit pay increases. For example, the present job performance of an employee is often the most significant consideration for determining whether to promote the person. While successful performance in the present job does not necessarily mean an employee will be an effective performer in a higher-level job, performance appraisals do provide some predictive information.

Performance appraisal information can also provide needed input for determining both individual and organizational training and development needs. For example, this information can be used to identify an individual employee's strengths and weaknesses. These data can then be used to help determine the organization's overall training and development needs. For an individual employee, a completed performance appraisal should include a plan outlining specific training and development needs.

Another important use of performance appraisals is to encourage performance improvement. In this regard, performance appraisals are used as a means of communicating to employees how they are doing and suggesting needed changes in behavior, attitude, skills, or knowledge. This type of feedback clarifies for employees the job expectations held by the manager. Often this feedback must be followed by coaching and training by the manager to guide an employee's work efforts②.

Finally, two other important uses of information generated through performance appraisals are (1) input to the validation of selection procedures and (2) input to human resource planning. Both of these topics were described in detail in earlier chapters.

A concern in organizations is how often to conduct performance appraisals. There seems to be no real consensus on how frequently performance appraisals should be done, but in general the answer is as often as necessary to let employees know what kind of job they are doing and, if performance is not satisfactory, the measures that must be taken for improvement. For many employees, this cannot be accomplished through one annual performance appraisal. Therefore, it is recommended that for most employees, informal performance appraisals be conducted two or three times a year in addition to an annual formal performance appraisal.

Determinants of Performance

Job performance is the net effect of an employee's effort as modified by abilities and role (or task) perceptions③. Thus, performance in a given situation can be viewed as <u>resulting from</u> the interrelationships among effort, abilities, and role perceptions.

Effort, which results from being motivated, refers to the amount of energy (physical and/or mental) an individual uses in performing a task. Abilities are personal characteristics used in performing a job. Abilities usually do not fluctuate widely over short periods of time. Role (task) perceptions refer to the direction(s) in which individuals believe they should channel their efforts on their jobs. The activities and behaviors people believe are necessary in the performance of their jobs define their role perceptions.

Environmental Factors as Performance Obstacles

Some of the more common potential performance obstacles include a lack of or conflicting demands on the employee's time, inadequate work facilities and equipment, restrictive policies that affect the job, lack of cooperation from others, type of supervision, temperature, lighting, noise, machine or equipment pacing, shifts, and even luck.

Environmental factors should be viewed not as direct determinants of individual performance but as modifying the effects of effort, ability, and direction. For example, poor ventilation or worn-out equipment may well affect the effort an individual expends. Unclear policies or poor supervision can also produce misdirected effort. Similarly, a lack of training can <u>result in</u> underutilized abilities. One of management's greatest responsibilities is to provide employees with adequate working conditions and a supportive environment to eliminate or minimize performance obstacles[④].

Appraisal Method

Whatever method of performance appraisal an organization uses, it must be job related. Therefore, <u>prior to</u> selecting a performance appraisal method, an organization must conduct job analyses and develop job descriptions.

Organizations belong to the American Management Association's human resources, finance, marketing, and information systems divisions explored the frequency of use of the various appraisal methods. The method most frequently mentioned was goal setting, followed by written essay statements, descriptions of critical incidents, graphic rating scales, weighted checklists, and behaviorally anchored rating scales. The methods used were paired comparisons, forced choice, and forced distribution. In recent years many firms have replaced traditional appraisal methods with various kinds of appraisal management, including goal setting and ongoing assessment.

Potential Errors in Performance Appraisals

Several common errors have been identified in performance appraisals. Leniency is the grouping of ratings at the positive end instead of spreading them throughout the performance scale[5]. Central tendency occurs when appraisal statistics indicate that most employees are appraised as being near the middle of the performance scale. Recency occurs when evaluations are based on work performed most recently-generally work performed one to two months prior to evaluation. Leniency, central tendency and recency errors make it difficult, if not impossible, to separate the good performers. In addition, these errors make it difficult to compare ratings from different raters. For example, it is possible for a good performer who is evaluated by a manager committing central tendency errors to receive a lower rating than a poor performer who is rated by a manager committing leniency errors.

Another common error in performance appraisals is the halo effect. This occurs when a rater allows a single prominent characteristic of an employee to influence his or her judgment on each separate item in the performance appraisal. This often results in the employee receiving approximately the same rating on every item.

Personal preferences, prejudices, and biases can also cause errors in performance appraisals. Managers with biases or prejudices tend to look for employee behaviors that conform to their biases. Appearance, social status, dress, race, and sex have influenced many performance appraisals. Managers have also allowed first impressions to influence later judgments of an employee. First impressions are only a sample of behavior; however, people tend to retain these impressions even when faced with contradictory evidence.

from: *Human Resource Management*, 7th Edition, 2007

Words and Expressions

confuse [kən'fju:z] *v.* 搞乱;使糊涂
perception [pə'sepʃən] *n.* 理解;感知
clarify ['klærifai] *v.* 澄清;阐明
layoff ['lei˛ɔ:f] *n.* 失业期
predictive [pri'diktiv] *adj.* 预言性的
identify [ai'dentifai] *v.* 识别
validation [væli'deiʃən] *n.* 确认
consensus [kən'sensəs] *n.* 一致同意;多数人的意见
modify ['mɔdifai] *v.* 修改
fluctuate ['flʌktjueit] *v.* 变动;波动
potential [pə'tenʃ(ə)l] *adj.* 潜在的;可能的
conflicting [kən'fliktiŋ] *adj.* 相冲突的
supervision [sju:pə'viʒən] *n.* 监督;管理
ventilation [venti'leiʃən] *n.* 通风
underutilize [ˌʌndə'ju:tilaiz] *v.* 未充分使用
eliminate [i'limineit] *v.* 排除;消除
prior ['praiə] *adj.* 优先的
frequency ['fri:kwənsi] *n.* 频率;周率
graphic ['græfik] *adj.* 图解的
anchor ['æŋkə] *v.* 锚定
prominent ['prɔminənt] *adj.* 卓越的;显著的
prejudice ['predʒudis] *n.* 偏见;成见
bias ['baiəs] *n.* 偏见;偏爱
overall training 全面培训
net effect 净效应
graphic rating scales 图表法
weighted checklist 权重核对表格法

behaviorally anchored rating scales 行为锚定等级评价法
halo effect 晕轮效应
central tendency 趋中效应

Difficult Sentences

① Performance refers to the degree of accomplishment of the tasks that make up an employee's job.
绩效指的是雇员完成任务即其工作构成的程度。

② Often this feedback must be followed by coaching and training by the manager to guide an employee's work efforts.
通常,为了对雇员的工作努力行为加以引导,反馈后必须随之进行的是由经理进行辅导和培训。

③ Job performance is the net effect of an employee's effort as modified by abilities and role (or task) perceptions.
工作绩效是经由能力和作用(任务)感知修正后的、雇员努力的净效应。

④ One of management's greatest responsibilities is to provide employees with adequate working conditions and a supportive environment to eliminate or minimize performance obstacles.
管理的最大责任之一是为雇员提供足够的工作条件和有利的环境,以消除或最小化工作阻力。

⑤ Leniency is the grouping of ratings at the positive end instead of spreading them throughout the performance scale.
从众效应是最后的评价归类,并非贯穿整个绩效评价。

Phrases and Patterns

1. connfused with... 与……混杂;对……困惑……
Often confused with effort, which refers to energy expended, performance is measured in terms of results.
绩效通常与努力混淆,后者是指经历的扩展,而前者却由工作成果来衡量。
The appraisal guidelines should be clear and easy-to-follow, so that the employees will not get confused with them.
评价指南应该清晰、易行,员工才不会感到困惑。

2. resulting from... 由……产生
Thus, performance in a given situation can be viewed as resulting from the interrelationships among effort, abilities, and role perceptions.
因而,给定条件下的绩效可以看成是产生于努力、能力和作用感知的相互作用。
Effort, which results from being motivated, refers to the amount of energy (physical and/or mental) an individual uses in performing a task.
努力,源于动机,是指个体在完成工作时所使用的精力的总量(体力上的和/或脑力上的)。

3. result in... 导致……
Similarly, a lack of training can result in underutilized abilities.
同样,培训短缺会导致对能力的开发利用不足。
This often results in the employee receiving approximately the same rating on every item.
这通常导致雇员的各个项目上的等级评价都大致相同。

4. prior to... 先于……
Therefore, prior to selecting a performance appraisal method, an organization must conduct job analyses and develop job descriptions.
因此,一个组织必须在进行绩效评估手段的选择之前,进行工作分析、开展工作描述。
Independence is prior to any other things in his work, just as it is for most professionals.
正如对于大多数的职业人士那样,工作中独立是最重要的。

5. conform to... 符合;遵照……

Managers with biases or prejudices tend to look for employee behaviors that conform to their biases.
心存偏见或成见的经理们趋向于寻找与其偏见相吻合的员工行为。

The career plans of both the company and it employees should conform to the overall mission and strategic goals of the business.
公司与其员工两者的职业计划都应该与企业的整体使命和战略目标一致。

7.2　Appraisal Methods
考核方法

Introduction

Whatever method of performance appraisal an organization uses, it must be job related. Therefore, prior to selecting a performance appraisal method, an organization must conduct job analyses and develop job descriptions. We will discuss lately each of the following performance appraisal methods:
- Goal setting or management by objectives (MBO).
- Multi-rater assessment or 360-degree feedback.
- The work standards approach.
- The essay appraisal method.
- The critical-incident appraisal method.
- The graphic rating scale method.
- The checklist method.
- Behaviorally anchored rating scale (BARS).
- Forced-choice rating.

Goal Setting or Management by Objectives (MBO)

The goal-setting approach to performance appraisal, or management by objectives (MBO) as it is more frequently called, is more commonly used with professional and managerial employees. Other names for MBO include management by results, performance management, results management, and work planning and review program.

The MBO process typically consists of the following steps: (1) Establishing clear and precisely defined statements of objectives for the work to be done by an employee. (2) Developing an action plan indicating how these objectives are to be achieved. (3) Allowing the employee to implement the action plan. (4) Measuring objective achievement. (5) Taking corrective action when necessary. (6) Establishing new objectives for the future.

For an MBO system to be successful, several requirements must be met. First, objectives should be quantifiable and measurable; objectives whose attainment cannot be measured or at least verified should be avoided where possible. Objectives should also be challenging yet achievable, and they should be expressed in writing and in clear, concise, unambiguous language.

MBO also requires that employees participate in the objective-setting process. Active participation by the employee is also essential in developing the action plan. Managers who set an employee's objectives without input and then ask the employee, "You agree to these, don't you?" are unlikely to get high levels of employee commitment.

A final requirement for the successful use of MBO is that the objectives and action plan must serve as a basis for regular discussions between the manager and the employee concerning the employee's performance[①]. These regular discussions provide an opportunity for the manager and employee to discuss progress and modify objectives when necessary.

Multi-rater Assessment, or 360-degree Feedback

One currently popular method of performance appraisal is called multi-rater assessment, or 360-degree feedback. With this method, managers, peers, customers, suppliers, or colleagues are asked to complete questionnaires on the employee being assessed. The person assessed also completes a questionnaire. The questionnaires are generally lengthy. Typical questions are: "Are you crisp, clear, and articulate? Abrasive? Spreading yourself too thin?" The human resources department provides the results to the employee, who in turn gets to see how his or her opinion differs from those of the group doing the assessment.

The Work Standards Approach

The work standards approach to performance appraisal is most frequently used for production employees and is basically a form of goal setting for these employees. It involves setting a standard or an expected level of output and then comparing each employee's performance to the standard. Generally, work standards should reflect the average output of a typical employee. Work standards attempt to define a fair day's output. Several methods can be used to set work standards.

An advantage of the work standards approach is that the performance review is based on highly objective factors. Of course, to be effective, the affected employees must view the standards as being fair. The most serious criticism of work standards is a lack of comparability of standards for different job categories.

The Essay Appraisal Method

The essay appraisal method requires that the evaluation describe an employee's performance in written narrative form. Instructions are often provided as to the topics to be covered. A typical essay appraisal question might be "Describe, in your own words, this employee's performance, including quantity and quality of work, job knowledge, and ability to get along with other employees. What are the employee's strengths and weaknesses?" The primary problem with essay appraisals is that their length and content can vary considerably, depending on the rater. For instance, one rater may write a lengthy statement describing an employee's potential and little about past performance; another rater may concentrate on an employee's past performance. Thus, essay appraisals are difficult to compare. The writing skill of the appraiser can also affect the appraisal. An effective writer can make an average employee look better than the actual performance warrants.

The Critical-incident Appraisal Method

The critical-incident appraisal method requires the evaluator to keep a written record of incidents as they occur. The incidents recorded should involve job behaviors that illustrate both satisfactory and unsatisfactory performance of the employee being rated[②]. As they are recorded overtime, the incidents provide a basis for evaluating performance and providing feedback to the employee.

The main drawback to this approach is that the rater is required to jot down incidents regularly, which can be burdensome and time-consuming. Also, the definition of a critical incident is unclear and may be interpreted differently by different people. This method may also lead to friction between the manager and employees when the employees believe the manager is keeping a "book" on them.

The Graphic Rating Scale Method

With the graphic rating scale method, the rater assesses an

employee on factors such as quantity of work, dependability, job knowledge, attendance, accuracy of work, and cooperativeness. Graphic rating scales include both numerical ranges and written descriptions.

The graphic rating scale method is subject to some serious weaknesses. One potential weakness is that evaluators are unlikely to interpret written descriptions in the same manner due to differences in background, experience, and personality. Another potential problem relates to the choice of rating categories. It is possible to choose categories that have little relationship to job performance or to omit categories that have a significant influence on job performance.

The Checklist Method

In the checklist method, the rater makes yes-or-no responses to a series of questions concerning the employee's behavior. The checklist can also have varying weights assigned to each question.

Normally the scoring key for the checklist method is kept by the human resource department; the evaluator is generally not aware of the weights associated with each question. But because raters can see the positive or negative connotation of each question; bias can be introduced. Additional drawbacks to the checklist method are that it is time-consuming to assemble the questions for each job category, a separate listing of questions must be developed for each job category, and the checklist questions can have different meanings for different rater[3].

Behaviorally Anchored Rating Scale (BARS)

The behaviorally anchored rating scale (BARS) method of performance appraisal is designed to assess behaviors required to successfully perform a job. The focus of BARS and, to some extent, the graphic rating scale and checklist methods is not on performance outcomes but on functional behaviors demonstrated on the job. The assumption is that these functional behaviors will result in effective job performance.

Most BARSs use the term job dimension to mean those broad categories of duties and responsibilities that make up a job. Each job is likely to have several job dimensions, and separate scales must be developed for each. Scale values, appear on the left side of the table and define specific categories of performance. Anchors, which appear on the right side, are specific written statements of actual behaviors that, when exhibited on the job, indicate the level of performance on the scale opposite that particular anchor[④]. As the anchor statements appear beside each scale value, they are said to "anchor" each scale value along the scale.

Rating performance using a BARS requires the rater to read the list of anchors on each scale to find the group of anchors that best describe the employee's job behavior during the period being reviewed[⑤]. The scale value opposite the group of anchors is then checked. This process is followed for all the identified dimensions of the job. A total evaluation is obtained by combining the scale values checked for all job dimensions.

BARSs are normally developed through a series of meetings attended by both managers and job incumbents. Three steps are usually followed: (1) Managers and job incumbents identify the relevant job dimensions for the job. (2) Managers and job incumbents write behavioral anchors for each job dimension. As many anchors as possible should be written for each dimension. (3) Managers and job incumbents reach a consensus concerning the scale values to be used and the grouping of anchor statements for each scale value.

The use of a BARS can result in several advantages. First, BARSs are developed through the active participation of both managers and job incumbents. This increases the likelihood that the method will be accepted. Second, the anchors are developed from the observations and experiences of employees who actually perform the job. Finally, BARSs can be used to provide specific feedback concerning an employee's job performance.

One major drawback to the use of BARSs is that they take considerable time and commitment to develop. Furthermore, separate forms must be developed for different jobs.

Many variations of the forced-choice rating method exist. The most common practice requires the evaluator to rank a set of statements describing how an employee carries out the duties and responsibilities of the job. The statements are normally weighted, and the weights generally are not known to the rater. After the rater ranks all of the forced-choice statements, the human resource department applies the weights and computes a score.

This method attempts to eliminate evaluator bias by forcing the rater to rank statements that are seemingly indistinguishable or unrelated⑥. However, the forced-choice method has been reported to irritate raters, who feel they are not being trusted. Furthermore, the results of the forced-choice appraisal can be difficult to communicate to employees.

When it becomes necessary to compare the performance of two or more employees, ranking methods can be used. Three of the more commonly used ranking methods are alternation, paired comparison, and forced distribution.

from: *Human Resource Management*, 7th Edition, 2007

Words and Expressions

implement ['implimənt] *v.* 贯彻;实现
quantifiable [kɔnti'faiəbl] *adj.* 可以计量的
verify ['verifai] *v.* 查证;核实

concise [kən'sais] adj. 简明的;简练的
unambiguous ['ʌnæm'bigjuəs] adj. 不含糊的;明确的
essential [i'senʃəl] adj. 基本的
crisp [krisp] adj. 脆的;易碎的
articulate [ɑː'tikjulit] adj. 发音清晰的
abrasive [ə'breisiv] adj. 研磨的
jot [dʒɔt] v. 略记
consume [kən'sjuːm] v. 消耗
illustrate ['iləstreit] v. 阐明
friction ['frikʃən] n. 摩擦;摩擦力
accuracy ['ækjurəsi] n. 精确性;正确度
omit [əu'mit] v. 省略;疏忽
connotation [ˌkɔnəu'teiʃən] n. 内涵
assemble [ə'sembl] v. 集合
assumption [ə'sʌmpʃən] n. 假定;设想
dimension [di'menʃən] n. 尺寸;维;数;度
incumbent [in'kʌmbənt] adj. 职责所在的;负有……义务的
considerable [kən'sidərəbl] adj. 相当大或多的
normally ['nɔːməli] adv. 正常地;通常地
irritate ['iriteit] v. 激怒;使急躁
alternation [ˌɔːltəː'neiʃən] n. 交替;轮流;间隔
distribution [ˌdistri'bjuːʃən] n. 分配;分发
goal setting, or management by objectives (MBO) 目标法
multi-rater assessment, or 360-degree feedback 多角度评价法或360度反馈法

the work standards approach 工作标准法
the essay appraisal method 文字叙述评价法
the critical-incident appraisal method 重大事件评价法
the graphic rating scale method 图表法
the checklist method 表格核对法

behaviorally anchored rating scale (BARS) 行为锚定等级评价法
forced-choice rating 迫选法

Difficult Sentences

① The final requirement for the successful use of MBO is that the objectives and action plan must serve as a basis for regular discussions between the manager and the employee concerning the employee's performance.
成功使用"目标法"的最后一个要求是目标与行动计划必须充当经理与雇员之间定期讨论后者工作绩效的基础。

② The incidents recorded should involve job behaviors that illustrate both satisfactory and unsatisfactory performance of the employee being rated.
记录的事件应该包括被评价人的正反两个方面的表现。

③ Additional drawbacks to the checklist method are that it is time-consuming to assemble the questions for each job category, a separate listing of questions must be developed for each job category, and the checklist questions can have different meanings for different rater.
表格法的其他缺点是为不同的工种准备不同的问题很耗时,每个不同的工种必须有单独的问题表,同时这些表格中的问题对于不同的评价人来说意义也不同。

④ Anchors, which appear on the right side, are specific written statements of actual behaviors that, when exhibited on the job, indicate the level of performance on the scale opposite that particular anchor.
右侧的锚定,是对实际行为的专门陈述,一旦用于工作,即指与之相对的等级评价中的成绩水平。

⑤ Rating performance using a BARS requires the rater to read the list of anchors on each scale to find the group of anchors that best describe the employee's job behavior during the period being reviewed.

使用行为锚定等级评价法要求评委通读评价单上的锚定表,找出能最佳描写评价期间雇员的工作表现的一组行为锚定。

⑥ This method attempts to eliminate evaluator bias by forcing the rater to rank statements that are seemingly indistinguishable or unrelated. 该办法尝试通过迫使评委把那些看似无法区别或毫不相关的陈述评分定等,以消除偏见。

Phrases and Patterns

1. provide...for/to... 提供……

   These regular discussions provide an opportunity for the manager and employee to discuss progress and modify objectives when necessary. 这些定期讨论为经理和雇员在必要时探讨进展和改进目标提供了机会。

   Finally, BARSs can be used to provide specific feedback concerning an employee's job performance to the evaluator. 最后,行为锚定等级评价法可以用来为评委提供关于雇员工作绩效的专门反馈。

2. jot down... 草草记下……

   The main drawback to this approach is that the rater is required to jot down incidents regularly, which can be burdensome and time-consuming. 该方法的主要缺点是要求评委定期对事件做记录,这既烦累又耗时。

   In the process of evaluation, some raters will jot down an employees potential competence and little about his past performance. 在评估过程中,一些评委会记下雇员的潜能,而对于其过去的表现却记之甚少。

3. be subject to... 常有;常患;常遭遇……

   The graphic rating scale method is subject to some serious weaknesses. 图示等级评价法易于导致一些严重的缺点。

Some evaluators are subject to prejudice.
一些评委易于产生偏见。
4. be aware of... 知道……
The evaluator is generally not aware of the weights associated with each question.
评委通常并不知道每个问题的权重。
The evaluators should be aware of the great difficulty of comparing essay appraisals for the same employee by different raters.
评委应该认识到对比不同的评价人对于同一员工的文字评价是很困难的。

7.3 Repertory Grid Procedure in Eliciting Personal Constructs of Appraisal Systems
循环坐标法在人事评估系统构建中的应用

Introduction

Each respondent was 'supplied' with nine representative appraisal system elements (as a common denominator) for construct elicitation. Rules for comparing grids require that either the elements or the constructs must remain constant. As our inquiry is concerned with how appraisers and appraisees construe/interpret their appraisal worlds, the decision to supply and keep the elements the same for all respondents was clear①. The elements were generated from two key sources. First, an extensive review of the relevant literature identified a wide spectrum of possible issues and activities involved with the examination of an entire performance appraisal system.② Second, 39 pre-pilot test interviews with practicing managers from the sample population (but not included in the grid interviews) revealed a list of about 60 core activities that constituted the make-up of a typical appraisal system (irrespective of the industry sector; all respondent organizations in the present study were medium to large sized organizations). Specifically, pilot test respondents were asked, "If you had to start from scratch what things would you include in your organization's appraisal system?" Of the list generated from this pre-pilot test, certain appraisal activities repeatedly occurred. These items were then double checked with the literature and the following nine appraisal system elements were identified for the present study:

E1: Attending performance appraisal (PA) training

E2: Attending/conducting the annual interview

E3: Reading appraisal guidelines and notes

E4: Attending/conducting progress reviews throughout the year

E5: Carrying out the performance criteria/standards used to appraise performance

E6: Reading/filling in the appraisal form (design of the form)

E7: Appraising yourself (formally or informally)

E8: Setting your own work goals

What is the E1 to E8

E1: Appraisal Training

As organizations become more competitive, they continue to inject more money into developing appraisal systems that will properly identify good and poor performance in individuals. In order for this to be achieved, proper training on the skills and knowledge of appraisals has become a critical part of any appraisal system. Companies (both private and public) are also investing in training provided to both appraisers and appraisees to ensure that all parties to the appraisal system are fully aware of their roles, duties, responsibilities, and the skill-sets needed to effectively carry out performance appraisals.

E2: Annual Interview

All appraisal systems incorporate this important aspect of

appraisals. It is perhaps the most crucial aspect where a formal dialogue about past performance is discussed, evaluated and developed, which in turn sets the scene for the forthcoming appraisal period. Hence whether a person is conducting or attending the interview, both parties to the discussion are exposed to this core activity of the system. A great deal of the appraisal literature also addresses this important aspect of the system.

E3: *Appraisal Guidelines and Notes*

Just as important as providing the necessary skills and discussing the performance of employees is the provision of clear and easy-to-follow appraisal guidelines and notes[3]. Both practicing managers and the appraisal literature make the importance very clear of having these instructions and communication materials in place in order that users of the system (both appraisers and appraisees) are fully aware of the process, the timing of appraisals, how appraisal information will be used, and what is required of employees as part of the overall system.

E4: *Progress Reviews*

Another integral part of any appraisal system is the constant feedback on staff performance throughout the year. All organizations in the pre-pilot test emphasized the importance of such reviews (even though some may not be carried out in a formal manner). Respondents advocated that one of the main reasons appraisals failed was because managers and staff do not sit down to discuss performance until that one time in the year where they are required to fill in the form. Such poor practices lead to resentments and distrust in the system. As a result, periodic monitoring and discussion of performance are seen as an important part of the entire system.

E5: *Performance Criteria and Standards*

These measures of performance or yardsticks from which performance is monitored form a key element of any appraisal system, without which appraisals become highly subjective. Appraisal systems if they are to be of any value to organizations and organizational performance must be linked to the overall mission and vision of the business. As such the importance of ensuring that the measures of performance (appraisal criteria and standards) are linked to business strategy has become a critical issue for appraisal system design. Not surprisingly, the obsessions with performance criteria and standards, the scales to use, inter alia, have been well documented in the literature.

E6: *The Appraisal Form*

Without doubt, the appraisal form is the backbone of the entire appraisal system as virtually everything hinges on it. People are evaluated in it, the criteria for assessment are stated in it, and key decisions about promotion, termination, training and development, inter alia, are based upon it. The appraisal form is the ultimate performance data capturer and, as such, a key element of any typical appraisal system. Though all appraisers must complete the form on their staff's performance, not all appraisees may be required to fill it in—perhaps the only requirement is a simple signature to confirm that such discussion had been documented. Nevertheless, the form is critical to both parties to the appraisal. Both appraisers and appraisees need to be fully conversant with the items stipulated in the form as they inevitably dictate the key competencies the organization (and the supervisor) will use in evaluating a staff member's performance[④].

E7: *Self-appraisal*

Another key aspect of appraisals as documented in the literature and identified by practicing managers is the importance of self-evaluation (albeit formally or informally). As more appraisal responsibility is shared between appraisers and appraisees, self-appraisals have become a key aspect of appraisal systems. It has become common practice for appraisees to take charge of their own careers and self-development (especially within the context of learning organizations and during economic downturn).

E8: Work Objectives

Both appraisers and appraisees set work objectives/goals as part of carrying out their jobs within the appraisal system. It is not just the performance criteria and standards that must be carried out as a measure of performance but also the work goals that are set on top of these measures that make up a key element of the performance appraisal system[5]. How well or how not well employees go about setting their work goals, along with how much of a say is offered in setting these work goals, has major impacts on the performance of their work objectives.

Result

Feedback sessions with the pre-pilot test group of practicing managers confirmed that all the short listed appraisal system elements apply to both appraisers and appraisees. Elements E2, E4, and E6 (annual interview, progress reviews, and the appraisal form, respectively) are carefully worded so that "conducting" applies to appraisers and "attending" applies to appraisees; a similar option is provided for reading/filling in the appraisal form. All appraisers and appraisees have their own views of what would constitute an effective system.

Each appraisal system element is triadically compared twice using different combinations to elicit as many personal constructs as possible about their appraisal experience. It is also important to note that all elements are given a roughly equal chance of being introduced in triads so that no particular one dominates the construct elicitation, which could distort the whole grid.

from: Mapping cognitions to better understand attitudinal and behavioral responses in appraisal research. *Journal of Organizational*

Behavior, 2004

Words and Expressions

repertory ['repətəri] *n.* 轮演;循环
grid [grid] *n.* 格子;坐标
elicit [i'lisit] *v.* 得出
respondent [ris'pɔndənt] *n.* 回答者
spectrum ['spektrəm] *n.* 光;光谱
scratch [skrætʃ] *n.* 乱写
incorporate [in'kɔ:pəreit] *v.* 合并
crucial ['kru:ʃiəl, 'kru:ʃəl] *adj.* 至关紧要的
forthcoming [fɔ:θ'kʌmiŋ] *adj.* 即将来临的
provision [prə'viʒən] *n.* 供应
integral ['intigrəl] *adj.* 完整的;整体的
constant ['kɔnstənt] *adj.* 不变的;坚决的
advocate ['ædvəkit] *v.* 提倡
resentment [ri'zentmənt] *n.* 怨恨
mission ['miʃən] *n.* 使命
obsession [əb'seʃən] *n.* 迷住;困扰
virtually ['və:tjuəli] *adv.* 事实上
termination [,tə:mi'neiʃən] *n.* 终止
capturer ['kæptʃərə] *n.* 捕获者
conversant [kən'və:sənt] *adj.* 亲近的;熟悉的
inevitably [in'evitəbli] *adv.* 不可避免地
stipulate ['stipjuleit] *v.* 规定;保证
context ['kɔntekst] *n.* 上下文;语境
respectively [ri'spektivli] *adv.* 分别地
deliberately [di'libərətli] *adv.* 故意地
benchmark ['bentʃmɑ:k] *n.* 基准
triad ['traiəd] *n.* 三个/人一组

repertory grid procedure 循环坐标法
personal constructs of appraisal systems 人事评估体系
common denominator 整体分母
the timing of appraisal 评价时耗
inter alia 和其他的事物(= among other things)
feedback sessions 反馈期
core appraisal system elements 评价体系的核心要素

Difficult Sentences

① As our inquiry is concerned with how appraisers and appraisees construe/interpret their appraisal worlds, the decision to supply and keep the elements the same for all respondents was clear.
由于我们的调查与评估双方如何解读/理解其评估内容有关,所以为所有答题者提供并保持同样的问题的决定就很好理解了。

② First, an extensive review of the relevant literature identified a wide spectrum of possible issues and activities involved with the examination of an entire performance appraisal system.
首先,对于相关文献的广泛阅览有助于识别大量的可能事件与活动,包括对整个评价体系的审查。

③ Just as important as providing the necessary skills and discussing the performance of employees is the provision of clear and easy-to-follow appraisal guidelines and notes.
与提供必要的技能和论述同样重要的是,提供雇员的成绩状况也是任何清晰、易行的评价指南的必备。

④ Both appraisers and appraisees need to be fully conversant with the items stipulated in the form as they inevitably dictate the key competencies the organization (and the supervisor) will use in evaluating a staff member's performance.
评价双方都应十分熟悉这些公示的条款,因为它们势必规定其组织(和管理者)将用之以评价雇员表现的主要能力。

⑤ It is not just the performance criteria and standards that must be carried out as a measure of performance but also the work goals that are set on top of these measures that make up a key element of the performance appraisal system.

不仅这些绩效标准必须作为绩效评价的尺度来执行,而且构成绩效评价体系关键成分之首的工作目标亦应如此(也必须作为绩效评价的尺度来执行)。

Phrases and Patterns

1. irrespective of... 不分……

   39 pre-pilot test interviews with practicing managers from the sample population (but not included in the grid interviews) revealed a list of about 60 core activities that constituted the make-up of a typical appraisal system (irrespective of the industry sector; all respondent organizations in the present study were medium to large sized organizations).

   39位前飞行员与抽样考察人员中的现任经理们的面试显示出一份大约由60个主要活动构成的典型评价体系的名单(不分工种,该研究中的所有受试人员均来自大中型企业)。

   The laws apply to everyone, irrespective of race, creed or colour.
   法律适用于所有的人,不分种族、信仰和肤色。

2. be linked to... 连接;联系……

   Appraisal systems if they are to be of any value to organizations and organizational performance must be linked to the overall mission and vision of the business.

   评价体系如果要有价值于组织和组织绩效,就必须与企业的整体任务和前景联系起来。

   As such the importance of ensuring that the measures of performance (appraisal criteria and standards) are linked to business strategy has become a critical issue for appraisal system design.

同样,确保绩效标准(评价标准)与企业战略相关联的重要性已经成为设计评价体系的一项极为关键的问题。

3. obsessions with... 迷住……;困扰……

The obsessions with performance criteria and standards, the scales to use, inter alia, have been well documented in the literature.

对于绩效标准、使用范围等等的困扰,在文献中都有很好地记载。

He had great obsessions with different essay appraisals for the same employee by different raters.

不同的评价人对于同一员工的文字评价竟然会有出入,他对此深感困惑。

4. take charge of 负责

It has become common practice for appraisees to take charge of their own careers and self-development.

受评人对其个人的事业以及自我发展负责早以成了常见的事实。

It will be better if the senior employees who take charge of conducting the evaluation have received this kind training.

如果负责评估的资深雇员受过此类训练会更好。

Questions

1. How often do you think performance appraisals should be conducted?
2. What performance appraisal method do you believe would best apply to the evaluation of a college professor or a sale manager in a computer company?
3. What's the relationship between self-appraisal and work objectives?
4. What's the logical order in the nine appraisal system elements?

8

Payment
薪 酬

【本章导读】 本章介绍有关薪金的一些问题。8.1 介绍有关薪金的发放水平以及影响薪金支付水平的诸多因素,如市场压力、身为资源的员工、细致全面的市场支付水平调研等。8.2 介绍员工们只能选择而无法随意改变的三种委托福利计划,即无业保险、社会安全和员工补偿。8.3 主要阐释薪金实际上仍然是激励员工最有效的手段。

8.1 Developing Pay Levels
不断改进的薪酬标准

Market Pressures

Any organization faces two important competitive market challenges in deciding what to pay its employees: product-market competition and labor-market competition.

Product-market Competition

First, organizations must compete effectively in the product market. In other words, they must be able to sell their goods and services at a quantity and price that will bring a sufficient return on their investment. Organizations compete on multiple dimensions (e.g., quality, service), and price is one of the most important dimensions. An important influence on price is the cost of production.

An organization that has higher labor costs than its product-market competitors will have to charge higher average prices for products of similar quality. Thus, for example, if labor costs are 30 percent of revenues at Company A and Company B, but Company A has labor costs that are 20 percent higher than those of Company B, we would expect Company A to have product prices that are higher by (.30 x .20) = 6 percent. At some point, the higher price charged by Company A will contribute to a loss of its business to competing companies with lower prices (like Company B). One study, for example, found that in 1991 the wage and benefit cost to produce a small car was approximately $1,700 for Ford Motor, $1,800 for Chrysler, and $2,400 for General Motors. Thus, if all other costs were equal, General Motors would have to sell the same quality car for $600 to $700 more than would Ford or Chrysler.

Therefore, product-market competition <u>places an upper bound on</u> labor costs and compensation. This upper bound is more constrictive when labor costs are a larger share of total costs and when demand for the product is affected by changes in price (i.e., demand is elastic)[①]. Although costs are only one part of the competitive equation (productivity is just as important), higher costs may result in a loss of business. <u>In the absence of</u> clear evidence on productivity differences, costs need to be closely monitored.

What components make up labor costs? A major component is the average cost per employee. This is made up of both direct payments (such as wages, salaries, and bonuses) and indirect payments (such as health insurance, Social Security, unemployment compensation, and so forth). A second major component of labor cost is the staffing level (i.e., number of employees). Not surprisingly, financially troubled organizations often seek to cut costs by focusing on one or both components. Staff reductions, hiring freezes, wages and salary freezes, and sharing benefits costs with employees are several ways of enhancing the organization's competitive position in the product market[2].

Labor-market Competition

A second important competitive market challenge is labor-market competition. Essentially, labor-market competition is the amount an organization must pay to compete against other companies that hire similar employees. These labor-market competitors typically include not only companies that have similar products but also those in different product markets that hire similar types of employees. If an organization is not competitive in the labor market, it will fail to attract and retain employees of sufficient numbers and quality. For example, even if a computer manufacturer offers newly graduated electrical engineers the same pay as other computer manufacturers, if automobile manufacturers and other labor-market competitors offer salaries $5,000 higher, the computer company may not be able to hire enough qualified electrical engineers. Labor-market competition places a lower bound on pay levels.

Employees as a Resource

Because organizations have to compete in the labor market, they should consider their employees not just as a cost but as a resource in which the organization has invested and from which it expects valuable returns. Although controlling costs has a direct effect on an organization's ability to compete in the product market, the organization's competitive position can be compromised if costs are kept low at the expense of employee productivity and quality[3]. Having higher labor costs than your competitors is not necessarily bad if you also have the best and most effective work force, one that produces more products of better quality.

Pay policies and programs are one of the most important human resource tools for encouraging desired employee behaviors and discouraging undesired behaviors. Therefore, they must be evaluated, not just in terms of costs, but in terms of what sort of returns they generate—how they attract, retain, and motivate a high-quality work force. For example, if the average revenue per employee in Company A is 20 percent higher than in Company B, it may not be important that the average pay in Company A is 10 percent higher than in Company B.

Deciding What to Pay

Although organizations face important external labor and product-market pressures in setting their pay levels, a range of discretion remains. How large the range is depends on the particular competitive environment the organization faces. Where the range is broad, an important strategic decision is whether to pay above, at, or below the market average. The advantage of paying above the market average is the ability to attract and retain the top talent available, which can translate into a highly effective and productive work force. The disadvantage, however, is the added cost.

So, under what circumstances do the benefits of higher pay outweigh the higher costs? According to efficiency wage theory, one circumstance is when organizations have technologies or structures that depend on highly skilled employees. For example, organizations that emphasize decentralized decision making may need higher-caliber employees. Another circumstance where higher pay may be warranted is when an organization has difficulties observing and monitoring its employees' performance. It may therefore wish to provide an above-market pay rate to ensure their incentive to put forth maximum effort. The theory is that employees who are paid more than they would be paid elsewhere will be reluctant to "shirk" (i.e., not work hard) because they wish to retain their good job.

Market Pay Surveys

Total quality management emphasizes the key importance of benchmarking, a procedure in which an organization compares its own practices against those of the competition. This notion is relevant in compensation management. Benchmarking against product-market and labor-market competitors is typically accomplished through the use of one or more pay surveys, which provide information on going rates of pay among competing organizations[④].

The use of pay surveys requires answers to several important questions:

(1) Which employers should be included in the survey? Ideally, they would be the key labor market and product market competitors.

(2) Which jobs are included in the survey? Because only a sample of jobs is ordinarily used, care must be taken that the jobs are representative in terms of level, functional area, and product market. Also, the job content must be sufficiently similar.

(3) If multiple surveys are used, how are all the rates of pay weighted and combined? Organizations often have to weight and combine pay rates because different surveys are often tailored toward particular employee groups (labor markets) or product markets. The organization must decide how much relative weight to give to its labor and product-market competitors in setting pay.

Several factors <u>come into play</u> when deciding how to combine surveys. Product-market comparisons that focus on labor costs are likely to deserve greater weight when (1) labor costs represent a large share of total costs, (2) product demand is elastic (i.e., it changes <u>in response to</u> product price changes), (3) the supply of labor is inelastic, and

(4) employee skills are specific to the product market (and will remain so). In contrast, labor-market comparisons may be more important when (1) attracting and retaining qualified employees is difficult and (2) the costs (administrative, disruption, etc.) of recruiting replacements are high.

As this discussion suggests, knowing what other organizations are paying is only one part of the story. It is also necessary to know what those organizations are getting in return for their investment in employees. To find that out, some organizations examine ratios such as revenues, employees and labor cost. The first ratio includes the staffing component of employee cost but not the average cost per employee. The second ratio, however, includes both. Note that comparing these ratios across organizations requires caution. For example, different industries rely on different resources (e. g. , labor and capital). So, comparing the ratio of revenues to labor costs of a petroleum company (capital intensive, high ratio) to a bank (labor intensive, low ratio) would be like comparing apples and oranges[⑤]. But within industries, such comparisons can be useful. Besides revenues, other return-on-investment data might include product quality, customer satisfaction, and potential work-force quality (e. g. , average education levels).

from: *Human Resource Management*: *Gaining a Competitive Advantage*, 1994

Words and Expressions

sufficient [sə'fiʃənt] *adj.* 充分的;足够的
charge [tʃɑːdʒ] *v.* 收费
revenue ['revinjuː] *n.* 收入;税收
bound [baund] *n.* 范围;限度
constrictive [kən'striktiv] *adj.* 紧缩的
equation [i'kweiʃən] *n.* 相等;平衡

average ['ævəridʒ] adj. 通常的;平均的
compromise ['kɔmprəmaiz] v. 妥协;折衷
external [eks'tə:nl] adj. 外部的
discretion [dis'kreʃən] n. 判断力
decentralized [di:'sentrəlaiz] v. 分散
caliber ['kælibə(r)] n. 才干
warrant ['wɔrənt] v. 保障
incentive [in'sentiv] n. 动机
reluctant [ri'lʌktənt] adj. 不顾的;勉强的
shirk [ʃə:k] v. 逃避;推卸
tailor ['teilə] v. 适应;适合
elastic [i'læstik] adj. 弹性的
disruption [dis'rʌpʃən] n. 瓦解;破坏
recruit [ri'kru:t] v. 使恢复;补充
caution ['kɔ:ʃən] n. 小心;谨慎
petroleum [pi'trəuliəm] n. 石油
intensive [in'tensiv] adj. 强烈的
Ford Motor 福特汽车制造商
Chrysler 克莱斯勒汽车制造商
General Motors 通用汽车制造商
health insurance 健康保险
social security 社会保障
unemployment compensation 失业补偿金
efficiency wage 计件工资;效率工资
higher-caliber employee 高质量员工
return-on-investment 投资回报
potential work-force quality 潜在的劳力质量

Difficult Sentences

① This upper bound is more constrictive when labor costs are a larger

share of total costs and when demand for the product is affected by changes in price (i. e. , demand is elastic).
当劳力成本在总成本中占有大份额、且产品需求受价格变化的影响(即,弹性需求)时,上限会更加紧缩。

② Staff reductions, hiring freezes, wages and salary freezes, and sharing benefits costs with employees are several ways of enhancing the organization's competitive position in the product market.
减员、雇用冻结、工薪冻结、与员工分享成本利润等是加强组织在产品市场中竞争地位的几种手段。

③ Although controlling costs has a direct effect on an organization's ability to compete in the product market, the organization's competitive position can be compromised if costs are kept low at the expense of employee productivity and quality.
尽管控制成本对于产品的市场竞争力有直接影响,但是如果保持低成本是以损害员工的生产力和质量为代价的话,其竞争地位将受到威胁。

④ Benchmarking against product-market and labor-market competitors is typically accomplished through the use of one or more pay surveys, which provide information on going rates of pay among competing organizations.
参照产品市场和劳工市场的竞争对手,典型的办法是进行一次或多次的支付调查,这将提供有关竞争对手的现时支付比率信息。

⑤ So, comparing the ratio of revenues to labor costs of a petroleum company (capital intensive, high ratio) to a bank (labor intensive, low ratio) would be like comparing apples and oranges.
比较一家石油公司(资金密集、高比率)的劳力成本收入与一家银行(劳力密集、低比率)的劳力成本收入,无异于比较苹果与柑橘。

Phrases and Patterns

1. in upper / a lower bound on... 上/下限

Therefore, product-market competition places an upper bound on labor costs and compensation.
因此,产品的市场竞争为劳力成本和补偿规定了一个上限。
Labor-market competition places a lower bound on pay level.
劳力成本为支付水准规定了一个下限。
2. in the absence of... 缺乏……时;当……不在时
In the absence of clear evidence on productivity differences, costs need to be closely monitored.
在缺乏明确的证据证明生产力有差异的情况下,需要密切监控成本。
In the absence of a thorough understanding of the mandated benefits programs, a company will not be able to decide a reasonable pay level.
对委托福利计划没有透彻的了解,公司将不能决定出合理的支付水准。
3. at the expense of... 在损害……的情况下;以……为代价
He built up a successful business, but it was all done at the expense of his health.
他创建了一个成功的企业,但这一切却损害了他的健康。
4. in response to... 响应;适应……
It changes in response to product price changes.
它随产品价格的变化而变化。
The average cost per employee will fluctuate in response to the changes of both direct payment and indirect payment.
每个员工的平均成本随直接支付与间接支付两者的变化而上下波动。

8.2 Mandated Benefits Programs
委托福利计划

Introduction

Three benefits programs offered by private and not-for-profit employers are mandated by federal and state governments. An employer has no choice about offering mandated benefits programs and cannot change them in any way without getting involved in the political process to change the existing laws. The three mandated programs are unemployment insurance, social security, and workers' compensation.

Unemployment Insurance

In the 1930s, when unemployment was very high, the government was pressured to create programs to take care of people who were out of work though no fault of their own. Unemployment insurance (UI) was set up in the United States as part of the Social Security Act of 1935. In July 1997, the average unemployment rate for the United States was approximately 5.0 percent.

Unemployment insurance was designed with several objectives:

(1) To provide periodic cash income to workers during short periods of involuntary unemployment.

(2) To help the unemployed find jobs.

(3) To encourage employers to stabilize employment.

(4) To stabilize the labor supply by providing benefits so that skilled and experienced workers are not forced to seek other jobs during short-term unemployment.

Unemployment insurance and allied systems for railroad, federal government, and military employees cover 95 percent of the labor force.

Major groups excluded from UI are self-employed workers, employees of small firms with less than four employees, domestics, farm employees, state and local government employees, and nonprofit employers such as hospitals①.

To be eligible for compensation, the employee must have worked a minimum number of weeks, be without a job, and be willing to accept a suitable position offered through a state Unemployment Compensation Commission. A Supreme Court decision granted unemployment insurance benefits to strikers after an eight-week strike period. The Court ruled that neither the Social Security Act nor the National Labor Relations Act specifically forbids paying benefits to strikers. Each state decides whether to permit or prohibit such payments.

Federal unemployment tax for employers in all states accounts for 0.8 percent of payroll. The tax pays for administrative costs associated with unemployment compensation, provides a percentage of benefits paid under extended benefits programs during periods of high unemployment, and maintains a loan fund for use when a state lacks funds to pay benefits due for any month②. Unemployment tax rates, eligibility requirements, weekly benefits, and duration of regular benefits vary from state to state.

Before benefits are paid, the reason for being unemployed must be assessed. An applicant can be disqualified for voluntarily quitting a job. On the other hand, a negotiated quit, that is, quitting to avoid discharge, is a legitimate reason for collecting unemployment benefits. Some states penalize employers who report such quits as voluntary. Discharge for work-related misconduct usually means the applicant is disqualified. Proper documentation is an employer's best protection in unemployment hearings.

The employee receives compensation for a limited period, typically a maximum of 26 weeks. In most states the weekly benefit amount is equal to 1/26 of the worker's average earnings, yielding a total benefit of 50 percent of earnings. Minimum and maximum benefit amounts are set by the federal government. Minimum benefits usually range from $5 to $50 per week, maximum benefits from $100 to $300, the average benefit is from $90 to $175.

Social Security

In 1935, the pension portion of the Social Security system was established under the Old-Age, Survivors, and Disability Insurance (OASDI) program. The goal of the pension portion was to provide income to retired people to supplement savings, private pensions, and part-time work. It was created at a time when the wealthy continued to live alone, the average person moved in with relatives, and the poor with no one to help them were put in a "poorhouse" or government-supported retirement home.

The basic concept was that the employee and employer were to pay taxes that would cover the retirement payments each employee would later receive in a self-funding insurance program. Initially, two goals were sought: adequate payments for all, and individual equity, which means that each employee was to receive what he or she and the employer had put into the fund. In the past 20 years, however, individual equity has lost out.

Social Security taxes are paid by employers and employees. Both pay a percentage of the employee's pay to the government. The percentage rose to 7.65 for both employee and employer in 1990. How much is paid by employee and employer is calculated on the average monthly wage (weighted toward the later years). Social Security payments make up about one-third of total federal outlays in the United States. Those receiving Social Security pensions can work part-time, up to a maximum amount that is increased each year to reflect inflation. Just about all employees except civilian federal government employees are eligible for Social Security coverage. Self-employed people must join the system. They paid 15.3 percent in 1995.

Employees become eligible to receive full benefits at age 65 or reduced benefits at age 62. Effective in 2027, an employee will not be able to retire with full benefits until age 67. If an employee dies, a family with children under 18 receives survivor benefits, regardless of the employee's age. An employee who is totally disabled before age 65 becomes eligible to receive insurance benefits. Under Medicare provisions of the Social Security system, eligible individuals aged 65 and older receive payments for doctor and hospital bills, as well as other related benefits and services.

Retirement benefits used to be tax-free, but in 1984 some benefits became taxable. For single people, up to 85 percent of Social Security benefits are taxable if they earn provisional income of $34,000 or more. Married couples filing jointly must pay taxes on provisional income of $44,000 or more. ("Provisional income" means adjusted gross income plus any tax-exempt interest from municipal bonds plus half of Social Security④.) It is possible to avoid these taxes by switching income to other types of assets.

The growth of international business has created another problem for companies dealing with Social Security payments. The United States has international Social Security agreements with several countries. If such an agreement does not exist, Social Security law requires contributions to be paid on earnings of United States citizens or residents working for American employers anywhere in the world. As a result, United States citizens may have to make double contributions—once to the American plan and once to the country in which they are employed. No contributions are necessary for United States citizens employed by a foreign company, however.

Because of the increasing numbers of Americans who spend at least part of their careers in more than one country, the United States has established agreements with other governments to coordinate Social Security benefits. The principal objectives of these agreements are to ensure equality of treatment, prevent duplicate contributions or gaps, provide that contributions are paid in the location where the worker is employed, and guarantee benefits to the employee's family when they have not accompanied the employee to the foreign assignment. Total benefits may not exceed the highest pension that the employee would have been paid if his or her entire career had been spent in a single country[5]. Benefits are administered by the state where the retired employee resides; a pensioner may have to wait two or three years to know what income he or she will receive.

    Social Security systems in many countries around the globe are in crisis, exacting a heavy financial burden while providing inadequate benefits. Employers worldwide must assume more responsibility for employee benefits as governments try to cut the cost of Social Security and national health insurance programs. Steps taken by foreign governments to meet this challenge include (1) reducing the level of future benefits and (2) increasing Social Security taxes. More private retirement provisions are being made, particularly in Europe.

    A number of changes in the Social Security system are being considered in an attempt to control future costs and benefits. Probable changes include (1) higher taxes on Social Security benefits; (2) participation of all state, local, and federal civil servants in the Social Security program; (3) beginning in the next three or four decades, longer work and later retirement; (4) dramatic changes in the Social Security, Medicare, and overall health care systems; and (5) reduction in benefits. A commission created by the Clinton administration has so far been unable to agree on an appropriate remedy. Probably the best way to save Social Security is to create a significant communication program to tell people the facts about retirement and Social Security. Everyone must understand these facts and comprehend how they apply to his or her own situation.

Workers' Compensation

Employees who incur expenses as a result of job-related illness or accidents receive a degree of financial protection from workers' benefits. The workers' compensation programs are administered individually by the various states. Employees pay the entire cost of workers' compensation insurance. The cost of premiums is tied directly to each employer's past experience with job-related accidents and illnesses.

All states plus the District of Columbia have workers' compensation laws, but New Jersey, South Carolina, and Texas do not require participation. Eligibility for benefits varies from state to state. A percentage of the disabled employee's weekly wage is provided for up to 26 weeks. Benefits range from from 20 to 66.23 percent of the average weekly wage. Workers' compensation claims have become increasingly expensive over the past 10 years, and these costs will escalate in the years ahead. Between 1980 and 1990 workers' compensation awards soared from $22.8 billion to $62 billion. By 2000, the bill could be over $200 billion. Workers' compensation costs are growing faster than health care insurance expenses because of several factors: escalating fraudulent claims, the expansion of "compensable injuries", and fewer restrictions to eligibility for benefits than in health care plans. Therefore, many states are modifying their existing legislation. For example, in 1992, four states provided workers' compensation through alternative sources (a combination of life, disability, accident, and health or other insurance). A number of states added deductibles to their plans: Kentucky, Minnesota, Mississippi, Missouri, and Colorado.

from: *Human Resource Management*, 1998

Words and Expressions

mandate ['mændeit] *v.* 委任统治
insurance [in'ʃuərəns] *n.* 保险
involuntary [in'vɔləntəri] *adj.* 自然而然的；无意的
stabilize ['steibilaiz] *v.* 稳定
allied ['ælaid] *adj.* 联合的；同盟的
federal ['fedərəl] *adj.* 联邦的；联合的
exclude [iks'klu:d] *v.* 排斥
domestic [də'mestik] *n.* 仆人
eligible ['elidʒəbl] *adj.* 符合条件的；合格的
grant [grɑ:nt] *v.* 同意；准予
prohibit [prə'hibit] *v.* 禁止；阻止
payroll ['peirəul] *n.* 薪水册
applicant ['æplikənt] *n.* 申请者；请求者
legitimate [li'dʒitimit] *adj.* 合法的；合理的
penalize ['pi:nəlaiz] *v.* 处罚
pension ['penʃən] *n.* 养老金；退休金
supplement ['sʌplimənt] *v.* 补充
outlay ['autlei] *n.* 费用
inflation [in'fleiʃənl] *n.* 通货膨胀；物价；暴涨
switch [switʃ] *v.* 转换
resident ['rezidənt] *n.* 居民
coordinate [kəu'ɔ:dinit] *v.* 调整
duplicate ['dju:plikeit] *adj.* 复制的；两重的
dramatic [drə'mætik] *adj.* 戏剧性的；生动的
commission [kə'miʃən] *n.* 委任；委托
incur [in'kə:] *v.* 招致
premium ['primjəm] *n.* 额外费用；奖金

soar [sɔː] v. 剧增

escalate ['eskəleit] v. 逐步升高

fraudulent ['frɔːdjulənt] adj. 欺诈的；骗得的

deductible [di'dʌktəbl] adj. 可扣除的

Unemployment insurance(UI) 失业保险

self-employed workers 自营工

Unemployment Compensation Commission 失业补偿委员会

Social Security Act 社会保障法

Nation Labor Relations Act 国家劳工关系法

work-related misconduct 失职

Old-age, Survivors, and Disability Insurance(OASD) 老年人、遗属及残疾保险

self-funding insurance program 自筹保险计划

individual equity 个人资产净值

survivor benefits 遗属补偿金

medicare provisions 医护规定

tax-exempt 免税

federal civil servants 联邦公务员

Difficult Sentences

① Major groups excluded from UI are self-employed workers, employees of small firms with less than four employees, domestics, farm employees, state and local government employees, and nonprofit employers such as hospitals.

失业保险拒绝投保的主要群体有：自营工、员工少于四人的小公司的雇员、仆人、州及地方政府雇员、非赢利雇主如医院。

② The tax pays for administrative costs associated with unemployment compensation, provides a percentage of benefits paid under extended benefits programs during periods of high unemployment, and maintains a loan fund for use when a state lacks funds to pay benefits due for any month.

与失业补偿相关的那部分管理成本的税务支出,为高失业率期间的扩展补偿计划提供了一定量的支付补偿金,也为地方政府缺钱支付随时到期的补偿金保存了一笔贷款备用。

③ Those receiving Social Security pensions can work part-time, up to a maximum amount that is increased each year to reflect inflation.
那些领取社会保障金的人可以兼职,其人数逐年增长,已接近最大值,反映出通货膨胀。

④ Married couples filing jointly must pay taxes on provisional income of $44,000 or more ("Provisional income" means adjusted gross income plus any tax-exempt interest from municipal bonds plus half of Social Security).
连带备案的已婚夫妇必须就 $44,000 或以上的临时收入纳税("临时收入"指的是调节后总收入+地方债券所免税额+半额的社会保障金)。

⑤ Total benefits may not exceed the highest pension that the employee would have been paid if his or her entire career had been spent in a single country.
补助金总额不得超过若其整个职业生涯都在同一国家度过的情况下应被支付的最高退休金。

Phrases and Patterns

1. ...so that... 以便……
To stabilize the labor supply by providing benefits so that skilled and experienced workers are not forced to seek other jobs during short-term unemployment.
提供补偿金以稳定劳力资源,以便熟练和富有经验的员工不会被迫在短期雇用期间另谋他职。
Employees must have a thorough understanding of the mandated benefit programs so that their benefit will not lose out.

员工们必须彻底了解委托福利计划,以便他们的利益不会受损。

2. accounts for... 占……

Federal unemployment tax for employers in all states accounts for 0.8 percent of payroll.

各州支付给雇员的联邦事业税占薪水总额的0.8%。

In most states, the weekly benefit amount accounts for nearly 30% of the workers average earnings.

在大多数州中,周津贴总量几乎占工人平均收入的30%。

3. lose out... 受损……

In the past 20 years, however, individual equity has lost out.

然而,在过去的20年里,个人资产净值已经受到损害。

If the pay levels are not studied and developed properly, the benefits of both employers and employees will be likely to lose out.

如果支付水准没有得到适当研发,双方的利益都有可能受损。

4. apply to... 应用于……

Everyone must understand these facts and comprehend how they apply to his or her own situation.

每个人都必须了解这些事实并理解它们如何适用于他或她自己的情况。

It's still not clear that which items can be applied to this situation.

还不清楚哪些条款可以适用于这种情形。

8.3 Gaps between What People Say and Do with Respect to Pay
人们关于薪酬问题的言行差异

When asked directly about the importance of pay, people tend to give it answers that place somewhere around fifth in lists of potential motivators. In contrast, meta-analytic studies of actual behaviors in response to motivational initiatives nearly always show pay to be the most effective motivator①. Indeed, after conducting the first such meta-analysis with respect to motivational interventions, Locke, Feren, McCaleb, Shaw, and Denny concluded: "Money is the crucial incentive... no other incentive or motivational technique comes even close to money with respect to its instrumental value". Subsequent research has continued to support their conclusion.

Why do such discrepancies occur, and how can psychological theories help us explain them? The common tendency for people to say one thing but do another is known as socially desirable responding: "the tendency to choose items that reflect societally approved behaviors". Social desirability stems from either a lack of self-insight or a lack of frankness. In the case of pay, people are likely to understate importance either because they misjudge how they might react to, say, an offer of a higher paying job, or due to social norms that view money as a less noble source of motivation than factors such as challenging work or work that makes a contribution to society.

Generally speaking, the more a particular question touches on strongly held social values, the less valid direct self-reports are likely to be②. In such cases, both managers and researchers must find additional ways of ferreting out more valid information. Recognizing this, some researchers have approached the topic of pay importance by examining how employees' behaviors (such as turnover or performance) change in response to changes in pay and other HR practices. These behavioral responses are far more compelling pieces of evidence than people's responses to surveys regarding what is "important" to them③. As Table I shows, on average, employees respond more effectively to monetary incentives than to any other motivational HR intervention.

The presence of socially desirable responding has been revealed using a number of other research techniques as well. For example, one common psychological research strategy is to adopt projective techniques (e.g., asking what people think others probably think or do, or asking them to create a motivational story from an ambiguous picture) to draw out sensitive or threatening information. A creative example of this approach was implemented by Jurgensen, who assessed the relative importance of ten job characteristics (including pay) to 50,000 job applicants over a 30-year period by asking them to "decide which of the following (job attributes) is most important to you". Based on these direct responses, males reported pay to be only the fifth most important factor, while women reported it to be even lower However, when Jurgensen asked the same men and women to rank the importance of the same ten attributes to "someone just like yourself—same age, education, and gender", pay jumped to first place among both men and women. In other words, job applicants seemed to believe that pay is the most important attribute to everyone except themselves!

A second creative technique, called "policy capturing", examines how people evaluate the attractiveness of holistic job alternatives (i.e., entire "bundles" of job characteristics, such as pay, location, type of work, and benefits) in order to tease out the relative contribution that pay and other characteristics make to their overall assessments[④]. The use of holistic job descriptions presents a situation much closer to the decisions job seekers actually make about prospective jobs than asking them to rate or rank a list of abstract, decontextualized job characteristics[⑤]. By measuring each job in terms of its underlying characteristics (i.e., level of pay, location, type of work, average time to promotion) and then comparing those characteristics with people's overall ratings of job attractiveness, the importance of each underlying job characteristic to overall attractiveness can be inferred without asking direct questions about importance.

In such studies, pay has generally been found to be a substantially more important factor when inferred via policy capturing than when assessed via people's direct reports⑥. For example, Feldman and Arnold found that pay was fourth out of six job attributes (opportunities to use important skills and abilities was first) when graduate business students were asked to rank them from "most preferred to least preferred". In contrast, when using policy capturing with "willingness to accept the position" as the outcome variable and the six job attributes as the predictor variables, they found that pay's "importance weight" was largest and nearly twice as large as that of the next job attribute⑦.

In summary, there is strong evidence that pay is a powerful motivator—perhaps the most powerful potential motivator—of performance. (We say "potential" motivator because in order to motivate, pay must be noticeably contingent on performance—a condition that does not hold in many organizations; more on this later.) However, the study by Rynes et al. suggests that managers do not believe pay is as important to employee behaviors as employees say it is, despite the fact that employees themselves appear to seriously underreport pay's importance to their actual behaviors! The systematic underestimation of pay's importance, both by managers and employees, is a puzzle that merits examination.

from: *The Importance of Pay in Employee Motivation. Human Resource Management*, 2004

Words and Expressions

motivational [ˌməutiˈveiʃənəl] *adj.* 动机的
initiative [iˈniʃiətiv] *n.* 主动性
intervention [ˌintə(ː)ˈvenʃən] *n.* 干涉
incentive [inˈsentiv] *n.* 激励;奖励
instrumental [ˌinstruˈmentl] *adj.* 仪器的
discrepancy [disˈkrepənsi] *n.* 差异;矛盾
stem [stem] *v.* 滋生

norm [nɔːm] n. 标准；规范
motivation [ˌməutiˈveiʃən] n. 动机
ferret [ˈferit] v. 搜出；搜索
valid [ˈvælid] adj. 有效的；正确的
turnover [ˈtəːnˌəuvə] n. 流通量；营业额
compelling [kəmˈpeliŋ] adj. 引人注目的
monetary [ˈmʌnitəri] adj. 货币的；金钱的
reveal [riˈviːl] v. 显示；揭示
adopt [əˈdɔpt] adj. 采用
projective [prəˈdʒektiv] adj. 投射的
ambiguous [æmˈbigjuəs] adj. 暧昧的；不明确的
threatening [ˈθretəniŋ] adj. 胁迫的；危险的
capture [ˈkæptʃə] v. 俘获；捕获
evaluate [iˈvæljueit] v. 评价
holistic [həuˈlistik] adj. 整体的；全盘的
tease [tiːz] v. 强求；找出
prospective [prəsˈpektiv] adj. 预期的
decontextualized [diˌkɔnˈtekstjuəlaizd] adj. 在脱离上下文中的情况下研究；无背景的
underlying [ˈʌndəˈlaiiŋ] adj. 根本的；潜在的
substantially [səbˈstænʃ(ə)li] adv. 充分地
via [ˈvaiə] prep. 通过；经由
attribute [əˈtribjuː(ː)t] n. 属性；特征
contingent [kənˈtindʒənt] adj. 可能发生的；附随的；暂时的
underreport [ˈʌndəriˈpɔːt] v. 少报；收入等；低估
underestimation [ˈʌndərestiˈmeiʃən] n. 低估
merit [ˈmerit] v. 有益于优点；价值
meta-analytic studies 隐含分析研究
instrumental value 利用价值
social norms 社会规范

valid information 确切信息
HR 人力资源
monetary incentives 货币激励
projective techniques 投射技术
policy capturing 政策
holistic job alternative 全盘的工作选择
decontextualized job characteristics 孤立的工作特性
underlying characteristics 潜在特征
job attribute 工作属性

Difficult Sentences

① In contrast, meta-analytic studies of actual behaviors in response to motivational initiatives nearly always show pay to be the most effective motivator.
相反,对于主动性引发的实际行为的隐含分析几乎总是表明薪水是最有效的激励因素。

② Generally speaking, the more a particular question touches on strongly held social values, the less valid direct self-reports are likely to be.
一般来说,某一特殊问题所涉及的固有社会价值越多,率直的自我报告的正确性就很可能越小。

③ These behavioral responses are far more compelling pieces of evidence than people's responses to surveys regarding what is "important" to them.
这些行为反应是远比人们对于调查什么"重要"的反应更引人注目的证据。

④ A second creative technique, called "policy capturing", examines how people evaluate the attractiveness of holistic job alternatives (i.e., entire "bundles" of job characteristics, such as pay, location, type of work, and benefits) in order to tease out the relative contribution that pay and other characteristics make to their overall assessments.

另一个创造性方法,称为"政策捕获",调查人们为了梳理出薪水和其他特性对于整体评估所做的相关贡献,是如何评价全盘工作选项(即,整"包"的工作特性,如薪水、场所、工种以及各种补贴)的魅力的。

⑤ The use of holistic job descriptions presents a situation much closer to the decisions job seekers actually make about prospective jobs than asking them to rate or rank a list of abstract, decontextualized job characteristics.

整体工作描述的使用所展示的情形,比要求他们评估一系列抽象、孤立的工作特性更接近于工作寻求者实际上就其预期工作所做的决定。

⑥ In such studies, pay has generally been found to be a substantially more important factor when inferred via policy capturing than when assessed via people's direct reports.

在这些研究中人们发现,与根据人们的自我报告而得来的评估相比,由政策获取推断得来的结论是薪水,通常是一个实质上更加重要的因素。

⑦ In contrast, when using policy capturing with "willingness to accept the position" as the outcome variable and the six job attributes as the predictor variables, they found that pay's "importance weight" was largest and nearly twice as large as that of the next job attribute.

相反,当使用的政策获取是以"接受岗位的主动性"为结果变量、以六个工作属性为预示变量的时,人们发现薪水的"重要性"最大,几乎两倍于下一个工作属性的重要性。

Phrases and Patterns

1. with respect to... 关于……

Indeed, after conducting the first such meta-analysis with respect to motivational interventions, Locke, Feren, McCaleb, Shaw, and Denny concluded: "Money is the crucial incentive... no other incentive or motivational technique comes even close to money with respect to its instrumental value".

确实,在进行首次有关动机干预的隐含分析研究后,Locke, Feren, McCaleb, Shaw, and Denny 断定:"金钱是至关重要的激励手段……就其工具性价值而言,没有其他的鼓励或激励手段能与之相比。"

2. ferret out... 发现;查获……

In such cases, both managers and researchers must find additional ways of ferreting out more valid information.

在这种情况下,经理和研究人员都必须找到其他获取正确信息的方法。

That people understate the importance of pay will make it difficult for managers and researchers to ferret out the top ones in holistic job alternatives.

人们低估薪资的重要性将使经理和研究人员难于发现整体工作选项中的最重要的因素。

Questions

1. Many factors will play an important role in deciding a reasonable pay level. What does each of them exert its influence?
2. Make a comparison between the different benefit systems in China and America.

9

Employee Relations
员工关系

【本章导读】 本章阐述的是劳动关系问题。9.1 介绍了劳动关系管理中的一个敏感问题——处罚。处罚的要点之一就是处罚的一致性。9.2 转而介绍工会产生的原因、建立过程和作用等,旨在说明工会在调节劳动关系中的重要作用。9.3 介绍员工与管理方及委托方(第三方)的关系问题,重在阐释在劳动合同存续期间,员工对于管理方的情感承诺和管理方所提供的服务性公民行为组织支持的感知效果。

9.1　Discipline in Employee Relations
　　　员工关系中的纪律

Introduction

　　Employee relation deals with the administration of discipline and grievance-handling procedure[①]. When a manager must take action against an employee for violating an organizational work rule or for poor performance, he or she uses the organization's disciplinary procedure to resolve the problem. When an employee has a complaint against the organization or its management, she or he normally uses the grievance procedure to resolve the problem. Some organizations have very formal discipline and grievance procedures, others are less formal, and some organizations have no set procedures at all. This chapter describes typical discipline and grievance-handling procedures.

Discipline Defined

Organizational discipline is action taken against an employee who has violated an organizational rule or whose performance has deteriorated to the point where corrective action is needed. Sixty years ago, a manager who objected to an employee's performance or behavior could simply say, "You're fired!" and that was it. Justification often played little, if any, part in the decision. At that time, managers had the final authority to administer discipline at will.

In applying organizational discipline, the primary question should be, "Why are employees disciplined?" Too many managers, when faced with a discipline problem in their organization, immediately think of what and how much: What should the penalty be? How severely should the employee be punished? The ultimate form of discipline is discharge, or organizational capital punishment as it is sometimes called. Organizations should use discharge in the case of repeated offenses or when the act committed is such that discharge is believed to be the only reasonable alternative.

Rather than an end in itself, discipline should be viewed as a learning opportunity for the employee and as a tool to improve productivity and human relations.

Generally disciplinary actions are taken against employees for two types of conduct: (1) Poor job performance or conduct that negatively affects an employee's job performance. Absenteeism, insubordination, and negligence are examples of behaviors that can lead to discipline. (2) Actions that indicate poor citizenship. Examples include fighting on the job or theft of company property.

The Discipline Process

The first step in the disciplinary process is the establishment of performance requirements and work rules. Performance requirements are normally established through the performance appraisal process. Work rules should be relevant to successful performance of the job. Because implementation of work rules partially depends on the employee's willingness to accept them, periodic review of their applicability is essential[2]. In addition, it is often desirable to solicit employee input either directly or indirectly when establishing work rules. Work rules are more easily enforced when employees perceive them as being fair and relevant to the job.

The second step in the process is to communicate the performance requirements and work rules to employees. This is normally handled through orientation and performance appraisal. Work rules are communicated in a variety of ways. Generally, an individual who is hired receives a manual that describes the work rules and policies of the organization. The human resource department or the new employee's supervisor explains these work rules and policies to the new employee during orientation. Furthermore, new employees may be required to sign a document indicating they have received and read the manual. In unionized organizations, work rules and the corresponding disciplinary actions for infractions are frequently part of the labor contract. Bulletin boards, company newsletters, and memos are also commonly used to communicate work rules. In any case, management bears the responsibility for clearly communicating all work rules to employees.

The final step in the disciplinary process is the application of corrective action (discipline) when necessary. Corrective action is needed when an employee's work performance is below expectations or when violations of work rules have occurred.

Prediscipline Recommendations

Before an employee is disciplined, management can take several steps to ensure that the action will be constructive and will not likely be rescinded by higher levels of management. Adequate records are of utmost importance in discipline cases. Written records often have a significant influence on decisions to overturn or uphold a disciplinary action. Past rule infractions and overall performance should be recorded.

Another key responsibility of management is the investigation. Things that appear obvious on the surface are sometimes completely discredited after investigation. Accusations against an employee must be supported by facts. Many decisions to discipline employees have been overturned due to an improper or less than thorough investigation. Undue haste in taking disciplinary action, taking the action when the manager is angry, and improper and incomplete investigations frequently cause disciplinary actions to be rescinded. An employee's work record should also be considered a part of the investigation. Good performance and long tenure with the organization are considerations that should influence the severity of a disciplinary action[3]. Naturally, the investigation must take place before any discipline is administered. A manager should not discipline an employee and then look for evidence to support the decision.

A typical first step in the investigation of the facts is for management to discuss the situation with the employee. Providing the employee with an opportunity to present his or her side of the situation is essential if a disciplinary system is to be viewed positively by employees.

Administering Discipline

Administering discipline should be analogous to the burn received when touching a hot stove. Often referred to as the hot-stove rule, this approach emphasizes that discipline should be directed against the act rather than the person. Other key points of the hot-stove rule are immediacy, advance warning, and consistency.

Immediacy refers to the length of time between the misconduct and the discipline. For discipline to be most effective, it must be taken as soon as possible but without involving an emotional, irrational decision. Notation of rules infractions in an employee's record does not constitute advance warning and is not sufficient to support disciplinary action. An employee must be advised of the infraction for it to be considered a warning. Noting that the employee was warned about the infraction and having the employee sign a form acknowledging the warning are both good practices. Failure to warn an employee of the consequences of repeated violations of a rule is one reason often cited for overturning a disciplinary action.

The hot stove burns immediately. Disciplinary policies should be administered quickly. There should be no question of cause and effect.

The hot stove gives a warning and so should discipline.

The hot stove consistently burns everyone who touches it. Discipline should be consistent.

The hot stove burns everyone in the same manner regardless of who they are. Discipline must be impartial. People are disciplined for what they have done and not because of who they are.

A key element in discipline is consistency. Inconsistency lowers morale, diminishes respect for management, and leads to grievances: Striving for consistency does not mean that past infractions, length of service, work record, and other mitigating factors should not be considered when applying discipline. However, an employee should believe that any other employee under essentially the same circumstances would receive the same penalty. Similarly, management should take steps to ensure that personalities are not a factor when applying discipline. The employee should understand that the disciplinary action is a consequence of what was done and not caused by his or her personality. A manager should avoid arguing with the employee and should administer the discipline in a straightforward, calm manner. Administering discipline without anger or apology and then resuming a pleasant relationship aids in reducing the negative effects of discipline[④]. A manager should also administer discipline in private. The only exception would be in the case of gross insubordination or flagrant and serious rule violations, where a public reprimand would help the manager regain control of the situation. Even in this type of situation, the objective should be to gain control and not to embarrass the employee.

Lower-level managers should be very reluctant to impose disciplinary suspensions and discharges. Usually discipline of this degree is reserved for higher levels of management. Even a lower-level manager who does not have the power to administer disciplinary suspensions or discharges, however, is nearly always the one who must recommend the action to higher management. Since discipline of this nature is more likely to be reviewed, more costly to the organization, and more likely to be reflected in overall morale and productivity, it is very important for lower-level managers to know when it should be recommended. Observing the hot-stove rule is essential for administering suspensions and discharges.

Management is expected to use corrective, or progressive, discipline whenever possible. Progressive, or corrective, discipline means the normal sequence of actions taken by management in disciplining an employee would be oral warning, written warning, suspension, and discharge. Some offenses, however, may justify discharge, such as stealing, striking a coworker or member of management, and gross insubordination. Management must be able to show, generally through the preponderance of evidence, that the offense was committed. Attention to the points covered regarding prediscipline recommendations is especially important in supporting a decision to discharge an employee⑤.

As in any lesser discipline, but even more essential in suspension and discharge, the employee has the right to a careful and impartial investigation. This involves allowing the employee to state his or her side of the case, gather evidence to support that side, and, usually, question the accuser. In the case of very serious offenses, the employee may be suspended pending a full investigation.

The suggestions outlined in the preceding paragraphs are designed to assist managers in applying discipline in a positive manner and with minimal application of the harsher forms of discipline. In the disciplinary procedure, observance of these suggestions should reduce the chance of a grievance or, if a grievance is filed, the chance of having the disciplinary action overruled⑥.

Legal Restrictions

The Civil Rights Act of 1964 and the Age Discrimination in Employment Act of 1967 as amended in 1978 changed an employer's authority in making decisions and taking actions involving employment conditions. Specifically, Title VII of the Civil Rights Act prohibits the use of race, color, religion, sex, or national origin as the basis of any employment condition. The Age Discrimination in Employment Act makes similar prohibitions involving persons over 40 years of age. Discipline is, of course, a condition of employment and is subject to these laws. Under these laws, employees have the right to appeal to the Equal Employment Opportunity Commission (EEOC) and to the courts any disciplinary action they consider discriminatory.

The landmark case guaranteeing employees this right was decided in 1974 by the Supreme Court in Alexander v. Gardner-Denver. In that case, the Supreme Court ruled that using the grievance procedure in an organization did not preclude the aggrieved employee from seeking redress through court action. Basically, the Court decided that the Civil Rights Act guar-anteed individuals the right to pursue remedies of illegal discrimination regardless of prior rejections in another forum.

from: *Human Resource Management*, 7th Edition, 2007

Words and Expressions

discipline ['disiplin] *n.* 处罚
grievance ['gri:vəns] *n.* 委屈;冤情;不平
deteriorate [di'tiəriəreit] *v.* 使……恶化
penalty ['penlti] *n.* 处罚;罚款
ultimate ['ʌltimit] *adj.* 最后的;最终的;根本的
insubordination [insəˌbɔ:di'neiʃən] *n.* 不顺从;反抗
negligence ['neglidʒəns] *n.* 疏忽
implementation [ˌimplimen'teiʃən] *n.* 执行
solicit [sə'lisit] *v.* 恳求
manual ['mænjuəl] *n.* 手册;指南
infraction [in'frækʃən] *n.* 违反;侵害
rescind [ri'sind] *v.* 废除
discredited [dis'kreditid] *adj.* 不足信的;不名誉的
accusation [ækju:'zeiʃən] *n.* 谴责
undue ['ʌn'dju:] *adj.* 不适当的
tenure ['tenjuə] *n.* 任期
irrational [i'ræʃənəl] *adj.* 无理性的;失去理性的

notation [nəu'teiʃən] n. 符号
impartial [im'pɑːʃəl] adj. 公平的
diminish [di'miniʃ] v. 使……减少；使……变小
mitigate ['mitigeit] v. 减轻
flagrant ['fleigrənt] adj. 不能容忍的；公然的
preponderance [pri'pɔndərəns] n. 优势；占优势
accuser [ə'kjuːzə] n. 原告
pending ['pendiŋ] adj. 未决的
discriminatory [di'skriminətɔːri] adj. 有辨识力的；有差别的
amend [ə'mend] v. 修正；改进
prohibit [prə'hibit] v. 禁止；阻止
preclude [pri'kluːd] n. 排除
aggrieved [ə'griːvd] adj. 受虐待的；权利受到不法侵害的
redress [ri'dres] n. 矫正；赔偿
rejection [ri'dʒekʃən] n. 拒绝
grievance-handling procedures 申诉处理程序
disciplinary procedure 惩罚程序
organizational capital punishment 组织性死刑
the hot-stove rule 趁热打铁原则
corrective, or progressive, discipline 矫正性或渐进性惩罚
normal sequence 正规序列
Civil Rights Acts 公民权利法案
the Age Discrimination in Employment Act 劳工法的年龄歧视
the Equal Employment Opportunity Commission (EEOC)
就业机会均等委员会

Difficult Sentences

①Employee relation deals with the administration of discipline and grievance-handling procedure.
雇员关系的主要内容是管理惩罚与申诉处理的程序。

② Because implementation of work rules partially depends on the employee's willingness to accept them, periodic review of their applicability is essential.

由于工作规章的执行部分地依赖于雇员是否愿意接受它们,定期复查其适用性很关键。

③ Good performance and long tenure with the organization are considerations that should influence the severity of a disciplinary action.

良好的业绩以及与企业长期的雇佣关系都是影响惩罚的严重性所要考虑的因素。

④ Administering discipline without anger or apology and then resuming a pleasant relationship aids in reducing the negative effects of discipline.

处罚而不带怒色或歉意,而后再重拾双方的愉快关系,有助于减少惩罚的负面影响。

⑤ Attention to the points covered regarding prediscipline recommendations is especially important in supporting a decision to discharge an employee.

在支持解雇员工的决定时,对于上述所荐有关惩罚前的种种加以关注尤为重要。

⑥ In the disciplinary procedure, observance of these suggestions should reduce the chance of a grievance or, if a grievance is filed, the chance of having the disciplinary action overruled.

在惩罚程序中,密切注视这些建议应该会降低申诉机会;或如果申诉已遭备案的话,也可减少否决惩罚的机会。

Phrases and Patterns

1. have a complaint against... 抱怨……

   When an employee has a complaint against the organization or its management, she or he normally uses the grievance procedure to resolve the problem.

当雇员对其组织或组织的管理不满时,正常情况下她或他会动用申诉程序以解决问题。

Employees have a complaint against that in the past 20 years their individual equity has lost out.

员工们抱怨他们的个人资产净值在过去的20年中受到损害。

2. be objected to... 反对……

Sixty years ago, a manager who objected to an employee's performance or behavior could simply say, "You're fired!" and that was it.

60年前,一位不满其雇员的表现或行为的经理只需简单地说声"你被解雇了"就万事大吉。

The management has tried its best to object to the organization of any kind of unions.

管理方尽全力反对组织任何形式的工会。

3. in the case of... 在……情况下

Organizations should use discharge in the case of repeated offenses or when the act committed is such that discharge is believed to be the only reasonable alternative.

只有在员工屡次冒犯或其行为如此严重只有解雇被认为是唯一理智的选择时,才应该动用解雇。

In any case, management bears the responsibility for clearly communicating all work rules to employees.

任何情况下,管理方都有责任告知员工所有的工作规则。

4. rather than... 而不是……

Rather than an end in itself, discipline should be viewed as a learning opportunity for the employee and as a tool to improve productivity and human relations.

惩罚本身并不是结束,而应视为是员工的一个学习的机会和改善生产力和人际关系的工具。

In applying organizational discipline, the primary question should be, "Why are employees disciplined?" rather than firing them on the spot.

在组织惩戒的过程中首要的问题是"员工为什么受到惩罚?"而不是当场将其解雇。

9.2 The Organizing Campaign
工会运动

Introduction

When employees are significantly dissatisfied with their situation in the workplace, union organizing is a possible outcome. Organizing is the process of forming a bargaining unit and petitioning the National Labor Relations Board for recognition. A bargaining unit is two or more employees who share common employment interests and conditions and may reasonably be grouped together. The right to organize in the private sector was established by the Wagner Act (National Labor Relations Act) and its amendments.

Conditions in the workplace that are most likely to trigger organizing are lack of job security, low wages, use of subcontracting, hostile supervisory practices, and inadequate health care or other benefits[①]. The AFL-CIO describes organizing as "the labor movement's lifeblood and the most critical element in the pursuit of our historic goal of helping working people secure justice, dignity, and a voice in the workplace and throughout society."

The organizing campaign determines who will represent or speak for whom in the collective bargaining process. The employees' representative can be a union (employee association) or a group of unions. Collective bargaining is the process by which unions and management establish the terms and conditions of employment. The process has three major functions:

to establish and revise the rules of the workplace through negotiation of a labor agreement (contract).

to administer the resulting labor agreement.

to establish a method for the settlement of disputes during the lifetime of the agreement.

Establishing the Bargaining Unit

A unit can exist only if workers prefer to be unionized. One of the first decisions that must be made is what group of employees should make up the individual bargaining unit. This important decision can be made by the employees, by management, or jointly by both. Labor and management often disagree as to which employees or groups of employees are eligible for inclusion in a particular proposed unit. Obviously, both sides want as much bargaining power as possible. The final determination of the appropriate bargaining unit is in the hands of the following agencies and individual(s):

· Private sector (for example, General Motors, Xerox, USX)—National Labor Relations Board (NLRB).

· Railway and airline sector (for example, Illinois Central, Delta)—National Mediation Board

· Postal sector—National Labor Relations Board (NLRB).

· Federal sector (for example, air traffic controllers)—Assistant Secretary of Labor—Management Relations.

· Public sector (for example, California Highway Patrol, New York Sanitation Department)—varies in accordance with state and local statutes.

In determining whether a proposed bargaining unit is appropriate, consideration is given to the history of collective bargaining in the organization and to the desires of the employees in the proposed unit. In general, the union will seek as large a unit as possible, while management will attempt to restrict the unit's size.

The Role of Unions

The union's intention is to convince employees that being a member will lead to important outcomes-better wages, fairer treatment from management, job security, and better working conditions. Unions attempt to stress issues that are meaningful, current, and obvious to employees.

In the 1990s, union organizers are finding a new kind of employee who is more difficult to organize. This employee accepts less, trusts less, and wants more. New issues are being addressed by unions. Insecurity is the most important issue facing nonunionized firms. Job retraining and advance notice of plant closings are pertinent issues. Traditional issues of grievance procedures, job security, improved benefits, and higher pay are still the issues most commonly stressed in organizing campaigns, however. Lack of sensitivity regarding employees' complaints, inept supervision, and poor communication are the most serious mistakes management can make that help pave the way for successful organizing campaigns.

The scope of the organizing campaign is changing. Unions are now trying to organize new bargaining units outside their traditional industries. The concept of jurisdiction is what is important here. Union jurisdiction refers to the territory within which a union organizes and engages in collective bargaining. In the past, a union stuck to organizing a single industry or specific types of jobs. With the decline of heavy industry, this kind of union organizing is no longer productive. In the 1990s, it is not unusual for unions to recruit new members from industries other than those defined as their primary jurisdictions[2].

The organizational and recruiting efforts of unions have varied according to changes in economic, social, and political conditions. New membership drives are taking place in the public sector, which includes military personnel, police, and fire-fighters; among professions, including teachers, medical personnel, athletes, and lawyers; and among employees in service industries. Another area that unions are attempting to unionize is agriculture. Organizing efforts are especially intense in the strawberry, grape, lettuce, citrus, and cotton regions of California.

The Role of Management

Research has shown that union organizing campaigns are often associated with significant declines in the profitability of firms. Therefore, most organizations prepare some type of campaign to oppose a union's move to organize workers. It is important to know that the NLRB forbids management actions to suppress the union and to intimidate employees considering unionization. These are considered unfair management practices. For example, firing a union supporter or disciplining a worker who is involved in organizing efforts may be considered an unfair management practice. If these actions are not supported with facts and are related to organizing efforts, management can become involved in lawsuits.

Normally, the HR department is responsible for presenting management's side of the story. Outside consultants or antiunion experts trained in preventing organizing often are used. One popular management approach is to emphasize that a union is run by outsiders. The outsider is pictured as being uninformed, uninterested, and unqualified. Management attempts to communicate clearly and forcefully to the employees about the advantages of remaining nonunionized[3]. Speeches, question-and-answer sessions, bulletin board postings, personal letters to employees, and articles in the company newspaper are used to promote the advantages of being nonunionized.

Three basic forms of opposition to unions have been identified: (1) positive labor relations without a union, (2) legal campaigns, and (3) unfair labor practices, sometimes called union busting. Organizations that have higher wages, better working conditions, more equitable supervisory practices, and generous benefits are less likely to commit unfair labor practices than firms with lower wages and less favorable working conditions. Strong opposition from management is an important factor contributing to the continuing decline in unionization.

The Role of the NLRB

The NLRB is a watchdog. Charges of unfair practices on the part of management or labor can be filed by the union, an employee, an employer, or any other person. A formal charge requires the NLRB to officially review the claim and decide whether a specific management or union tactic was fair under the guidelines of the law. As previously mentioned, the NLRB can also be called on by either side to be sure the bargaining unit is appropriate. The NLRB is responsible for conducting the election and certifying the results of organizing efforts in the private and public sectors. It pays particular attention to the following areas:

Concerning the Employer

· NLRB makes sure that questioning of employees about union membership is done in a fair and nonintimidating manner.

· NLRB checks to see if the information provided to employees about unions is truthful.

· NLRB does not allow any final presentations within 24 hours preceding the election.

Concerning the Union

· NLRB makes sure that no threats or intimidations are used to gain votes.

· NLRB guards the employees against the union's promises of

special treatment for votes if the union wins.

· No final presentations are allowed within 24 hours preceding the election.

Once the appropriate bargaining unit has been determined or agreed upon, the next step is the representation election process, including the authorization card campaign.

Authorization Card Campaign

An authorization card is a document indicating that an employee wants to be represented by a union (employee association) in collective bargaining. It is the union's way of finding out how many workers are in favor of unionization. When signed by an employee, the card authorizes the union to represent that employee during negotiations. At least 30 percent of the employees in a bargaining unit must sign before the NLRB can be petitioned to hold a representation election. However, if over 50 percent of the unit's employees sign up, the union can ask the company directly that it be named representative without a certification election.

There are three other ways that a union can be certified. If the union can demonstrate that it represents a majority of the firm's employees, management can recognize the union as the exclusive bargaining representative voluntarily. This out come is not very typical, however. Most unions achieve recognition through petitioning the National Labor Relations Board for a certification election after the authorization cards demonstrate employees' interest. The NLRB will conduct a secret-ballet election. Certification elections are usually held within 45 days of the initial request. If the union receives a simple majority (50 percent plus one vote), the NLRB certifies the union as the exclusive bargaining representative, and collective bargaining begins. If the union fails to get the majority of votes cast, it cannot represent the employees. No new representation election can be held for that bargaining unit for one year.

The third way that a union can be recognized is for the NLRB to direct the employer to recognize the union without an election. This happens when the employer engages in serious unfair labor practices during the union organizing campaign. The conclusion here is that it would be impossible to hold a fair, impartial election because of the employer's previous unethical antiunion practices. The NLRB has actually ordered collective bargaining rights in about 1% of all cases.

If a union legally wins an organizing election, it is recognized as the exclusive bargaining representative of a unit. The NLRB requires that both the elected union and management bargain in good faith. This requirement is spelled out in the Taft-Hartley Act as follows:

For the purposes of this section, to bargain collectively is the performance of the mutual obligation of the employer and representative of the employees to meet at reasonable times and confer in good faith with respect to wages, hours, and other terms and conditions of employment, or the negotiation of an agreement, or any question arising thereunder, and the execution of a written contract incorporating any agreement reached if requested by either party, but such obligation does not compel either party to agree to a proposal or require the making of a concession[4].

Occasionally, the NLRB conducts a decertification election. A decertification election is the opposite of the certification election. If employees decide they no longer need a union, either between contracts or when the union fails to negotiate an initial contract during the first 12-month period, decertification elections can be held. If a simple majority decides in favor of management, the union is no longer the official bargaining representative. Decertification elections increased in frequency in the 1990s and unions lost them more frequently.

Antiunion consultants, or union busters, have had significant success in keeping unions out and helping management encourage employees to decertify unions. The AFL-CIO has identified 520 consulting and law firms that assist companies in warding off unions. The unions' feeling about these consultants is that they prevent employees from exercising their rights. Management, however, feels that they are important in helping organizations use legal means to remain union-free or to decertify unions.

from: *Human Resource Management*, 1998

Words and Expressions

petition [pi'tiʃən] *v.* 请求;恳求
amendment [ə'mendmənt] *n.* 改善;改正
trigger ['trigə] *v.* 引发;引起;触发
subcontract [sʌb'kɔntrækt] *n.* 转包合同
hostile ['hɔstail] *adj.* 敌对的
dignity ['digniti] *n.* 尊严;高贵
revise [ri'vaiz] *v.* 修订
sanitation [sæni'teiʃən] *n.* 卫生;卫生设施
statute ['stætjuːt] *n.* 法令;条例
pertinent ['pəːtinənt] *adj.* 有关的
convince [kən'vins] *v.* 使确信;使信服
jurisdiction [ˌdʒuəris'dikʃən] *n.* 权限
suppress [sə'pres] *v.* 抑制
intimidate [in'timideit] *v.* 胁迫
consultant [kən'sʌltənt] *n.* 顾问
session ['seʃən] *n.* 会议;开庭
bust [bʌst] *v.* 打碎
equitable ['ekwitəbl] *adj.* 公正的;平衡法的
certify ['səːtifai] *v.* 证明;保证
exclusive [iks'kluːsiv] *adj.* 独占的;唯一的

unethical [ˈʌnˈeθikəl] adj. 不道德的
confer [kənˈfəː] v. 协商;交换意见
thereunder [ðɛərˈʌndə] adv. 在那下面;依据
execution [ˌeksiˈkjuːʃən] n. 实行;完成;执行
incorporate [inˈkɔːpəreit] v. 合并
compel [kəmˈpel] v. 强迫;迫使
concession [kənˈseʃən] n. 让步
buster [ˈbʌstə] n. 非凡的人或物
decertify [diːˈsəːtifai] v. 收回……的证件;拒绝承认
National Labor Board 美国国家劳工委员会
The Wagner Act 瓦格纳法案
National Labor Relation Act 美国国家劳工关系法案
AFL (American Federation of Labor) 美国劳工联合会
CIO (Congress of Industrial Organizations) 美国产业会联合会
National Mediation Board 美国国家调解委员会
California Highway Patrol 加州高速公路巡警
New York Sanitation Department 纽约卫生部
nonunionized firm 非工会化公司
primary jurisdiction 优先税收管辖权
exclusive bargaining representative 独家协商代理
a secret-ballet election 不记名选举
Taft-Hartley Act 塔夫脱-哈特利法案

Difficult Sentences

① Conditions in the workplace that are most likely to trigger organizing are lack of job security, low wages, use of subcontracting, hostile supervisory practices, and inadequate health care or other benefits. 工作场所中极易引发组织工会的情况有工作安全不足、低工资、使用转包合同、恶意监管、卫生保健或其他待遇不充分。

② In the 1990s, it is not unusual for unions to recruit new members from industries other than those defined as their primary jurisdictions.

20 世纪 90 年代,常见的情况是工会从产业行业而不是从那些被规定为具有优先税收管辖权的行业吸收新成员。

③ Management attempts to communicate clearly and forcefully to the employees about the advantages of remaining nonunionized.

管理方尝试尽全力清晰而强烈到告知员工保持非工会化大有好处。

④ For the purposes of this section, to bargain collectively is the performance of the mutual obligation of the employer and representative of the employees to meet at reasonable times and confer in good faith with respect to wages, hours, and other terms and conditions of employment, or the negotiation of an agreement, or any question arising thereunder, and the execution of a written contract incorporating any agreement reached if requested by either party, but such obligation does not compel either party to agree to a proposal or require the making of a concession.

为此,共同协商是雇佣双方代表的义务体现,双方应适时举行会议,真诚探讨下列事宜:工薪、工时、雇佣的其他条款及状况,商讨协议的有关问题。同时,只要一方提出要求,就应该对附含任一协议的书面合同的执行情况进行协商,但并不强迫任何一方同意某一提议或做出让步。

Phrases and Patterns

1. in the pursuit of... 追求;寻求……

The AFL-CIO describes organizing as "the labor movement's lifeblood and the most critical element in the pursuit of our historic goal of helping working people secure justice, dignity, and a voice in the workplace and throughout society."

美国劳工联合会-美国产业工会联合会把组织工会这一活动称为"是劳工运动的生命源泉,是追求帮助劳动人民获得正义、尊严这

—历史目标的关键因素,是来自工作场所和整个社会的声音"。
The NLRB is always in the pursuit of communication in good faith between management and unions.
美国国家劳资关系委员会一直追求的是管理方与工会的真诚交流。

2. pave the way for... 为……铺平道路;为……做好准备
Lack of sensitivity regarding employees' complaints, inept supervision, and poor communication are the most serious mistakes management can make that help pave the way for successful organizing campaigns.
对员工的不满反应迟钝、监管不当以及缺乏交流是管理上可能犯的最严重的错误,却能为成功地组织大型活动创造条件。
Poor conditions in workplaces are most likely to pave the way for unions to manifest themselves.
不良的工作条件最有可能导致工会的出现。

3. engage in... 从事于……;参加……
Union jurisdiction refers to the territory within which a union organizes and engages in collective bargaining.
工会司法是指组织工会和进行集体协商的范围。
They have engaged in bargaining of who is eligible for inclusion in the particular union.
他们正忙于协商谁有资格入选这一特殊的工会。

4. stick to... 坚持……
In the past, a union stuck to organizing a single industry or specific types of jobs.
过去工会坚持组织一个单独的行业或几个特殊的工种。
The management stuck to that decertification election should be conducted at that time.
管理方当时坚持认为应该举行选举,拒绝承认工会。

9.3 Exploring the Employment Relationship of Contracted Employees (background and results)
基于劳动合同的雇佣关系探讨

Introduction

Although growth has occurred in contract employment arrangements both in the public and private sectors, scant research has been conducted on the organizations and employees affected by these arrangements. This study examines the employment relationship of long-term contracted employees using a social exchange framework. Specifically, we examine the effects of employee perceptions of organizational support from contracting and client organizations on their (a) affective commitment to each organization and (b) service-oriented citizenship behavior[1]. We also examine whether felt obligation toward each organization mediates this relationship. Our sample consists of 99 long-term contracted employees working for four contracting organizations that provide services to the public on behalf of a municipal government. Results indicate that the antecedents of affective commitment are similar for the client and contracting organization. Employee perceptions of client organizational supportiveness were positively related to felt obligation and commitment to the client organization. Client felt obligation mediated the effects of client perceived organizational support (POS) on the participation dimension of citizenship behavior[2]. Our study provides additional support for the generalizability of social exchange processes to nontraditional employment relationships. Implications for managing long-term contracted employees are discussed.

Background

Organizations increasingly are positioning their human resources in work arrangements that create new forms of employment relationships. One of the fastest-growing forms involves the use of external or contracted employees. Contract arrangements are themselves highly variable. Contingent contract arrangements may entail, for example, self-employed individuals who sell their services to a client organization for a specified time or project, seasonal employment arrangements, or temporary employment through in-house or intermediate agencies where hours may be nonsystematic.

Less contingent, more permanent contract arrangements are rapidly evolving, where a third-party body (e. g., a contractor or professional employer organization) agrees to handle a set of work responsibilities for a client organization at their work location(s) or as assigned. The contractor supplies the employees and is the legal employer of record. The client organization has, in effect, outsourced some operations to the contractor. The contractor supplies the employees and is the legal employer of record. The client organization has, in effect, outsourced some operations to the contractor. Stated differently, the contractor and the client organization have negotiated a shared employer relationship vis-a-vis the contracted employee, creating a triangular system of employment relations[3]. What differentiates this work arrangement from others is the multiple-agency aspect of the work, wherein a worker simultaneously fulfills obligations to more than one employer through the same act or behavior.

A second difference between this and other contingent contract arrangements is that this arrangement assumes a longer time horizon and tends to entail more relational exchanges between employees and the client organization. Lepak and his associates describe this type of employment relationship as an alliance or partnership. Employees who work under these arrangements, whom we refer to as long-term contracted employees, are the focus of this study.

The popularity of outsourcing as a business practice is reflected in a substantial increase in the size of the contractor industry and growth in the number of long-term contracted employees. NAPEO estimates that 2-3 million Americans are currently coemployed in long-term contracted arrangements. The growth in contract work has been even stronger in Australia and Europe, especially in the United Kingdom. Despite this expansion, long-term contracted employees have received scant research attention, and little guidance has been provided to practitioners seeking to manage these unique employees. They are quite different from other nonstandard employee groups such as temporary employees or independent contractors because they are embedded in a more secure and permanent employment context.

Moreover, client organizations often regard such employees as front-line service representatives who possess firm-specific knowledge that can build customer loyalty over the long run. Hence, relying on empirical research comparing standard and various other types of nonstandard employees is insightful but not adequate. Clearly, more intense examination of long-term contracted workers is warranted. It would be beneficial to know, for example, if the same underlying psychological processes that govern standard employees' organizational behavior are replicated among long-term contracted employees. As Liden, Wayne, Kraimer, and Sparrowe point out, working for two organizations simultaneously makes understanding contracted employees more complex than the study of standard employees.

To this end, this study sets out to explore the extent to which long-term contracted employees develop social exchange relationships with their contracting and client organizations. More specifically, we investigate how perceived support and felt obligation associated with the two organizations manifest themselves in the expression of commitment attitudinally (affective organizational commitment) and behaviorally (service-oriented organizational citizenship behaviors)④. The model depicted in Figure 1 outlines expected relations. A second purpose of this study is to compare whether the social exchange processes associated with contractor and client organizations operate similarly in explaining affective organizational commitment and citizenship behaviors. In doing so, this study contributes to the employment relationship literature by exploring the extent to which a social exchange framework is applicable to contracted employees⑤.

Results

In summary, perceived organizational supportiveness is positively related to employees' felt obligation toward the target of the support. Second, employees' felt obligation toward their contract organization partially mediated the effect of contractor POS on contractor affective commitment and on loyalty citizenship behaviors. Third, employees' felt obligation toward the client partially mediated the effect of client POS on client affective commitment and fully mediated the effect of client POS on participation citizenship behaviors.

from: Serving Two Organizations: Exploring The Employment Relationship of Contracted Employees from Human Resource Management, 2006

Words and Expressions

scant [skænt] *adj.* 不足的
obligation [ˌɔbli'geiʃən] *n.* 义务;职责
mediate ['miːdiit] *v.* 仲裁;调停
municipal [mju(ː)'nisipəl] *adj.* 市政的;地方性的

antecedent [ˌænti'siːdənt] n. 先辈
contingent [kən'tindʒənt] adj. 可能发生的；附随的；暂时的
entail [in'teil] v. 使必需
evolving [i'vɔlviŋ] adj. 进化的；展开的
differentiate [ˌdifə'renʃieit] v. 区别；区分
simultaneously [siməl'teiniəsly] adv. 同时地
associate [ə'səufieit] n. 合作人；同事
alliance [ə'laiəns] n. 联盟；联合
substantial [səb'stænʃəl] adj. 充实的
embed [im'bed] v. 使插入；使嵌入
loyalty ['lɔiəlti] n. 忠诚；忠心
adequate ['ædikwit] adj. 适当的；足够的
beneficial [beni'fiʃəl] adj. 有益的；受益的
manifest ['mænifest] v. 表明；证明
attitudinally [ˌæti'tjuːdinəli] adv. 根据或表示个人态度地
depict [di'pikt] v. 描述
applicable ['æplikəbl] adj. 可适用的；可应用的
perceived organizational support 感知组织支持
non-traditional employment relationship 非传统性雇佣关系
long-term contracted employee 长期合同工
client organization 客户
time horizon 时间范围
National Association of Professional Employer Organizations (NAPEO) 美国职业雇主组织国家联合会

Difficult Sentences

① Specifically, we examine the effects of employee perceptions of organizational support from contracting and client organizations on their (a) affective commitment to each organization and (b) service-oriented citizenship behavior.

我们尤其调查了员工对来自于合同方与委托方作用于其(a)对于任一方的情感承诺和(b)服务性公民行为的组织支持的感知效果。

② Client felt obligation mediated the effects of client perceived organizational support (POS) on the participation dimension of citizenship behavior.
客户感觉到的义务对于其感知组织支持作用于公民参与行为的效果进行了调节。

③ Stated differently, the contractor and the client organization have negotiated a shared employer relationship vis-a-vis the contracted employee, creating a triangular system of employment relations
换言之,承包商与客户已经商定了一个共同的与合同工的雇佣关系,创造了一个雇佣关系的三角体系。

④ More specifically, we investigate how perceived support and felt obligation associated with the two organizations manifest themselves in the expression of commitment attitudinally (affective organizational commitment) and behaviorally (service-oriented organizational citizenship behaviors).
更确切地说,我们调查的是与两个组织相关的感知支持与感觉义务是如何以态度性承诺(情感性组织承诺)和行为性承诺(服务性组织的公民行为)的方式出现。

⑤ This study contributes to the employment relationship literature by exploring the extent to which a social exchange framework is applicable to contracted employees.
该研究通过对"社会互换框架适用于合同工的程度"这一问题的探索丰富了雇佣关系文献。

Phrases and Patterns

1. on behalf of... 代表……

Our sample consists of 99 long-term contracted employees working for four contracting organizations that provide services to the public on behalf of a municipal government.

我们抽样调查中的99名身为长期合同工的代表来自于四家合同企业，它们服务于公众并代表地方政府。

They are going to do some amendment to the old appraisal system on behalf of their company.

他们将代表公司对旧的评估体系做一些改进。

2. in effect... 实际上……

The client organization has, in effect, outsourced some operations to the contractor.

实际上，委托方已经把一些项目的运作转包给了承包商。

Longer term contracted employees have, in effect, received scant research attention.

长期合同工实际上只得到少量的研究关注。

3. set out to... 开始……

To this end, this study sets out to explore the extent to which long-term contracted employees develop social exchange relationships with their contracting and client organizations.

该研究开始探索长期合同工与其合同单位以及委托单位发展社会互换关系的程度。

They set out to conduct the research on the organizations and employees affected by these arrangements.

他们开始研究受这些约定影响的组织和雇员。

Questions

1. Two employees violate the same work rule. One is above average in performance and has been with your company for eight years. The other employee is an average performer who has been with your company for a little over a year. Should these employees receive the same discipline? Why or why not?

2. What conditions in the workplace are most likely to trigger a union organizing campaign? Why?
3. Compare and contrast the role of each of the following in the organizing process: employees, union, management, and the NLRB.
4. Discuss the employment relationship of contracted employees.

PART TWO　CASE

第二部分　案例

1. Daimler Has to Steer the Chrysler Merger
戴姆勒与克莱斯勒的并购之路

When Chrysler Corp. and Daimler Benz announced their megamerger—the largest international corporate marriage in history—it looked to be further evidence that globalisation cannot be stopped. But unlike fluid flows of money and technology across borders, the links between companies of different nationalities can be quite brittle. Remember how Renault was unable to hang on to American Motors or how Matsushita had to disgorge Universal Studios? Unless tough decisions are quickly made to overcome deeply ingrained differences of strategy and culture, global combinations can easily fall apart. Indeed, the survival of Daimler Chrysler is already at risk.

The new company will face massive challenges. Daimler Chrysler will still be only the fifth-largest car company, behind General Motors, Ford, Toyota and Volkswagen. Its product line, ranging from an US $11,000 Dodge to a US $130,000 Mercedes, could foster a confused image and culture. The German corporate governance system in which labour and banks hold board seats in order to take a longer-term view could collide with the obsession of American shareholders with immediate returns. Compensation philosophies could be irreconcilable: just compare Chrysler Chairman and CEO Robert J. Eaton's 1997 pay package of US $16 million with that of Daimler chief Jurgen E. Schrempp's US $1.9 million. And politically explosive decisions are sure to arise about how to apportion layoffs between America and Germany when downsizing occurs because of the overcapacity in the global auto industry.

To make this deal work, Daimler—which has been subtly identified by both parties as the controlling partner, despite all the talk about this being "a merger of equals"—needs to take complete charge, quickly and decisively. But in public statements, both Eaton and Schrempp have gone to great lengths to underline the "evolutionary" process of integrating the two companies. This slow-fuse approach—joint CEOs for a few years; headquarters in both Stuttgart and Detroit; separate operations for engineering, manufacturing and marketing—could unleash powerful centrifugal forces among competing departments.

In fact, Daimler ought to study another set of deals involving a high-profile takeover by an admired foreign company of prized American assets: Sony Corp's acquisition of both CBS Records Inc. and Columbia Pictures in the late 1980s. Sony started off mistakenly thinking that it could oversee its freewheeling American companies from afar and with a light touch. It failed to put its own strong management structure in theUnited States. It neglected to build links between Sony's American subsidiaries on the two coasts. It lost control of expenses and, by 1994, Sony was forced to take a US＄2.7 billion write-off.

But lessons were learned. The following year a new president, Nobuyuki Idei, put the Sony stamp on itsUnited States operations. He replaced top management in America with highly professional United States executives, such as Howard Stringer, former president of CBS Broadcast Group, who supported Sony's tradition of teamwork and its goals of integrating its operations in the United States and around the world. Top Japanese executives were placed in New York and Los Angeles. Idei came to the United States once a month to oversee the business and to network with such American counterparts as Bill Gates and Andy Grove.

Sony went from a loss of US＄1.8 billion in 1995 to a pretax profit of US＄3.4 billion in 1997, helped in part by its enormous success with computer video games. A leader in the United States-based digital revolution, Sony has even marshalled the resources of its music subsidiary inNew York, its movie business in Los Angeles and its electronics expertise in Tokyo to produce European movies in local languages out of Germany.

Sony and Daimler are in different businesses, of course, and no one blueprint applies to all big international mergers. But the most successful global companies, such as Nestle, ABB Asea Brown Boveri and General Electric, have put their unambiguous imprint on all their operations by imposing one strong corporate culture with central management for the most critical functions. Someone must articulate overall philosophy and values and establish companywide investment priorities. Someone must set financial and operational performance requirements, compensation policies and development paths for senior executives. Unless Daimler takes charge of these kinds of tasks immediately, do not be surprised if the deal comes unwound. Announcing a big global merger is nothing compared to making it succeed.

from: *Jeffrey E. Garten, Daimler Has to Steer the Chrysler Merger, Business Week,* 20 *July* 1998, *p.* 20.

Questions

1. One way to expand business globally is to merge with another company to create a powerful international corporation. The challenge of mergers is to unite two different companies with distinct business processes, strategies and cultures. Mergers are even more challenging when they involve companies from different countries (such as the Chrysler-Daimler Benz merger). Executives need to review operational, financial and people processes to develop a common set of rules, practices and procedures for the "new" company. What HRM issues do Chrysler Corporation and Daimler Benz have to resolve to

make the merger successful?
2. How might Chrysler and Daimler Benz decide which HRM practices to adopt companywide (globally)?

More Knowledge

克莱斯勒(Chrysler)汽车公司是美国第三大汽车工业公司,创立于 1925 年,创始人名叫沃尔特·克莱斯勒。该公司在全世界许多国家设有子公司,是一个跨国汽车公司。公司总部设在美国底特律。1924 年沃尔特·克莱斯勒离开通用汽车公司进入威廉斯·欧夫兰公司,开始生产克莱斯勒牌汽车。1925 年他买下破产的马克斯维尔公司组建自己的公司。凭借自己的技术和财力,他先后买下道奇、布立格和普利茅斯公司,逐渐发展成为美国第三大汽车公司。

随着经营的扩大,克莱斯勒开始向海外扩张,先后在澳大利亚、法国、英国、巴西建厂和收买当地汽车公司股权,购买了意大利的马沙拉蒂公司和兰伯基尼公司,从而使公司成为一个跨国汽车公司。在 20 世纪 30 年代它的黄金时期,曾一度超过福特公司。20 世纪 70 年代,公司因管理不善濒于倒闭,著名企业家李·雅柯卡接管了该公司。雅柯卡上任后大胆启用新人,裁减员工,争取政府资助,并把主要精力投入市场调研和产品开发上,在产品广告上出奇制胜。在 80 年代初,克莱斯勒又奇迹般地活了过来,继续排在世界前 5 名汽车大公司行列。

进入 90 年代,因日本汽车公司的进攻,克莱斯勒再次陷入困境,它在汽车公司排名中一降再降,甚至降到日产美国分公司(美国市场)之下。克莱斯勒汽车公司有道奇、顺风、克莱斯勒轿车部以及道奇载重车、零部件部等。现行汽车新产品则有"行可达"轻型货车、"太阳舞"轿车以及"幽灵"和"道奇 600"、"顺风快帆船"等汽车产品。

奔驰(Benz)公司是世界上资格最老的厂家,也是经营风格始终如一的厂家,是世界十大汽车公司之一,德国按销售额为第一大汽车公司,按产量则居第二。创立于 1926 年,创始人是卡尔·本茨和戈特利布·戴姆勒。它的前身是1886年成立的奔驰汽车厂和戴姆勒汽车厂。1926年两厂合并后，叫戴姆勒—奔驰(Daimler Benz)汽车公司，中国翻译简称奔驰汽车公司。现在，奔驰汽车公司除以高质量、高性能豪华汽车闻名外，它也是世界上最著名的大客车和重型载重汽车的生产厂家。

1998年5月6日，享誉全球的德国戴姆·奔驰汽车公司和美国三大汽车公司之一的克莱斯勒公司共同发表声明，宣布它们已签署一项总额高达380亿美元的合并协议。这成为历年来汽车制造业最大的一起合并。两家公司将以换股方式进行合并，合并后的公司取名戴姆勒—克莱斯勒公司，由大众公司董事长施仁普和克莱斯勒董事长伊顿共同执掌。

全球的汽车制造业格局在并购浪潮中发生了不小的变化；奔驰与克莱斯勒的合并起到推波助澜的作用，使业内巨头们不得不再次调整战略，以保证自己的竞争优势。

2. What's Next for E-HRM?
电子化人力资源管理的未来之路

Second generation B2E is upon us. Increasingly, companies are recognising the imperative to integrate their legacy systems, as intranets, extranets and external websites expand and diversify—often in an adhoc way—creating an environment of increasing complexity, where information systems are potentially unable to talk to each other.

Enter the people manager—the go-between who recognises the importance of people in the process of technological change. It is these HR practitioners, consultants and software providers who are standing out in the crowded marketplace of technological innovation, where vendors jostle in the Australian market.

"Workplace relations and organisational culture are more important to employees than technology," argues Steven Melville, managing director of Ingena, a business to employee (B2E) consultancy and solutions provider, "When organisations start by looking at technology solutions, they inevitably stray into issues about employee satisfaction and cultural workplace issues. And they should."

Is B2E just another fashionable term in the most jargon-laden industry in history? Or is it, as Melville argues, leading a new business philosophy by empowering people in an organisation with the knowledge and information they want, in a format they can use?

Australia has positioned itself well, according to the Economist Intelligence Unit and Pyramid Research, coming in second to the US in "e-readiness", placing it among the 13 countries considered e-business leaders, and ahead of the hundred others relegated to the categories of "contenders", "followers" and "laggards".

In the financial services, telecommunications and utilities sectors in particular, Australian companies are implementing some of the most innovative B2E solutions in the world.

Market research commissioned by Corechange, a global provider of e-business software that entered the Australian market in 2000, found that at the beginning of 2001, 37 percent of a surveyed 157 companies with more than 1,000 employees had a portal infrastructure project underway. The vast majority (73 percent) said they were implementing a B2E portal for the benefit of employees.

There is a clear distinction made between first and second generation B2Es. According to Ericsson's Kate Raulings, most corporate intranets are only a first generation internet application. "An important distinction between a standard intranet and a portal is that, with the latter, the appropriate processes are in place at the backend and they react in a timely manner." she says.

B2E portals enable employee self-service—applications like Peoplesoft's HRMS give employees control over their own personal details. For example, employees can update their own bank account details, triggering a "workflow" that goes through to the payroll manager. Raulings reports that annual leave requests are now approved within 24 hours at Ericsson, a clear winner for many employees.

In contrast, most first generation intranets are generally only central document repositories that are designed in an organisation-centric, rather than user-centric, way.

"Take travel, for example," says Raulings, "In the early days, an employee had to know they needed to look under 'HR' to find our travel policy, and under 'finance' to get a copy of the travel expenses claim form. Now Ericsson employees can start with 'I need travel', and run through each step of the workflow."

Tim Drinkall, formerly management and development consultant at call centre company UCMS, and now training analyst at United Energy, notes that "UCMS's adoption of a B2E portal is still in its infancy. At the moment, it's really only an intranet that sits on the desktop as an icon. Making it 'the' desktop will qualify it as a true portal".

"In 12 months, the Australian market has matured significantly." Raulings observes. In the early days, companies were concerned with demonstrating the return on investment and arguing the business case for moving away from the first generation intranet towards a more sophisticated portal. "I think that argument has largely been won now, and that the focus is shifting to understanding how we can harness the technology to enable personalisation, customisation and wireless access."

Corechange's research study supports Raulings' claim. It found that the most commonly sought benefit among 157 large Australian companies implementing B2E was the ability for a "single sign-on". Using one password, single sign-on provides a single point of access to all appropriate content and applications.

Perhaps more importantly, single sign-on paves the way for role-based access control architecture, where all information relevant to each employee's role within the enterprise is dynamically gathered and presented to them. It's a user-centric approach because it also enables each employee to customise the arrangement and display of content to suit their own needs.

"With the evolution of B2E, the 'top down' push of information is a thing of the past. Employees now have the opportunity to choose the learning and development path they want, at a pace they feel comfortable, and in a format they desire." says Ingena's Steven Melville, "A B2E portal site dynamically customises itself to present information and resources according to the personal needs of the employee. There needs to be more than one paradigm. People understand things in different ways. Generally, we give people three or four ways to navigate and they usually settle on one."

In addition to providing personalised access, using an internet architecture enables portability—users can log in from anywhere in the world. This is why many Australian companies implementing B2E portals are not only focusing on the technology, but are also thinking about the future of their physical workplace.

Although the uptake of B2E technology is high in a global sense, at an operational level, few companies are using the term B2E, or taking a long term, wholistic approach to the technology. instead, there is a tendency to think more in the short term, with references to the individual disciplines B2E enables, such as learning, knowledge management or records processing, or to its corporate brand—such as MX at ANZ, Inside EPA at Ericsson, Telstra's E-Campus, andAdvisor University at MLC.

But according to Steve Goldberg, vice president, Global HRMS Product Management, at Peoplesoft Inc., "just about any HR function, business process or transaction is handled more efficiently over the internet as long as business process workflow/rules are properly defined up-front."

Melville concurs: "A B2E portal is suitable for any company with a critical mass in user numbers. It could be as low as 300~400 employees in a call centre environment for example."

"Potentially, a B2E portal can be many things to many people, but in reality most companies start small, with solutions limited to specific business units that can demonstrate quick wins, which both encourage employee uptake and benefit the bottom line." he says.

Goldberg says most of Peoplesoft's clients aim to build up a groundswell by starting with the basics—such as enabling employees to manage their own personal profile or enrol in courses online.

"Then they can move further up the HR food chain to functions like performance management and job transfers. Given that many of the more complex HR functions are interdependent with other business processes, it takes time to build trust and acceptance."

There is ready consensus among technology consultants and HR practitioners about what makes B2E portals work effectively. Global business technology consultancy the Gartner Group says that the majority of e-business initiatives have been executed as IT projects, rather than strategic business initiatives, which is why many have failed.

Melville agrees: "I routinely come across companies implementing a knowledge management system where the vendor is only interested in selling user licences. When you think about the physical workplace, a generic 'one size fits all' floor plan is not going to meet the needs of an entire workforce. Nor is a one size fits all technology solution going to work."

"A complete and robust solution requires an investment that doubles the spend on software. My advice is that only 50 per cent of the budget should be spent on technology and that it needs to matched by an equal investment in research, change management and communication."

"Tying the B2E solution into core business functions maximises potential uptake," he advises, "The primary benefit of a B2E portal is the fact that you are working with a captive audience. If employees have to access the B2E portal to request important information and perform mandatory HR functions, they will also be exposed to optional learning, information and communication tools on a regular basis."

"But you need to thoroughly understand the needs of end users. In my experience, this is one of the biggest stumbling blocks. Many companies fail to grasp the importance of involving the user from the outset. They think they understand what their employees need."

Kate Raulings agrees, "The introduction of a B2E portal requires a complete re-engineering of an entire workflow. It only succeeds when everyone involved in that workflow plays a role in saying how it can work better and you need to allow employees to make decisions. It's a great way to bring employees on board if you can actually demonstrate how they've had input and influenced its design."

Perhaps the most critical factor in the maximisation of user uptake is the management of the change process. While the implementation of a B2E portal can support cultural change, it can't drive the process alone. A combination of road shows, tutorials, user support and integrated help ensures effective communication and education of the user population throughout all stages of the system lifecycle.

Walking in and switching on a shrink-wrapped portal solution is clearly not going to work, says Melville, adding that Ingena's approach is based on a combination of change management consultancy and technology development.

As a pure technology vendor, Peoplesoft has adopted a slightly different approach. While Goldberg observes that some organisations' HR functions or business architecture are traditionally very closed, centralised and non-collaborative, "our focus is on enabling an organisation to have open, distributed and collaborative HR business processes. Clients plot their own course and there are other domain experts who can assist with change management".

But both Melville and Goldberg agree that the other vital ingredients for successful deployment include a first-class IT&T infrastructure, good comfort levels with new technology and integration with enterprise-wide business processes.

"HR should be at the strategic end of the business. It's not a separate supply chain," observes Goldberg.

B2E portals are particularly suited to companies with a high number of knowledge workers with internet access at home, and Melville argues that uptake will be better if access at home is provided. "A B2E portal solution particularly appealed to Telstra, for example, because their team leaders wanted home access to career development."

Drinkall notes that at home access is planned for stage two of UCMS's portal. "At the moment, remote access is somewhat limited because we use a rich multimedia environment for online training delivery, which is difficult to deliver over a dial-up connection."

According to Jupiter Media Metrix, only about three percent of internet users in metropolitan areas are using cable, ADSL or satellite (and a tiny one percent outside the capital cities).

Whether performance management can be achieved in an online environment has caused some debate in the industry.

Peoplesoft, which conducts on average three to four focus groups every week somewhere in the world to inform product development, thinks it will work. The company has spent 27 percent of revenue on research and development leading up to the introduction of Peoplesoft 8 on the market. Its Enterprise Performance Management is a new product line, "designed to help businesses to carve out a performance score card."

However, Adrian Cropley, internal communications manager at Ericsson, says he is "wary about online performance management, which would only be suitable in rare circumstances."

"While we tend to think of our B2E portal as a base upon which to build, I think performance management has to start with face-to-face communication (or phone or video conferencing at the very least). The portal then becomes a platform for the next steps in the process, but not the first."

Melville agrees: "You have to be very careful about removing the whole range of face-to-face communication, even in the learning arena. Blended training delivery is important."

Kate Raulings believes the implementation of "personalisation" is still 12 months away at Ericsson. The technology is available, but understanding the needs of users takes time. Ericsson is equally focused on making its B2E portal ready for wireless delivery, and in this it is not alone.

Corechange's director of business development, Gari Johnson, says the research they conducted showed a surprisingly high number of organisations are looking to deploy wireless mobile devices.

The number of organisations that consider wireless access an important feature of enterprise portals can be expected to double to around 42 percent by early 2002. What most companies today might call a B2E portal won't be recognised as such in coming years.

from: K. Sunderland, *Portal power*, HR Monthly, August 2001, pp. 18-26.

Questions

1. What are the likely challenges or problems for Australian organisations considering using B2E technology for human resource management purposes?
2. Does information technology enhance or conflict with the role of human resource managers as strategic business partners?

More Knowledge

B2E 是英文 B(business), 代表的是买卖双方; E 是拉丁字母中的第 5 个字母。它来源于一个与它形状和功能相像的希腊字母 Epsilon (E, ε), 代表的是全新商业模式的五大系统平台的聚合体。B2E 是对现有 B2B 和 B2C 商业模式的一次升级, 针对大宗商品市场更有针对性的创造出五大系统平台聚合体, 解决的大宗商品市场中存在的交易、物流、仓储、金融、信息等全方位的问题。

传统的企业间的交易往往要耗费企业的大量资源和时间, 无论是销售和分销还是采购都要占用产品成本。通过 B2E 的交易方式买卖双方能够在网上完成整个业务流程,从建立最初印象,到货比三家,再到讨价还价、签单和交货,最后到客户服务。B2E 使企业之间的交易减少许多事务性的工作流程和管理费用,降低了企业经营成本。网络的便利及延伸性使企业扩大了活动范围,企业发展跨地区跨国界更方便,成本更低廉。

  B2E 不仅仅是建立一个网上的买卖者群体,它也为企业之间的战略合作提供了基础。任何一家企业,不论它具有多强的技术实力或多好的经营战略,要想单独实现 B2E 是完全不可能的。单打独斗的时代已经过去,企业间建立合作联盟逐渐成为发展趋势。网络使得信息通行无阻,企业之间可以通过网络在市场、产品或经营等方面建立互补互惠的合作,形成水平或垂直形式的业务整合,以更大的规模、更强的实力、更经济的运作真正达到全球运筹管理的模式。

3. Paul Anderson's BHP Experiment: Will It Work?
保罗安德森的必和必拓经验：这些经验可行吗？

In just two years BHP has gone from basketcase to unprecedented corporate laboratory. Paul Anderson, the former second-in-charge at a middle-sized gas pipeline business in the United States called Duke Energy is producing a revolution in the corporate culture of BHP that is as dramatic and interesting as anything this country has ever seen. Don Argus, the former CEO of National Australia Bank, is doing the same thing in the BHP boardroom.

The result is a remarkable experiment in corporate governance and management, its two architects emboldened by the fact that they could not have made things any worse.

Argus is also working actively to find a successor for Anderson, whose contract runs for exactly four years and eleven months (because his American assets and income will start to be taxed by Australia after five years of living here). Unless something goes wrong, Anderson's chief financial officer, Chip Goodyear, also an American, will probably take over as CEO in October 2003.

But at this stage everything is going far from wrong. The Paul Anderson experiment has pulled the share price up from $12 to $20, produced a record profit of $2 billion, cleaned up and refocused the asset portfolio and replaced most of the senior management team. Given the financial mess he inherited, turning the financials around was the easy part. What has been more significant, and more profound, is the cultural change he is bringing about.

The personality of BHP is changing completely, and if Chip

Goodyear gets the top job in three years, BHP will be totally unrecognisable within five years. That's because Goodyear is likeAnderson, only more so.

Up to now Anderson and Goodyear have been fixing the company up, as they put it, but they now must put BHP on a growth path to keep faith with the stockmarket. On Monday, Anderson forecast a doubling of earnings per share within three years, and bidding $830 million for QCT Resources with Mitsubishi Developments this week is seen as the start of an aggressive acquisition phase. But given that the financial disasters that engulfed BHP in the 1990s came from deep systemic flaws within the company, there is no doubt that Anderson's most important task now is to ensure that the cultural change he is bringing about is a permanent one.

Some of the symbols of change are very obvious. At the analysts briefing on Monday, there were five people on stage, includingAnderson, and not one Australian accent. Anderson, Goodyear, chief strategic officer, Brad Mills, and head of corporate finance, Anna-Lou Fletcher, are all Americans, and the head of human resources, Tom Brown, is a Scot.

Brown said afterwards: "You must realise BHP is not really an Australian company any more, that's the point. It's just a resource company that happens to be based inAustralia."

Moreover, the fact that the HR chief was briefing financial analysts at all was significant. He reported to them that sixty percent of John Prescott's executive leadership group had now gone, that many of the departures had resulted from a penetrating external assessment of the top 150 managers by Egon Zehnder and that all managers now have two-thirds of their salary tied directly to performance.

No-one in BHP wears a tie any more: it's permanent casual clothes throughout the company. That's not too unusual in theUnited States these days, but it's unique for a top-50 Australian corporation. And considering that in the old days BHP executives had to put on their jackets, not just a tie, before attending a meeting with the managing director, it is an especially big change for this company.

Anderson and Goodyear usually eat lunch in the staff cafeteria. At first they were given a wide berth by the rest of the staff, but now juniors and senior executives alike eat their focaccias together, and "Paul"s' and "Chip's" tables are as open as any. Previously all meetings between executives were set up by their secretaries; now managers are encouraged to just walk into Paul Anderson's office, and often do. From being the stiffest, most formal organisation in the country, BHP is becoming the least formal. Was it planned, or is this just the way Paul Anderson is?

Don Argus says it's just the way he is, which is why he wanted to hire him. "He's just an average Joe," says Argus, "It's really true. He'd go to the pub and have a beer with anyone."

But Anderson's response suggests some planning went into it, too. "One of the things that struck me at BHP when I first got here was that it was a very formal organisation, there were a lot of barriers, there were a lot of gatekeepers and when you walked in you felt like you were entering the lobby of a substantial company with a very significant presence and as you would come up to the forty-ninth floor here were all the trappings that would say 'yes, this is an important place'. That can be useful, I suppose, in negotiating or in positioning the company, but it can also be very off-putting in terms of getting a free flow of communication."

But he agrees it's also the way he is. "I'm probably more informal than the average person out there. I hate black-tie functions, I'd much rather wear a T-shirt and jeans to something. If you want to get me to come to a function, tell me that it's totally informal and I'd love to come. If it's black tie, I'll only come under duress, but, you know, other people like to dress up."

He introduced casual dress at Duke Energy before he left, but not without controversy. "There was quite a debate over whether it would lead to sloppy work as opposed to a more open flow of information and it was very successful there, so I was just replicating (at BHP) the environment that we had there."

Another huge change in BHP has been with cars. Executives' eyes go quite dreamy when they talk about BHP's old car policy. The whole corporate culture and hierarchy was given expression in the executive carpark. Each promotion came with a certain type of car, starting with a Ford Futura and rising to a top-of-the-range Mercedes. The carpark was a perfectly ordered display of graduated status. Says HR manager, Tom Brown: "They actually differentiated between various models of the same car for different levels of the company, so you could stand at the gate and tell exactly what level each person was on as they drove through." Needless to say that's all gone. The BHP executive carpark looks like a public carpark now.

Paul Anderson says: "I think that the informality is energising a lot of people, they don't feel constrained any more. So my bias is that if the organisation stays informal we'll be much more effective, efficient and flexible, which I think is really critical."

Source from: Alan Kohler, *Paul Anderson's BHP Experiment: Will It Work?*, *Australian Financial Review*, 2 September 2000, p. 21.

Questions

1. The article about BHP (now BHP-Billiton) identifies a number of changes made to improve BHP's financial performance. What changes do you think influenced employee performance and how do you think this occurred?
2. A process of 360-degree review has been introduced in BHP as a

basis for performance assessment and the information contributes to reward decisions. Explain some of the advantages of this review process and discuss ways in which some of the errors associated with performance review could be overcome.

More Knowledge

BHP BILLITON(必和必拓公司)由两家巨型矿业公司合并而成,现在已经是全球最大的采矿业公司。其中,BHP 公司成立于 1885 年,总部设在墨尔本,是澳大利亚历史最悠久、规模最庞大的公司之一。Billiton(比利登)是国际采矿业的先驱,于 1860 年成立,曾经以不断创新和集约式运营方式而闻名。

2001 年,两家公司合并,组成 BHP BILLITON 矿业集团,BHP 持股 58%,比利登持股 42%。该公司在全球 20 多个国家开展业务,合作伙伴超过 90 个,员工约 3.5 万人,遍及世界各地,主要产品有煤、铁矿砂、铜、铝、镍、石油、液化天然气、镁、钻石等。2003~2004 财年,总收入 340.87 亿澳元,总市值 1,363.5 亿澳元,雇佣员工 3.5 万人,成为全球第二大矿业集团公司。2004~2005 财年,该公司实现净利润 80 亿澳元,相比去年翻了一倍。同年,公司成功收购西部矿业公司(WMC),奠定了其全球采矿业"龙头"老大地位。公司市值现在已高达 882.74 亿美元,雄踞澳大企业名单之首。该公司在澳大利亚、伦敦和纽约的股票交易所上市。

必和必拓公司与中国关系源源流长,早在 1891 年就开始向中国出口铅矿。该公司在北京设有代表处,在上海等地设有工厂。在过去十几年中,其在中国的勘探和开发的费用达到 2,600 万美元。

4. "Hello, Welcome to..."
"哈喽,欢迎拨打……"

Telstra's front-line sales force is plagued by high absenteeism and low morale and is deeply dissatisfied with its own management, according to a confidential study commissioned byAustralia's most profitable company.

Employees believe that their management is not committed to high-quality customer service, they do not trust management to keep its word and they doubt their own competence, the study by Professor Stephen Deery and Dr Roderick Iverson of theUniversity of Melbourne found.

Their report, obtained by The Australian Financial Review, shows that the vast majority of employees at Telstra's telephone-based sales centres perceive themselves as underskilled and overworked.

Eighty per cent said they lacked the necessary skills to do the full range of tasks required in their job and ninety-two per cent said their workload was excessive.

Employee perceptions of management's commitment to high-quality customer service were very negative, with some forty per cent strongly disagreeing and thirty-two per cent disagreeing that Telstra's senior management had a high regard for the company's customers.

More than seventy per cent had little faith that Telstra would fulfil obligations and promises made to employees.

Commissioned by Telstra to examine the reasons for absenteeism in call centres—averaging more than 12.7 days per employee, mostly in the form of one- and two-day absences—the study appears to paint a portrait of a low-trust workplace dogged by problems of performance and morale.

But this was strongly denied by Telstra's managing director, commercial and consumer sales, Mr Andrew Day. He said that morale was strong, that absenteeism was not high by industry standards and that feedback from customers contradicted employees' negative perceptions about management commitment to service quality.

Staff were equating quality service with the length of time they spent on the phone to a customer, but the company had to balance this against the need to answer calls promptly with limited labour resources.

"People who are close to the action don't always understand the full picture," he said.

Ninety-eight percent of the more than 500 employees surveyed judged some colleagues as unsuited to sales centre work, suggesting that they were finding it hard to adapt to the sales culture demanded in a competitive market.

Telstra last month implemented a new performance regime in its call centres under which employees can face dismissal for failing to meet performance measures.

Sales consultants ranked unacceptable on any two of six management process measures will be sacked if their performance fails to improve within two months after counselling and training.

Mr Day said staff would benefit from clear, fair and open guidelines on what was expected from them under the performance targets. Measures focus on sales in dollars, winning back custom from competitors, employees' average handling time on calls, adherence to work schedules, supervisors' assessments of service quality and minimising unplanned absences.

"We are adopting recognised commercial practice," he said, "The driver on the business side is the external environment—increased competition and customers expecting more—and we have to operate a commercial business."

But the Community and Public Sector Union intends to challenge any disciplinary action taken under Telstra's new sales management process. At stop-work meetings last week, CPSU members condemned the new performance management for overturning restrictions on the use of computer-generated statistics for dismissal of employees. Under a previous enterprise agreement, performance measures could only be used for coaching and staff development.

"Telstra's unilateral imposition of minimum accountabilities is unacceptable," a CPSU organiser in NSW, Mr Sean Mountford, said, "We have no problem with properly negotiated and agreed measures, but if management proceed to link an arbitrary process to dismissal they can be assured we will contest their action."

The negative employee feedback at Telstra is consistent with a role conflict—identified in management literature—between the employees' desire to help customers and their need to sell. It is also consistent with the stress experienced by workers caught between demands for quality customer interactions and benchmarks designed to minimise labour costs. TheUniversity of Melbourne study correlated absenteeism at Telstra to employee perceptions that their jobs were becoming "routinised" and repetitive, and to burnout experienced by employees who perceived their work as emotionally draining.

Source from: S. Long, *Telstra sales crew unhappy with bosses*, The Australian, 1 February 1999, p. 5.

Questions

1. Why is absenteeism high in call centres, such as the one described in this article?
2. What specific factors are identified that may contribute to absenteeism?
3. What strategies would you suggest?

(a) If you were Telstra management?
(b) If you were representing the Community and Public Sector Union members?
(c) If you were representing the researchers? Explain and justify your recommendations.

More Knowledge

澳电讯公司(Telstra)是澳大利亚最大的电讯公司,全称澳大利亚电信公司,是澳大利亚联邦拥有的唯一的国有企业,其历史可以追溯至1901年。1995年公司正式使用名称Telstra。1997年10月澳政府通过向机构投资者和个人投资者出售49.9%的股权,所获得的收入被用于实施"全国联网计划",由此称为"T1计划"。该公司实行部分私有化,政府仍持有50.1%的股份。1999年,澳政府再次将澳讯16.6%的股权售出,仅保持公司50.1%的绝对控股地位。澳政府将所获得的收入用于环保和电讯发展项目,此为"T2计划"。2006年,澳联邦已将公司的31%股份出售,完成澳讯公司的私有化。

澳大利亚电讯是世界上盈利情况最好的电信公司之一,是澳大利亚领先的全业务电讯运营商,业务横跨有线通信、ADSL、HFC、卫星、CDMA和GSM数字移动网络等,并且是澳大利亚领先的ISP。它的市场资本在世界电信业排名第11,在世界最大公司排名榜上,名列第49位。是澳大利亚、新西兰和纽约股市的上市公司。

澳大利亚电讯公司是搜房网的大股东。搜房网成功实现了其扩张计划,百城战略的实施反映了中国经济的强劲表现和互联网市场的持续增长。目前搜房每月有超过8,000万在线访客,月均页面浏览达14亿,是全球访问量最高的房地产网站。

2011年的销售利润达到250.304亿澳元。净利润达到30.231亿澳元,公司总资产达到370.913亿澳元而净资产达到120.074亿澳元。2012年财富世界500强排行榜排名第438位。

PART THREE
ACADEMIC INFORMATION

第三部分 专业学术信息

1. Academic Journals
专业学术期刊

1.1 国外专业学术期刊

以下列出的国外专业学术期刊,可以通过因特网直接登录并了解各自的稿件要求。

Academy of Management Journal
　　管理学会杂志
Academy of Management Review
　　管理学会评论
Academy of Marketing Science Review
　　营销学学会评论
Accounting Organization and Society
　　会计、组织与社会
Administrative Science Quarterly
　　行政学季刊
Agricultural Economics
　　农业经济学
American Economic Review
　　美国经济评论
American Journal of Agricultural Economics
　　美国农业经济学杂志
American Journal of Economics and Sociology
　　美国经济学和社会学杂志
Applied Economics
　　应用经济学
Asia-Pacific Economic Review

亚太经济评论
Asia Pacific Journal of Management
亚太管理杂志
Asian Case Research Journal
亚洲案例研究杂志
Asian Economic Journal
亚洲经济杂志
Asian Journal of Marketing
亚洲营销杂志
Asian Survey
亚洲调查
Asian-Pacific Economic Literature
亚太经济文献
Atlantic Economic Journal
太平洋经济杂志
Australian Economic Review
澳大利亚经济评论
Australasian Marketing Journal
澳大利亚营销杂志
Australian Journal of Management
澳大利亚管理杂志
The Banker
银行家
Brazilian Electronic Journal of Economics
巴西经济学电子杂志
British Journal of Industrial Relations
英国劳资关系杂志
Brookings Papers on Economic Activity
布鲁金斯经济活动论文集
Bulletin of Economic Research

经济调查简报
Bulletin of Indonesian Economic Studies
印度尼西亚经济研究简报
Business Strategy and the Environment
商业策略与环境
Business Week
商业周刊
California Management Review
加利福尼亚管理评论
Cambridge Journal of Economics
剑桥经济学杂志
Canadian Journal of Economics
加拿大经济学杂志
China Economic Review
中国经济评论
Commercial Carrier Journal
商业运输期刊
Comparative Economic Studies
比较经济研究
Computational Economics
计算经济学
Contemporary Economic Policy
当代经济政策
Corporate Reputation Review
公司声誉评论
Development & Change
发展与变化
Development Policy Review
发展政策评论
Eastern Economic Journal

东方经济杂志
East European Politics and Societies
东欧政治和社会
Ecological Economics
生态经济学
Econometric Reviews
计量经济评论
Econometric Theory
计量经济理论
Econometrica
计量经济学
Econometrics Journal
计量经济杂志
Economic Analysis and Policy
经济分析和政策
Economic and Industrial Democracy
经济和工业民主
Economic & Political Weekly
经济与政治周刊
Economic Development and Cultural Change
经济发展与文化变革
Economic Development Quarterly
经济发展季刊
Economic History Review
经济史评论
Economic Inquiry
经济探究
Economic Issues
经济问题
Economic Journal

经济学杂志
Economic Outlook
　经济展望
Economic Policy
　经济政策
Economic Record
　经济记录
Economic Systems Research
　经济体制研究
Economic Theory
　经济理论
Economy and Society
　经济和社会
Economics and Philosophy
Economics Journals
　经济学杂志
Economics Letters
　经济学快报
Economy and Society
　经济与社会
European Review of Agricultural Economics
　欧洲农业经济学评论
Financial Counseling and Planning
　财政咨询和规划
Forbes
　福布斯
Fortune
　财富
Fuzzy Economic Review
　模糊经济评论

Games and Economic Behavior
  对策与经济行为
Global Business and Economics Review
  全球商业和经济评论
Global Economy Quarterly
  全球经济季刊
Harvard Business Review
  哈佛商业评论
Human Resource Management
  人力资源管理
IE: Money Magazine
  个人理财杂志
Industrial & Labor Relations Review
  劳资关系评论
Industrial Marketing Management
  工业销售管理
Information Economics and Policy
  信息经济学和政策
Innovation Management Journals
  创新管理杂志
Insurance: Mathematics & Economics
  保险:数学与经济学
International Business Review
  国际商业评论
International Economic Review
  国际经济评论
International Finance
  国际财政
International Game Theory Review
  国际对策理论评论

International Journal of Auditing
  国际审计杂志
International Journal of Electronic Commerce
  国际电子商务杂志
International Journal of Forecasting
  国际预测杂志
International Journal of Game Theory
  国际对策论杂志
International Journal of Industrial Organization
  国际产业组织杂志
International Journal of Service Industry Management
  国际服务业管理杂志
International Journal of Social Economics
  国际社会经济学杂志
International Marketing Review
  国际营销评论
International Organization
  国际组织
Journal of Applied Psychology
  应用心理学杂志
Journal of Business
  商业杂志
Journal of Business & Economic Statistics
  商业与经济统计学杂志
Journal of Business Research
  商业研究杂志
Journal of Business Strategies
  商业策略杂志
Journal of Business Venturing
  商业风险杂志

Journal of Comparative Economics
　　比较经济学杂志
Journal of Consumer Research
　　消费者研究杂志
Journal of Consumer Psychology
　　消费者心理杂志
Journal of Development Economics
　　发展经济学杂志
Journal of Development Studies
　　发展研究杂志
Journal of Econometrics
　　经济计量学杂志
Journal of Economic Behavior & Organization
　　经济行为与组织杂志
Journal of Economic Dynamics & Control
　　经济动力学与控制杂志
Journal of Economic Education
　　经济教育杂志
Journal of Economic History
　　经济史杂志
Journal of Economic Issues
　　经济问题杂志
Journal of Economic Literature
　　经济文献杂志
Journal of Economic Perspectives
　　经济展望杂志
Journal of Economic Theory
　　经济理论杂志
Journal of Environmental Economics & Management
　　环境经济学与环境管理杂志

Journal of Finance
　金融杂志
Journal of Financial & Quantitative Analysis
　财务分析与定量分析杂志
Journal of Financial Economics
　金融经济学杂志
Journal of Financial Intermediation
　金融媒介杂志
Journal of Financial Markets
　金融市场杂志
Journal of Health Economics
　卫生经济学杂志
Journal of Human Resources
　人力资源杂志
Journal of Industrial Economics
　工业经济学杂志
Journal of Institutional & Theoretical Economics
　制度与经济理论杂志
Journal of International Economics
　国际经济学杂志
Journal of International Money & Finance
　国际货币与金融杂志
Journal of Labor Economics
　劳动经济学杂志
Journal of Law & Economics
　法律与经济学杂志
Journal of Law, Economics & Organization
　法律、经济学与组织学杂志
Journal of Macroeconomics
　宏观经济学杂志

Journal of Marketing Management
营销管理杂志
Journal of Marketing Research
市场营销研究杂志
Journal of Mathematical Economics
数学经济学杂志
Journal of Monetary Economics
货币经济学杂志
Journal of Money, Credit & Banking
货币、信贷和银行业务杂志
Journal of Policy Analysis and Management
政策分析和管理杂志
Journal of Political Economy
政治经济学杂志
Journal of Population Economics
人口经济学杂志
Journal of Product Innovation Management
产品革新管理杂志
Journal of Productivity Analysis
生产率分析杂志
Journal of Public Economics
公共经济学杂志
Journal of Real Estate Finance & Economics
不动产、金融和经济学杂志
Journal of Regional Science
区域学杂志
Journal of Regulatory Economics
管制经济学杂志
Journal of Retailing
零售杂志
Journal of Risk & Insurance

风险与保险杂志
Journal of Risk & Uncertainty
　　风险和不确定性杂志
Journal of Rural Studies
　　农村研究杂志
Journal of Technology Transfer
　　技术转让杂志
Labour Economics
　　劳动经济学
Long range planning
　　长远规划
Management Decision
　　管理决策
Management Science
　　管理科学
Marketing Education Review
　　营销教育评论
Marketing Research On-Line
　　网络营销调查
New Generation Journal
　　新一代杂志
New Political Economy
　　新政治经济
Organization Science
　　组织学
Oxford Bulletin of Economics & Statistics
　　牛津经济学与统计学通报
Oxford Economics Papers
　　牛津经济论文集
Oxford Review of Economic Policy
　　牛津经济政策评论

Pacific Economic Bulletin
太平洋经济简报
Pacific Economic Review
太平洋经济评论
Public Administration and Development
公共管理和发展
Public Choice
公共选择
Public Opinion Quarterly
公共舆论季刊
Quarterly Journal of Economics
经济学季刊
Rand Journal of Economics
兰德经济学杂志
R&D Management
研发管理
Real Estate Economics
房地产经济学
Regional Science & Urban Economics
区域科学和都市经济学
Regional Studies
区域研究
Review of Development Economics
发展经济学评论
Review of Economic Studies
经济研究评论
Review of Economics & Statistics
经济学与统计学评论
Review of Financial Studies
金融研究评论
Review of Income and Wealth

收入和财富评论
Scandinavian Journal of Economics
　　斯堪的纳维亚经济学杂志
Service Industries Journal
　　服务业杂志
Social Science Journal
　　社会科学杂志
Scottish Journal of Political Economy
　　苏格兰政治经济学杂志
Sloan Management Review
　　斯隆管理评论
Southern economic journal
　　南部经济学杂志
Tax Policy and the Economy
　　税收政策和经济
Theory and Decision
　　理论和决策
Telecommunications Policy
　　电信政策
Urban Studies
　　城市研究
Review of World Economy
　　世界经济文献
World Development
　　世界发展
World Economy
　　世界经济
World Economy and China
　　世界经济和中国

1.2 国内专业学术期刊

国内人力资源管理学术期刊主要指《中国人力资源开发》、《中国人才》、《人力资本》等。同时,将有影响的相关期刊也分类列出(见下表),仅供参考。

全国中文重点核心期刊投稿指南(社科)

序号	刊名	主办单位	刊期	编辑部电话	邮编	编辑地址	投稿信箱
1	中国人力资源开发	中国人力资源开发研究会	月	010-88363175	100037	北京市西城区百万庄子区38号	zbs_zzs@cass.org.cn
2	中国人才	中国人事报社	月	010-84626925	100101	北京市朝阳区育慧里5号	zhgrc@163.com
3	人力资本	中国国际贸易促进委员会、中国国际商会	月	010-8807533	100860	北京复兴门外大街1号	hccz@51job.com
4	中国社会科学	中国社会科学院	双月	010-64076113	100720	北京鼓楼西大街甲158号	zbs_zzs@cass.org.cn
5	新华文摘	人民出版社	半月	010-65132880 010-65255159	100706	北京朝阳门内大街166号	wzhuyz@263.net wzjial@263.net
6	人民日报	中共中央	日	010-65368383 010-65368407	100733	北京朝阳门外金台西路2号 上海浦东新区世纪大道777号	rm@peopledaily.com.cn
7	求是	中共中央	半月	010-64037005 010-64037122	100722	北京市东城区北河沿大街甲83号	qiushi@qsjournal.com.cn
8	管理世界	国务院发展研究中心	月	010-62112235 010-62115760	100098	北京海淀区大钟寺8号东楼3层	该刊暂不授理E-mail投稿

续表

序号	刊名	主办单位	刊期	编辑部电话	邮编	编辑地址	投稿信箱
9	经济研究	中国社会科学院经济研究所	月	010-68034153	100836	北京市西城区月坛北小街2号	erj@cass.org.cn 该刊暂不授理E-mail投稿
10	经济日报	国务院	日	010-58393509 010-58393569	100054	北京市宣武区白纸坊东街2号	jjrbtg@ced.com.cn
11	光明日报	光明日报报业集团	日	010-67078650 010-67078800	100062	北京市崇文区珠市口东大街5号	gmzbs@gmw.cn
12	中共中央党校学报	中共中央党校	季	010-62805375	100091	北京市海淀区大有庄100号	Luntan588@yahoo.com.cn
13	哲学研究	中国社会科学院哲学研究所	月	010-85195528	100732	北京市建国门内大街5号	Zhexueyanjijbjb-1@sina.com
14	世界经济	中国世界经济学会等	月	010-85195790	100732	北京市建国门内大街5号	jwe@cass.net.cn
15	社会学研究	中国社会科学院社会研究所	双月	010-65122608	100732	北京市建国门内大街5号	sbjb@sociology.cass.org.cn
16	中国法学	中国法学会	双月	010-66139120	100034	北京西城区兵马司胡同63号	www.clol.com.cnzgfxzzs@sina.com
17	历史研究	中国科学院世界历史研究所	双月	010-64076113	100006	北京鼓楼西大街甲158号	isyj@agazin.cass.net.cn
18	政治学研究	中国社会科学院政治学研究所	季	010-65136660	100732	北京市东城区建国门内大街5号	http://chinaps.cass.cn
19	当代世界与社会主义	中央编译局世界所 中国国际共运史学会	双月	010-66509501 010-66509531	100032	北京市西单西斜街36号	ddsj@vip.sina.com

续表

序号	刊名	主办单位	刊期	编辑部电话	邮编	编辑地址	投稿信箱
20	中国图书馆学报	中国图书馆学会 中国国家图书馆	双月	010-88545141	100081	北京市中关村南大街33号	tsgxb@nlc.gov.cn
21	中国工业经济	中国社科院工业经济研究所	月	010-68047499	100836	北京市阜成门外月坛北小街2号	gjbjb@sina.com
22	中国农村经济	中国社科院农村发展研究所	月	010-85195649	100732	北京市建国门内大街6号	ruraleconomy@cass.org.cn
23	中共党史研究	中共中央党校研究室	双月	010-82615330	100080	北京市8799信箱（海淀区北四环路69号）	ds8799@sina.com
24	中国软科学	科技部政策法规与体制改革司	月	010-58882532 010-58882961	100038	北京市海淀区复兴路15号532室	www.cssm.com. cncopyright@cssm.com.cn
25	外语教学与研究	北京外国语大学	双月	010-88819339		北京西三环北路2号	weirq@fltrp.com
26	党建研究	中共中央组织部党建研究杂志社	月	010-58586946	100815	北京市西长安街80号	postmaster@zgdjyj.com
27	北京大学学报	（哲社版）北京大学	双月	010-62756706 010-62751216	100871	北京市海淀区北京大学德斋205号	xbna@pku.edu. cnjournal@pku.edu.cn
28	复旦学报	（社科版）复旦大学	双月	021-65642669	200433	上海市邯郸路220号	fdxb@chinajournal.net.cn
29	北京师范大学学报	北京师范大学	双月	010-62207848	100875	北京新街口外大街19号	wkxb@bnu.edu.cn
30	中国人民大学学报	中国人民大学	双月	010-62511499	100080	北京市中关村大街59号	rdxb@263.net zrdx@chinajournal.net.cn
31	中国社会科学文摘	中国社会科学研究院	双月	010-64076113	100720	北京鼓楼西大街甲158号	zbs_zzs@cass.org.cn

续表

序号	刊名	主办单位	刊期	编辑部电话	邮编	编辑地址	投稿信箱
32	国家行政学院学报	国家行政学院	季	010-68929341 010-68929345	100089	北京市海淀区长寿桥路6号	xuebao@163bj.com xuebao@nsa.gov.cn
33	南京大学学报	（哲社版）南京大学	双月	025-3594656 025-3592704	210093	南京市汉口路22号	xbnse@netru.nju.edu.cn
34	经济理论与经济管理	中国人民大学	月	010-62511022	100080	中国人民大学出版社大楼805号	etbm@263.net
35	科学社会主义	中国科学社会主义学会	双月	010-62805237 010-62809964	100091	北京市海淀区大有庄100号	sszydx@sina.com
36	马克思主义研究	中国社科院马列所	双月	010-65138265	100732	北京建国门内大街5号	stud@chinajournal.net.cn
37	中国人力资源开发	中国人力资源开发研究会	月	010-88363163	100037	北京西城区百万庄子区38号	hrdchina@263.net
38	哲学动态	中国社会院哲学研究所	月	010-65137954	100732	北京建国门内大街5号	zxdt@chinajournal.net.cn
39	自然辩证法研究	中国自然辩证法研究会	月	010-62103265	100081	北京市海淀区学院南路86号	zrbz@chinajournal.net.cn zrbzfyjzz@263.net
40	中国人力资源开发	中国人力资源开发研究会	月	010-88363175	100037	北京市西城区百万庄子区38号	zbs_zzs@cass.org.cn
41	道德与文明	天津市社会科学院 中国伦理学会	双月	022-23075124	300191	天津市南开区迎水道7号	ddym@chinajournal.net.cn
42	经济学动态	中国社科院经济研究所	月	010-68051607	100836	北京市阜成门外月坛北小街2号	jjxdt_jjs@css.org.cn

续表

序号	刊名	主办单位	刊期	编辑部电话	邮编	编辑地址	投稿信箱
43	当代经济科学	西安交通大学	双月	029-5222048	710061	西安市纬二街,西安交通大学财经校区0068信箱	djkx @ xjtu.edu.cn
44	企业管理	中国企业联合会	月	010-68414646	100044	北京市海淀区紫竹院南路17号	qyglzz @ 263.net.cn
45	中国经济问题	厦门大学经济研究所	双月	0592-2184570　0529-2184571	361005	福建省厦门市厦门大学内厦大经济研究所	jjs@ xmu.edu.cn　cnjjsb @ xmu.edu.cn
46	世界经济与政治	中国社会科学院世界经济与政治研究所	月	010-85195784	100732	北京市建国门内大街5号	jzbjb @ cass.org.cn
47	中国科技论坛	中国科学技术促进发展研究中心	双月	010-68252469　010-68252453	100038	北京市海淀区普惠北里8号楼C座(北京3814信箱)	zgkjlt @ china.com
48	教育研究	中央教育科学研究所	月	010-62011873	100088	北京市北三环中路46号	jyyjzz@ 263.net
49	理论前沿	中央党校邓小平理论研究中心	半月	010-62805185　010-62807201	100091	北京市海淀区大有庄100号中共中央党校校刊社	llqy @ ccps.gov.cn　lilunqianyan@ 126.com
50	江海学刊	江苏省社会科学院	双月	025-83715429	210013	南京市虎踞北路12号	jhxk @ jlonline.com
51	学术月刊	上海市社科联	月	021-53069080　021-53060399	200020	上海市淮海中路622弄7号(乙)	xuesyka @ public3.bta.net.cn
52	国外社会科学	中国社会科学院文献信息中心	双月	010-65137749	100732	北京市建国门内大街5号	guowaisheke @ yahoo.com.cn

续表

序号	刊名	主办单位	刊期	编辑部电话	邮编	编辑地址	投稿信箱
53	学习与探索	黑龙江省社会科学院	双月	0451-86242279	150001	哈尔滨市南岗区联发街62号	xxts@chinajournal.net.cn
54	社会科学	上海社会科学院	月	021-53602234	200020	上海市淮海中路622弄7号	shkx@sass.org.cn
55	社会科学战线	吉林省社会科学院	季	0431-4638362	130031	吉林省长春市自由大路187号	shzx@chinajournal.net.cn
56	马克思主义与现实	中央编译局马克思主义研究所	双月	010-66509601	100032	北京市西城区西斜街36号	mkszy@vip.sina.com
57	改革	重庆市社会科学院	双月	023-67761226	400020	重庆市江北区桥北村270号	reform@cta.cq.cn
58	华东师范大学学报	（哲社版）华东师范大学	双月	021-62232305	200062	上海市中山北路3663号	xbzs@xb.ecnu.edu.cn
59	南开学报	（哲社版）南开大学	双月	022-23508374 022-23501681	30071	天津市卫津路94号南开大学内	该刊暂不受理E-mail投稿
60	厦门大学学报	（哲社版）厦门大学	季	0592-2182366	361005	福建省厦门市厦门大学	xdxbs@jingxian.xmu.edu.cn
61	中国社会科学院研究生院学报	中国社会科学院研究生院	双月	010-64722354 010-64753231	100102	北京市朝阳区望京中环南路1号	xb-yjsy@cass.org.cn
62	江苏社会科学	江苏省哲学社会科学界联合会	双月	025-83321531 025-86638356	210009	江苏省南京市山西路120号国贸大厦16层	3701531@sohu.com
63	欧洲研究	中国社会科学院欧洲研究所	双月	010-65135017	100732	北京建国门内大街5号1453室	europe-ed@ies.cass.net.cn
64	江苏行政学院学报	江苏省行政学院	双月	025-84200709	210004	南京市建邺路168号	jsxyxb@263.net
65	教学研究	燕山大学	季	0355-8057043	066004	河北省秦皇岛市海港区河北大街西段438号	jxyj@ysu.edu.cn

续表

序号	刊名	主办单位	刊期	编辑部电话	邮编	编辑地址	投稿信箱
66	青年研究	中国社会科学院社会学研究所		010-85195565	100732	北京建国门内大街5号	
67	学习时报	中共中央党校	周		100092	北京市海淀区大有庄100号	xxsb@263.net
68	农业经济问题	中国农业银行经济学会		010-68918705	100081	北京市中关村南大街12号	nyjjwt@cass.net.cn
69	心理学报	中科院心理研究所中国心理学会	月	010-64850861	100101	北京市中国科学院心理研究所内	xuebao@psych.ac.cn
70	现代国际关系	中国现代国际关系研究院	月	010-88547315 010-88547316	100081	北京市海淀区万寿寺甲2号	cir@cicir.ac.cn
71	世界历史	中国社科院世界历史研究所	双月	86-10-6524-8571	100006	北京市东城区东王府井大街东厂胡同1号	szhyjb-sjlss@cass.org.cn
72	体育科学	中国体育科学学会	双月	010-87182586 010-87182585	100061	北京市崇文区体育馆路9号	office@cass.cn
73	微计算机应用	中科院声学研究所	双月	010-62554573	100080	北京市海淀区北四环西路21号中科院声学所	weiji@dsp.ac.cn
74	科学学与科学技术管理	天津市科学学研究所等		022-24437122 022-24324911	300011	天津市河东区新开路138号科技创新大厦5楼	该刊暂不授理E-mail投稿
75	中国党政干部论坛	中共中央党校		010-62805370	100091	北京市海淀区大有庄100号	lutan588@yahoo.com.cn
76	党建	中共中央宣传部	月		100051	北京市宣武区南新华街甲1号	djjj@chinajournal.net.cn

资料来源：当代教育论文网(www.x5dj.com)

2. Academic Conferences and Organizations
专业学术会议与组织

（1）人力资源学术会议，目前还只限于国内，国际会议尚处于开发阶段。以下所列的人力资源管理专业学术会议是目前较有影响的。在这些学术会议上，主办方将所收集到的论文经过筛选后制成会议论文集，对文章质量特别高的论文，主办方将向国内的学术权威机构推荐。

（2）中国人力资源管理专业教学改革研讨会

（3）中国人力资源管理教学与实践年会

（4）中美创业研究与教育国际研讨会

（5）管理科学与工程国际学术会议

（6）中国人力资源开发研究会年度学术研讨会（由中国人力资源开发研究会主办，由会员单位协办或承办，会议论文由主办方整理后评选成集。）

（7）美国人力资源开发学会（美国较有影响的人力资源管理学术团体，是 Personnel Magazine 的主办方。）

（8）中国管理科学学会人力资源管理专业委员会与中国劳动学会企业人力资源管理与开发专业委员会是国内将有影响的专业学术团体，有自己的学术期刊。前者研究的重点是人力资源开发与管理，后者研究的重点是企业内人员的组织与开发管理问题。

（9）地方性人力资源学会或协会，如吉林市人力资源管理学会。

3. Academic Websites
专业学术网站

3.1　国外人力资源管理相关网站

人力资源管理协会
　　http://www.shrm.org

工业和组织心理学协会
　　http://www.siop.org

工作团队研究中心
　　http://www.workteams.unt.edu

劳动力研究中心
　　http://www.workorceonline.com

培训、培训资源、沟通和网络信息
　　http://www.trainingsupersite.com/

美国教育统计中心
　　http://www.ed.gov/NCES

培训信息和网络培训
　　http://www.multimediatraining.com/

创新领导中心
　　http://www.ccl.org/

工作与生活问题
　　http://www.workfamily.com/

学习研究学院
　　http://www.irl.org/

职业生涯
　　http://www.careermosaic.com/

Monster 委员会
　　http://www.monster.com/

美国国家科学基金会(NSF:National Science Foundation)
http://cos.gdp.org/best/feedfund/nsf-intro.html
全球互联网虚拟图书馆
http://www.w3.org/

3.2 国内人力资源管理相关网站

中国人力资源管理在线
http://www.hrdm.net/
人力资源管理与开发
http://www.hrm21cn.com/
人力资源管理软件
http://www.sowan.com/
人力资源在线
http://www.hrtocom.com/

PART FOUR GLOSSARY

第四部分 专业词汇

A

abrasive [ə'breisiv] adj. 研磨的
absenteeism [æbsən'tiːiz(ə)m] n. 旷工
absorb [əb'sɔːb] v. 吸收
accommodate [ə'kɔmədeit] v. 考虑
accompanying [ə'kʌmpəniŋ] adj. 附随的
accomplish [ə'kɔmpliʃ] v. 完成；实现
accrue [ə'kruː] v. 自然增加；产生
accuracy ['ækjurəsi] n. 精确性；正确度
accusation [ækju(ː)'zeiʃən] n. 谴责
accuser [ə'kjuːzə] n. 原告
acknowledge [ək'nɔlidʒ] v. 承认
acquisition [ˌækwi'ziʃən] n. 获得
actualization [ˌæktjuəlai'zeiʃən] n. 实现
adapt [ə'dæpt] v. 使适应；改编
additional [ə'diʃənl] adj. 另外的
address [ə'dres] v. 把注意力集中于
adept ['ædept] adj. 熟练的
adequate ['ædikwit] adj. 适当的；足够的
adjourning [ə'dʒəːniŋ] n. 解散期；解散阶段
adjustment [ə'dʒʌstmənt] n. 调节适应
administer [əd'ministə] v. 执行
administrative [əd'ministrətiv] adj. 行政的
adopt [ə'dɔpt] adj. 采用
adversely ['ædvəːsli] adv. 不利地；负面地
advocate ['ædvəkit] v. 提倡
affirmative [ə'fəːmətiv] adj. 肯定的
aforementioned [ə'fɔːˌmenʃənd] adj. 上述的
aggregate ['ægrigeit] v. 合计

aggressive [əˈgresiv] adj. 积极进取的
aggrieved [əˈgriːvd] adj. 受虐待的;权利受到不法侵害的
agreeableness [əˌgriːˈeiblnis] n. 令人愉悦
alliance [əˈlaiəns] n. 联盟;联合
allied [ˈælaid] adj. 联合的;同盟的
alternately [ɔːlˈtəːnitli] adv. 或者
alternation [ˌɔːltəːˈneiʃən] n. 交替;轮流;间隔
alternative [ɔːlˈtəːnətiv] adj. 选择性的;二中择一的
alumni [əˈlʌmnai] n. 男校友(alumnus 的复数)
ambient [ˈæmbiənt] adj. 周围的
ambiguous [æmˈbigjuəs] adj. 暧昧的;不明确的
amend [əˈmend] v. 修正;改进
amendment [əˈmendmənt] n. 改善;改正
amnesty [ˈæmnest] n. 赦免
ample [ˈæmpl] adj. 充足的;丰富的
analogous [əˈnæləgəs] adj. 类似的
analyst [ˈænəlist] n. 分析家
anchor [ˈæŋkə] v. 锚定
antecedent [ˌæntiˈsiːdənt] n. 先例
anticipate [ænˈtisipeit] v. 预期;期望
apparently [əˈpærəntli] adj. 显然地
applicable [ˈæplikəbl] adj. 可适用的;可应用的
applicant [ˈæplikənt] n. 申请者请求者
apply [əˈplai] v. 应用
appraisal [əˈpreizəl] n. 评价
appreciate [əˈpriːʃieit] v. 意识到
apprenticeship [əˈprentisˌʃip] n. 学徒身份
approach [əˈprəutʃ] v. 着手处理
aptitude [ˈæptitjuːd] n. 天资;智能
arithmetic [əˈriθmətik] n. 算术

articulate [ɑːˈtikjulit] adj. 发音清晰的
artifact [ˈɑːtifækt] n. 典型产物
assemble [əˈsembl] v. 集合
assessment [əˈsesmənt] n. 估价
associate [əˈsəuʃieit] n. 合作人;同事
assumption [əˈsʌmpʃən] n. 假定;设想
assurance [əˈʃuərəns] n. 断言;保证
attitudinally [ˌætiˈtjuːdinəli] adv. 根据或表示个人态度地
attorney [əˈtəːni] n. 律师
attribute [əˈtribju(ː)t] n. 属性特征
attribution [ˌætriˈbjuːʃən] n. 归因
automation [ɔːtəˈmeiʃən] n. 自动化
autonomy [ɔːˈtɔnəmi] n. 自主性
avenue [ˈævinjuː] n. 方法;途径
average [ˈævəridʒ] adj. 通常的;平均的
a high priority 高优先性
a mid career crisis 职业中期危机
a paucity of 少量
a secret-ballet election 不记名选举
a telephone verification 电话确认系统
AAR—after action review 行动后学习机制
ability of manager 管理者的能力
ability test 能力测试
absence management 缺勤管理
absence rate 缺勤率
absent with leave 因故缺勤;(被)许可缺勤
absent without leave 无故缺勤擅离职守
accelerating premium 累进奖金制
accident rates 意外补偿
accident frequency 事故频率

accident insurance 意外伤害保险
accident investigation 事故调查
accident loss 事故损失
accident prevention 事故预防
accident proneness 事故(频发)倾向
accident severity 事故严重程度
accident severity rate 事故严重率
accident work injury 工伤事故
achievement need 成就需求
achievement test 成就测试
acoustical wall material 墙体消音材料
action teams 行动队
action learning 行动(为)学习法
action research 行动研究
active practice 自动实习
administrative level 管理层次
administrative line 直线式管理
ADR—alternative dispute resolution 建设性争议解决方法
adventure learning 探险学习法
adverse impact 负面影响
advertisement recruiting 广告招聘
affective commitment 情感认同
affiliation need 归属需求
affirmative action 反优先雇佣行动
AFL (American Federation of Labor) 美国劳工联合会
age composition 年龄结构
age discrimination 年龄歧视
age retirement 因龄退休
agreement content 协议内容
alternative ranking method 交替排序法

American Telephone and Telegraph 美国电信
amoeba management 变形虫式管理
an aging population 老龄化人口
an isolated incident 孤例
analytic approach 分析法
annual bonus 年终分红
annual leave 年假
applicant-initiated recruitment 自荐式招聘
application blank 申请表
appraisal feedback 考评反馈
appraisal interview 考评面谈
appraisal standardization 考评标准化
appraiser training 考评者培训
apprenticeship training 学徒式培训
apprenticeship training 学徒式培训
arbitration/mediation 仲裁
as such 同样地
assessment center 评价中心
At & T 美国电话电报公司
ATS—applicant tracking system 求职跟踪系统
attendance incentive plan 参与式激励计划
attendance rate 出勤率
attitude survey 态度调查
attribution theory 归因理论
audiovisual instruction 视听教学
autonomous work groups 自主工作组
availability analysis 可获性分析
availability forecast 供给预测

B

baffle ['bæfl] *n.* 隔音板
balance ['bæləns] *n.* 余额
benchmark ['bentʃmɑːk] *n.* 基准
beneficial [beni'fiʃəl] *adj.* 有益的;受益的
bias ['baiəs] *n.* 偏见;偏爱
billboard ['bilbɔːd] *n.* 广告牌
biographical [baiəu'græfikəl] *adj.* 传记的
blueprint ['bluːˌprint] *n.* 蓝图;计划
blur [bləː] *v.* 涂污;污损(名誉)等
bonus ['bəunəs] *n.* 奖金
booth [buːθ] *n.* 售货亭
bound [baund] *n.* 范围;限度
brainstorm ['breinˌstɔːm] *v.* 脑力激荡
bricklayer ['brikleiə(r)] *n.* 砖匠
budget ['bʌdʒit] *n.* 预算
bureau ['bjuərəu] *n.* 办公署
burnout ['bəːnaut] *n.* 精疲力尽
bust [bʌst] *v.* 打碎
buster ['bʌstə] *n.* 非凡的人或物
background investigation 背景调查
balance-sheet approach 决算表平衡法
bargaining issue 谈判问题
basic skill 基础技能
behavior modeling 行为模拟
behavior modification 行为矫正疗法
behavioral predispositions 行为的本质特征
behavioral description interview 工作方式介绍面试
behavioral rating 工作方式考核法

behaviorally anchored rating scale (BARS) 行为锚定等级评价法
BEI——behavior event interview 行为事件访谈法
benchmark job 基准职位
benchmarking management 标杆管理
benefit plan 福利计划
BFOG——bona fide occupational qualification 实际职业资格
biological approach 生物型工作设计法
board interview 会议型面试
BOS——behavior observation scale 行为观察量表
bounded rationality 有限理性
brainstorm ideas 头脑风暴法

C

caliber ['kælibə(r)] n. 才干
capture ['kæptʃə] v. 给与重视;俘获;捕获
capturer ['kæptʃərə] n. 捕获者
cardiovascular [ˌkɑːdiəu'væskjulə] adj. 心脏血管的
career [kə'riə] n. 事业
catastrophe [kə'tæstrəfi] n. 大灾难
categorize ['kætigəraiz] v. 加以类别
causal ['kɔːzəl] adj. 因果关系的
caution ['kɔːʃən] n. 小心;谨慎
cede [siːd] v. 让与
certify ['səːtifai] v. 证明;保证
charge [tʃɑːdʒ] v. 收费
circulate ['səːkjuleit] v. 使散布
citizenship ['sitizənʃip] n. 公民权
civic ['sivik] adj. 公民的
claim [kleim] v. 索赔
clarify ['klærifai] v. 澄清;阐明

clerical ['klerikəl] n. 牧师
coefficient [kəui'fiʃənt] n. （数）系数
coextensive [,kəuiks'tensiv] adj. 同时包括的
cognitive ['kɔgnitiv] adj. 认知的；认识的
collegial [kə'li:dʒiəl] adj. 大学之组织的
collegiality [kə,li:dʒi'æliti] n. 共同掌权
combat ['kɔmbət] v. 战斗；搏斗；抗击
commission [kə'miʃən] n./v. 佣金；委托；委任
compel [kəm'pel] v. 强迫；迫使
compelling [kəm'peliŋ] adj. 引人注目的
compensation [kɔmpen'seiʃən] n. 赔偿
competence ['kɔmpətəns] n. 能力
competent ['kɔmpitənt] adj. 有能力的
competitive [kəm'petitiv] adj. 竞争的
compilation [,kɔmpi'leiʃən] n. 编辑
compliance [kəm'plaiəns] n. 顺从
component [kəm'pəunənt] n. 成分
compound ['kɔmpaund] v. 使增加
comprehensive [,kɔmpri'hensiv] adj. 全面的
compromise ['kɔmprəmaiz] v. 妥协；折衷
concession [kən'seʃən] n. 让步
concise [kən'sais] adj. 简明的；简练的
conduct ['kɔndəkt] n. 引导；管理
confer [kən'fə:] v. 协商；交换意见
confidentiality [kənfi,denʃi'æliti] n. 机密性
confirm [kən'fə:m] v. 确定
conflicting [kən'fliktiŋ] adj. 相冲突的
confuse [kən'fju:z] v. 搞乱；使糊涂
congruence ['kɔŋgruəns] n. 一致
connotation [,kɔnəu'teiʃən] n. 内涵

conscientiousness [ˌkɔnʃi'enʃəsnis] n. 谨慎
consensus [kən'sensəs] n. 一致同意；多数人的意见
consequently [kɔnsikwəntli] adv. 从而；因此
considerable [kən'sidərəbl] adj. 相当大或多的
consistency [kən'sistənsi] n. 一致性
consistent [kən'sistənt] adj. 一致的；调和的
consistently [kən'sistəntli] adv. 始终如一地
constant ['kɔnstənt] adj. 不变的；坚决的
constitute ['kɔnstitju:t] v. 组成
constraint [kən'streint] n. 约束措施
constrictive [kən'striktiv] adj. 紧缩的
consultant [kən'sʌltənt] n. 顾问
consume [kən'sju:m] v. 消耗
contact ['kɔntækt] n. 熟人
contender [tən'tendə(r)] n. 竞争者
content [kən'tent] n. 内容
contingent [kən'tindʒənt] adj. 可能发生的；附随的；暂时的
conversant [kən'və:sənt] adj. 亲近的；熟悉的
convey [kən'vei] v. 传达
conviction [kən'vikʃən] n. 定罪
convince [kən'vins] v. 使确信；使信服
coordinate [kəu'ɔ:dinit] v. 协调
coordination [kəuˌɔ:di'neiʃən] n. 协调性
core [kɔ:] n. 核心
cost-effective ['kɔstiˌfektiv] adj. 有成本效益的
counselor ['kaunsələ] n. 顾问
covariate [kə'vɛəriit] n. 协方差
coverage ['kʌvəridʒ] n. 范围
criminal ['kriminl] adj. 刑事的
crisp [krisp] adj. 脆的；易碎的

criteria [kraɪˈtɪərɪə] n. （复数）标准
crucial [ˈkruːʃɪəl; ˈkruːʃəl] adj. 至关紧要的
curriculum [kəˈrɪkjʊləm] n. 课程
cycle [ˈsaɪkl] n. 周期；循环
cafeteria-style benefit 自助式福利
california Highway Patrol 加州高速公路巡警
campus recruiting 校园招聘
candidate-order error 候选人次序错误
capital-intensive 资本密集型的
career insight 职业洞察力
career management 职业生涯管理
career plateau 职业发展停滞
career resilience 职业张力
career anchors 职业锚/职业动机
career counseling 职业咨询
career curve 职业曲线
career cycle 职业周期
career development method 职业发展方法
career path 职业途径
career path information 职业途径信息
career planning 职业规划
career stage 职业阶段
career training 专业训练职业训练
career-long employment 终身雇佣制
case study training method 案例研究培训法
CBT—computer based training 以计算机为载体的培训
central tendency 居中趋势
chief executive 首席执行官
CIO（Congress of Industrial Organizations） 美国产业会联合会
CIT—critical incident technique 关键事件技术

citizenship behavior 组织公民行为
Civil Rights Acts 公民权利法案
classification method 分类法
classroom training 课堂培训
client organization 客户
closed shop 闭门企业
co-determination 共同决策制
coercive power 强制权力
cognitive aptitude test 认知能力测试
colleague appraisal 同事考评
collective bargaining 劳资谈判
common denominator 整体分母
comparable worth 可比价值
comparative appraisal method 比较评估法
compensable factor 报酬要素
compensation & benefit 薪酬福利
compensation committee 报酬委员会
compensatory time off 补假
competence-based interview 基于能力的面试
competency assessment 能力评估
competency model 胜任特征模型
competency-based education and training 能力本位教育与训练
competency-based pay/skill-based pay 技能工资
competitive advantage 竞争优势
comprehensive training 综合培训
compressed workweek 压缩工作周
compulsory binding arbitration 强制性仲裁
computerized career progression system 电脑化职业生涯行进系统
computerized forecast 电脑化预测
conceptual skill 概念性技能

concurrent validity 同期正当性
conference method 会议方法
conflict management 冲突管理
construct validity 结构效度
constructive discharge 事实上的解雇
content validation 内容的正确性
content validity 内容效度
contextual performance 关系绩效
contractual right 契约性权利
contrast error 比较性错误
contributory plan 须付费的退休金计划
coordination training 合作培训
core appraisal system elements 评价体系的核心要素
core competency 核心竞争力
core value 核心价值观
core worker 核心员工
core workforce 核心工作团队
corporate culture 企业文化
corporate identity 企业识别
corporate image 企业形象
correlation analysis 相关分析
cost per hire 单位招聘成本
course credit hours 课程学分
crew turnover 员工周转率
criterion-related validity 标准关联效度
critical job dimension 关键性工作因子
cross training 交叉培训
cross-functional training 跨功能训练
cross-training 岗位轮换培训
culture shock 文化冲突

cumulative trauma disorder 累积性工伤
cutoff score 录用分数线
cyclical variation 循环变动

D

decentralized [di:'sentrəlaiz] v. 分散
decertify [di:'sə:tifai] v. 收回……的证件;拒绝承认
declarative [di'klærətiv] adj. 陈述的
decompose [ˌdi:kəm'pəuz] v. 分解
decontextualized [ˌdiˌkɔn'tekstjuəlaizd] adj. 在脱离上下文中的情况下研究的;无背景的
decry [di'krai] v. 谴责
deductible [di'dʌktəbl] adj. 可扣除的
delegate ['deligit] v. 委派……为代表
deliberate [di'libəreit] adj. 深思熟虑的
deliberately [di'libərətli] adv. 故意地
demanding [di'mændiŋ] adj. 苛求的
demographic [deməˈgræfik] adj. 人口统计学的
demonstrate ['demənstreit] v. 示范;证明;论证
depict [di'pikt] v. 描述
deprive [di'praiv] v. 剥夺
derive [di'raiv] v. 获得
desirable [di'zaiərəbl] adj. 值得要的
desist [di'zist] v. 终止
deteriorate [di'tiəriəreit] v. 使……恶化
determinant [di'tə:minənt] adj. 决定性的
deterrent [di'terənt] n. 威慑手段
detrimental [ˌdetri'mentl] adj. 有害的
diagnostic [ˌdaiəgˈnɔstik] adj. 诊断的
differential [ˌdifəˈrenʃəl] n. 工资级差

differentiate [ˌdifə'renʃieit] v. 区别;区分
dignity ['digniti] n. 尊严;高贵
dimension [di'menʃən] n. 尺寸;维;数;度
diminish [di'miniʃ] v. 使……减少;使……变小
directive [dai'rektiv] n. 命令或指示
discharge [dis'tʃɑːdʒ] v. 解雇
discipline ['disiplin] n. 处罚;学科
discredited [dis'kreditid] adj. 不足信的;不名誉的
discrepancy [dis'krepənsi] n. 差异;矛盾
discretion [dis'kreʃən] n. 判断力
discrimination [disˌkrimi'neiʃən] n. 歧视
discriminatory [di'skriminətɔːri] adj. 有辨识力的;有差别的;歧视的
disparate ['dispərit] adj. 完全不同的
disruption [dis'rʌpʃən] n. 瓦解;破坏
disseminate [di'semineit] v. 散布
distraction [dis'trækʃən] n. 分心的事物
distribution [ˌdistri'bjuːʃən] n. 分配;分发
domestic [də'mestik] n. 仆人
downsize ['daunˌsaiz] v. 缩减
dramatic [drə'mætik] adj. 戏剧性的;生动的
drawback ['drɔːˌbæk] n. 缺点
duplicate ['djuːplikeit] adj. 复制的;两重的
dynamic [dai'næmik] adj. 有活力的;动态的
decontextualized job characteristics 孤立的工作特性
defined benefit plan 固定收益制
dependent relationship 依赖型关系
differential piece rate 差额计件工资
demission interview 离职面谈
demission rate 离职率
disciplinary procedure 惩罚程序

disciplinary action 纪律处分
discriminant analysis 判别分析
dismissal reason 解雇理由
disparate impact 异质影响
disparate treatment 异质对待
disparate impact 差别性影响
disparate treatment 差别性对待
distribute bonus/profit sharing 分红
distributive bargaining 分配式谈判
distributive justice 分配公正
diversity management 多样性管理
diversity training 多样化培训
division structure 事业部结构
document examination 记录审查
double-loop learning 双环学习
downward pattern 自上而下的模式
DTI—decision tree induction 决策树归纳法
dual career path 双重职业途径

E

edge [edʒ] *n.* 优势
efficiently [i'fiʃəntli] *adv.* 有效率地
elastic [i'læstik] *adj.* 弹性的
elicit [i'lisit] *v.* 得出
eligibility [ˌelidʒə'biliti] *n.* 合格
eligible ['elidʒəbl] *adj.* 符合条件的;合格的
eliminate [i'limineit] *v.* 取消;淘汰;排除
embed [im'bed] *v.* 使……插入;使……嵌入
embody [im'bɔdi] *v.* 包含
empirical [em'pirikəl] *adj.* 完全根据经验的

encompass [in'kʌmpəs] v. 包含
endurance [in'djurəns] n. 耐久性
enforce [in'fɔːs] v. 执行
enhance [in'hɑːns] v. 提高;增强
ensure [in'ʃuə] v. 保证;保证得到
entail [in'teil] v. 使必需
entrepreneur [ˌɔntrəprə'nəː] n. 企业家;主办人
equation [i'kweiʃən] n. 相等;平衡
equitable ['ekwitəbl] adj. 公正的;平衡法的
equitably ['ekwitəbli] adv. 公正地
ergonomics [ˌəːgəu'nɔmiks] n. 工效因素
escalate ['eskəleit] v. 逐步升高
essential [i'senʃəl] adj. 基本的
esteem [is'tiːm] n. 尊敬;尊重
etiology [ˌiːti'ɔlədʒi] n. 病因
evaluate [i'væljueit] v. 评价
eventually [i'ventjuəli] adv. 最后;终于
evident ['evidənt] adj. 明显的;显然的
evolving [i'vɔlviŋ] adj. 进化的;展开的
exclude [iks'kluːd] v. 排斥
exclusive [iks'kluːsiv] adj. 独占的;唯一的
ex-convict [ˌekskən'vikt] n. 从前曾被判刑的人
execution [ˌeksi'kjuːʃən] n. 实行;完成;执行
exhaust [ig'zɔːst] v. 使……枯竭
exhaustible [ig'zɔːstəbl] adj. 可穷尽的
exhort [ig'zɔːt] v. 劝诫
expel [iks'pel] v. 开除
expertise [ˌekspəː'tiːz] n. 专家的意见;专门技术
exposure [iks'pəuʒə] n. 揭露
extension [iks'tenʃən] n. 延伸

extensive [iks'tensiv] *adj.* 大量的
external [eks'tə:nl] *adj.* 外部的
extrapolate [eks'træpəleit] *v.* 推断
extrinsic [eks'trinsik] *adj.* 非本质的
extroversion [ˌekstrəu'və:ʃən] *n.* 外向
exude [ig'zju:d] *v.* 洋溢
EAP—employee assistance program 员工帮助计划
early retirement 提前退休
early retirement factor 提前退休因素
early retirement window 提前退休窗口
economic strike 经济罢工
education subsidy 教育津贴
EEOC—equal employment opportunity commission 公平就业机会委员会
EEO—equal employment opportunity 公平就业机会
effect factors of career planning 职业规划影响因素
effective coaching technique 有效的训练方法
effective working hour 有效工时
efficiency wage 计件工资;效率工资
efficiency of labor 劳动效率
efficiency wage 效率工资
election campaign 选举活动
electronic meeting 电子会议
emotional appeal 感召力
employee attitude surveys 员工态度调查
employee career management 员工职业生涯管理
employee consultation services 员工咨询服务
employee equity 员工公平
employee involvement 员工参与
employee leasing 员工租借
employee manual 员工手册

employee orientation 员工向导
employee ownership 员工所有制
employee polygraph protection act《雇员测谎保护法案》[美]
employee potential 员工潜能
employee referral 在职员工推荐
employee retirement income security act《职工退休收入保障法》[美]
employee safety and health 员工安全和健康
employee security 员工安全
employee security measures 员工安全措施
employee services benefits 员工服务福利
employee skill 员工技能
employee stock ownership trust 企业员工持股信托
employee surplus 员工过剩
employee survey 员工测评
employee training method 员工培训方法
employee turnover rate 员工流动率
employee under training 受训员工
employee-centered job redesign 以员工为中心的工作再设计
employees bonus 雇员红利
employer sanction 雇主制裁
employer unfair labor practices 雇主不当劳动行为
Employment Act 雇用法案
employment advertising 招聘广告
employment agency 职业介绍所
employment authorization 工作许可证
employment application form 应聘申请表
employment at will 自由就业
employment consultant 招聘顾问
employment contract renewal 雇用合同续签
employment diseases 职业病

employment history 工作经历
employment objective 应聘职位
employment offer/enrollment 录用
employment relationship 员工关系
employment separation certificate 离职证明书
EPA—equal pay act《平等工资法案》
equal pay for equal work 同工同酬
equity theory 公平理论
ERM—employee relationship management 员工关系管理
ERP—enterprise resource planning 企业资源计划
ESOP—employee stock ownership plan 员工持股计划
essay method 叙述法
ETS—environmental tobacco smoke 工作场所吸烟问题
evaluation criterion 评价标准
exclusive bargaining representative 独家协商代理
executive search firms 猎头公司
executive ability 执行力
executive compensation 管理层薪资水平
executive development program 主管发展计划
executive director 执行董事
executive management 行政管理
executive marketing director 市场执行总监
executive recruiters 高级猎头公司
executive salaries 管理层工资
exempt employee 豁免员工
exit interview 离职面谈
expectancy theory 期望理论
expected salary 期望薪水
experimental method 实验法
experimental research 试验调查

expiry of employment 雇用期满
exploit of HR 人力资源开发
external costs 外部成本
external employment 外部招聘
external environment of hr 人力资源外部环境
external equity 外部公平
external labor supply 外部劳力供应
external recruiting sources 外部招聘来源
external recruitment environment 外部招聘环境
extra work 加班
extrinsic rewards 外部奖励

F

facially ['feiʃəli] adv. 表面上
facilitate [fə'siliteit] v. 推动;帮助;促进
facility [fə'siliti] n. 设备
factual ['fæktjuəl] adj. 事实的
fare [fεə] v. 进展
fatal ['feitl] adj. 致命的
fatigue [fə'ti:g] n. 疲乏
federal ['fedərəl] adj. 联邦的;联合的
ferret ['ferit] v. 搜出;搜索
fine [fain] n. 罚款
flagrant ['fleigrənt] adj. 不能容忍的;公然的
flat [flæt] adj. 平坦的;扁平的
flexibility [ˌfleksə'biliti] n. 弹性
flextime ['flekstaim] n. 弹性上班制
fluctuate ['flʌktjueit] v. 变动;波动
forthcoming [fɔ:'θkʌmiŋ] adj. 即将来临的
forum ['fɔ:rəm] n. 论坛

fraudulent ['frɔːdjulənt] *adj.* 欺诈的;骗得的
frequency ['friːkwənsi] *n.* 频率;周率
friction ['frikʃən] *n.* 摩擦;摩擦力
frustration [frʌs'treiʃən] *n.* 挫败;挫折
face validity 表面效度
factor comparison method 因素比较法
fair labor standards act《公平劳动标准法案》
family and medical leave act《家庭和医疗假期条例》
federal civil servants 联邦公务员
feedback sessions 反馈期
first impression effect 初次印象效应
five-day workweek 每周五天工作制
fixed term appointment 固定期聘用
fixed term contract 固定任期合同
fixed term staff 固定期合同工
FJA—functional job analysis 功能性工作分析法
flat organizational structure 扁平化组织结构
flex place 弹性工作地点
flex plan 弹性工作计划
flex time 弹性工作时间
flexible benefits program 弹性福利计划
flow of the training program 训练流程
focus group 核心小组
forced distribution method 强制分配法
forced-choice rating 迫选法
Ford Motor 福特汽车制造商
formal organization 正式组织
from scratch 从零开始
front-line manager 基层管理人员
function of HRM 人力资源管理职能

functional conflict theory 冲突功能理论
functional department 职能部门
funeral leave 丧假

G

generalizability [ˈdʒenərəˌlaizəˈbiliti] n. 普遍性
generalize [ˈdʒenərəlaiz] v. 归纳
generate [ˈdʒenəˌreit] v. 产生；发生
generically [dʒinəˈrikəli] adv. 一般地
geographic [ˌdʒiəˈgræfik] adj. 地理的
grant [grɑːnt] v. 同意；准予
graphic [ˈgræfik] adj. 图解的
grid [grid] n. 格子；坐标
grievance [ˈgriːvəns] n. 委屈；冤情；不平
gain-sharing plan 收益分享计划
Gang boss 领班/小组长
GATB—general aptitude test battery 普通能力倾向成套测验
GE Capital Services 美国通用电气金融事业公司（通用公司的子公司）
General Mills 通用磨坊（大型跨国食品公司）
General Motors 通用汽车制造商
general union 总工会
given role playing 角色定位演示法
glass ceiling 玻璃天花板
goal setting; or management by objectives (MBO) 目标法
goal conflict 目标冲突
GOJA—guidelines oriented job analysis 指导性工作分析
golden handshake 黄金握别
government body 政府机构
graphic rating scales 图表法
graphic rating scale 图尺度评价法

grievance rates 抱怨补偿
grievance mediation 抱怨调解
grievance procedure 抱怨程序
grievance-handling procedures 申诉处理程序
gross pay/total payroll 工资总额
group appraisal 小组评价
group congeniality/cohesiveness 群体凝集力
group life insurance 团体人寿保险
group pension plan 团体退休金计划
group piece work 集体计件制
group/team bonus 团体/小组奖金
growing pains 个人;企业等发展初期所遇的困难
guaranteed employment offer 雇用信

H

handle ['hændl] v. 处理
haphazard ['hæp'hæzəd] adj. 偶然的;随便的
haunt [hɔːnt] v. 使困窘
hierarchical [ˌhaiəˈrɑːkikəl] adj. 分等级的
highlight ['hailait] v. 强调
Hispanic [his'pænik] n. 美籍西班牙人
hold [hold] v. 认为
holistic [həu'listik] adj. 整体的;全盘的
hostile ['hɔstail] adj. 敌对的
humidity [humidity] n. 湿度
halo effect 晕轮效应
hands-on 实习
handwriting analysis 笔迹分析法
health insurance 健康保险
helping behavior 助人行为

help-wanted ads 招聘广告
hierarchy of needs theory 需要层次理论
high performance organization 高绩效组织
higher-caliber employee 高质量员工
high-performance work system 高绩效工作系统
HMO—health maintenance organization 健康维护组织
holiday pay 假日薪水
holistic job alternative 全盘的工作选择
home/family leave 探亲假
horizontal career path 横向职业途径
hospitality suite 比较安静的度假酒店套房
housing/rental allowance 住房补贴
HR—human resources 人力资源
HR generalist 人力资源通才
HR information system 人力资源信息系统
HR manager 人力资源经理
HR officer 人力资源主任
HR policy 人力资源政策
HRCI—human resource certification institute 人力资源认证机构
HRD appraisal 人力资源开发评价
HRD intermediary 人力资源开发媒介
HRD process 人力资源开发过程
HRD—human resource development 人力资源开发
HRM—human resource management 人力资源管理
HRP—human resource planning 人力资源规划
human relations movement 人际关系运动
hygiene factor 保健因素

I

identical [aiˈdentikəl] *adj.* 同一的

identify [ai'dentifai] v. 识别
identity [ai'dentiti] n. 身份;同一性;一致
idiosyncratic [ˌidiəusin'krætik] adj. 特殊的
illustrate ['iləstreit] v. 阐明
image ['imidʒ] n. 形象
impact ['impækt] n. 影响;效果
impart [im'pɑːt] v. 传授;告知
impartial [im'pɑːʃəl] adj. 公平的
impede [im'piːd] v. 妨碍
implement ['implimənt] v. 贯彻;实现
implementation [implimen'teiʃən] n. 实施;执行
implication [ˌimpli'keiʃən] n. 隐含的意义
incentive [in'sentiv] n. 激励;奖励;诱因
incidence ['insidəns] n. 发生频率
incorporate [in'kɔːpəreit] v. 合并
incumbent [in'kʌmbənt] n./adj. 任职者;职责所在的;负有…义务的
incur [in'kəː] v. 招致
index ['indeks] n. 目录
Indianapolis ['indiə'næpəlis] n. 印第安纳波利斯[美国印第安纳州首府]
indispensable [ˌindis'pensəbl] adj. 不可缺少的
individuality [ˌindiˌvidju'æliti] n. 个人;个性
inevitably [in'evitəbli] adv. 不可避免地
infancy ['infənsi] n. 幼年
inflation [in'fleiʃən] n. 通货膨胀;物价;暴涨
infraction [in'frækʃən] n. 违反;侵害
initial [i'niʃəl] adj. 最初的
initiative [i'niʃiətiv] n. 开始;进取心;主动性
innovative ['inəuveitiv] adj. 创新的
innuendo [ˌinju'endəu] n. 暗讽的话;影射的话
input ['input] n. 输入

inquisitiveness [inkwi'zaitivnis] n. 好奇
instrumental [ˌinstru'mentl] adj. 仪器的
insubordination [ˌinsəˌbɔːdi'neiʃən] n. 不顺从；反抗
insurance [in'ʃuərəns] n. 保险
integral ['intigrəl] adj. 完整的；整体的；必须的
integrity [in'tegriti] n. 正直
intelligent [in'telidʒənt] adj. 显示出可靠的判断和推理的
intensive [in'tensiv] adj. 强烈的
intentional [in'tenʃənəl] adj. 故意的
intern ['in'təːn] n. 实习生
interaction [ˌintər'ækʃən] n. 交互作用
internship ['intəːnʃip] n. 实习期
interpretation [inˌtəːpri'teiʃən] n. 解释
intersection [ˌintə(ː)'sekʃən] n. 交叉点
interval ['intəvəl] n. 间隔
intervention [ˌintə(ː)'venʃən] n. 干涉
intimidate [in'timideit] v. 胁迫
intranet [intrə'net] n. 企业内部互联网
intrinsic [in'trinsik] adj. 本质的
invent [in'vent] v. 发现
inventory ['invəntri] n. 清查；对能力的评估
involuntary [in'vɔləntəri] adj. 自然而然的；无意的
irrational [i'ræʃənəl] adj. 无理性的；失去理性的
irritate ['iriteit] v. 激怒；使急躁
ill-health retirement 病退
immediate post training knowledge 训后知识
in conjunction with 与……协力
in excess of 超过
in lieu of 替代
in the face of 面对

in-basket test 公文筐测验
in-basket training 篮中训练
incentive compensation/reward payment/premium 奖金
incentive plan 激励计划
incentive-suggestion system 奖励建议制度
incident process 事件处理法
independent contractor 合同工
indirect financial compensation 间接经济报酬
individual democracy 个人民主
individual equity 个人资产净值
individual incentive plan 个人奖金方案
individual income tax 个人所得税
individual interview 个别谈话
individual retirement account 个人退休账户
industrial injury compensation 工伤补偿
industrial union 产业工会
informal communication 非正式沟通
informal organization 非正式组织
in-house training 在公司内的培训
initial interview 初试
inside moonlighting 内部兼职
instrumental value 利用价值
insurance benefit 保险福利
Intel Corporation 英特尔公司
inter alia 和其他的事物(= among other things)
internal environment of HR 人力资源内部环境
internal equity 内部公平
internal growth strategy 内部成长战略
internal job posting 内部职位公开招聘
internal recruitment 内部招聘

internal recruitment environment 内部招聘环境
interpersonal skill 人际交往能力
interview appraisal 面谈考评
interview content 面试内容
interview method 访谈法
interview objective 面试目标
interview planning list 面试计划表
intrinsic reward 内在奖励

J

jeopardize [ˈdʒepədaiz] v. 危害
jot [dʒɔt] v. 略记
jurisdiction [ˌdʒuərisˈdikʃən] n. 权限
just [dʒʌst] adj. 公正的
JAP—job analysis program 工作分析程序法
JAS—job analysis schedule 工作分析计划表
job attribute 工作属性
job design 工作设计
job element 工作要素
job fairs 招聘会
job rotation 工作轮换
job account 工作统计
job action 变相罢工（如怠工、放慢速度等）
job aid 工作辅助
job analysis 工作分析
job analysis formula 工作分析公式
job analysis information 工作分析信息
job analysis methods 工作分析方法
job analysis process 工作分析流程
job assignment 工作分配

job attitude 工作态度
job bidding 竞争上岗
job card 工作单
job characteristic 工作因素
job characteristics model 工作特性模式
job classification 职位分类
job clinic 职业问题咨询所
job code 工作编号；职位编号
job context 工作背景
job description 职位描述；工作说明
job design 工作设计
job enlargement 工作扩大化
job enrichment 工作丰富化
job evaluation 工作评估
job identification 工作识别
job inventory 工作测量表
job involvement 工作投入
job knowledge test 业务知识测试
job morale 工作情绪
job performance 工作表现
job plan 工作计划
job posting 公开招聘
job pricing 工作定价
job qualification and restriction 工作任职条件和资格
job redesign 工作再设计
job rotation 工作轮换
job satisfaction 工作满意度
job scope 工作范围
job security 工作安全感
job sharing 临时性工作分担

job specialization 工作专业化
job specification 工作要求细则
job standard 工作标准
job stress 工作压力
job surrounding 工作环境
job time card 工作时间卡
job vacancy 职业空缺；岗位空缺
job-family 工作群
job-hop 跳槽频繁者
job-posting system 工作告示系统
Johnson & Johnson 美国强生公司
JTPA—job training partnership act《职业培训协作法》
junior employee 初级雇员
junior board 初级董事会
just cause 正当理由

K

knowledgeable ['nɔlidʒəbl] adj. 有……丰富知识的
KSAs—knowledge, skills, abilities and other characteristics 知识；技能；态度和其他的特征
karoshi 过劳死
knowledge database 知识数据库
knowledge management 知识管理
KPI—key process indication 企业关键业绩指标

L

latent ['leitənt] adj. 潜伏的
lateral ['lætərəl] adj. 横向的
layoff ['lei,ɔ:f] n. 失业期
legality [li(:)'gæliti] n. 合法性

legislation [ˌledʒisˈleiʃən] n. 立法
legitimate [liˈdʒitimit] adj. 合法的；合理的
libel [ˈlaibəl] n. 诽谤罪
lieu [ˈljuː] n. 替代
litigation [ˌlitiˈgeiʃən] n. 诉讼
logo [ˈlɔgəu] n. 标识语
loyalty [ˈlɔiəlti] n. 忠诚；忠心
labor unions 工会
labor clause 劳工协议条款
labor condition 劳动条件
labor contract 劳动合同；雇佣合同
labor contract renewal 劳动合同续签
labor cost 劳动成本
labor demand forecast 劳动力需求预测
labor discipline 劳动纪律
labor dispute 劳动纠纷
labor exchange/employment agency 职业介绍所
labor handbook 劳动手册
labor insurance 劳保
labor laws 劳动法
labor management relations act 《劳动关系法》
labor market 劳动力市场
labor protection 劳动保护
labor rate variance 工资率差异
labor redundancy 劳动力过剩
labor relation 劳动关系
labor relation consultant 劳工关系顾问
labor relations process 劳工关系进程
labor reserve 劳动力储备
labor shortage 劳动力短缺

labor stability index 人力稳定指数
labor wastage index 人力耗损指数
labor/working hour 人工工时
lateral communication 横向沟通
lateral thinking 横向思维
layoff process 临时解雇程序
leader attach training 领导者匹配训练
leaderless group discussion 无领导小组讨论法
leader-member exchange theory 领导者-成员交换理论
leader-member relation 上下级关系
leader-participation model 领导参与模式
learning curve 学习曲线
learning organization 学习型组织
learning performance test 学习绩效测试
legal compliance 守法
legitimate power 合法权力
level-to-level administration 分级管理
lie detector 测谎器
life cycle theory of leadership 领导生命周期理论
life insurance 人寿保险
lifetime employment 终生雇佣
likes and dislikes survey 好恶调查表
line manager 生产线管理人员
line authority 直线职权
line manager 直线经理
line structure 直线结构
line-staff relationship 直线参谋关系
locus of control 内外控倾向
long-term trend 长期趋势
long-distance education 远程教育

long-range strategy 长期策略
long-term contracted employee 长期合同工
lower management 基层管理
lower-order need 低层次需求
lump sum bonus/pay incentive 绩效奖金
lump-sum merit program 一次性总付绩效报酬计划

M

machinist [mə'ʃiːnist] n. 机械师
magnify ['mægnifai] v. 夸大
magnitude ['mægnitjuːd] n. 大小；数量
maintenance [meintinəns] n. 维护；保持
managerial [ˌmænə'dʒiəriəl] adj. 管理的
mandate ['mændeit] v. 委任统治
mandatory ['mændətəri] adj. 强制性的；必须的
manifest ['mænifest] v. 表明；证明
manual ['mænjuəl] n. 手册；指南
marginal ['mɑːdʒinəl] adj. 边际效用的
matrix ['meitriks] n. 母体；发源地；矩阵
maxim ['mæksim] n. 格言；座右铭
mean [miːn] adj. 平均的
mediate ['miːdiit] v. 仲裁；调停
memo ['meməu] n. 备忘录
mentor ['mentɔː] n. 贤明的顾问；指导者
merit ['merit] v. 有益于优点；价值
methodology [meθə'dɔlədʒi] n. 方法
miniaturize ['miniətʃəraiz] v. 使微型化
minimum ['miniməm] adj. 最低的
minority [mai'nɔriti] n. 少数；少数民族
mission ['miʃən] n. 使命

mitigate ['mitigeit] v. 减轻
modify ['mɔdifai] v. 修改
monetary ['mʌnitəri] adj. 金钱的
monetary ['mʌnitəri] adj. 货币的；金钱的
monitor ['mɔnitə] v. 监控
monitoring ['mɔnitəriŋ] n. 监测
motivated ['məutiveitid] adj. 有动机的
motivation [ˌməuti'veiʃən] n. 动机
motivational [ˌməuti'veiʃənəl] adj. 动机的
multi-attribute ['mʌltə'tribju(ː)t] n. 多种属性
municipal [mju(ː)'nisipəl] adj. 市政的；地方性的
mutual ['mjuːtjuəl] adj. 相互的；共有的
managed care 有控制的医疗保健
management turnover 管理层周转率
management as porpoise 海豚式管理
management assessment center 管理评价中心
management by walking about 走动管理
management development 管理层开发
management of human resource development 人力资源开发管理
management psychology 管理心理学
management right 管理权
management risk 管理风险
management tool 管理工具
management training 管理培训
managerial art 管理艺术
managerial authority 管理权威
managerial function 管理职能
managerial grid theory 管理方格理论
mandated benefit 强制性福利
mandatory bargaining issue 强制性谈判项目

marital status 婚姻状况
market price 市场工资
marriage leave 婚假
massed practice 集中练习;集中学习
matrix structure 矩阵结构
MBA（Master of Business Administration）工商管理硕士
MBO—management by objective 目标管理
MCDA（Multi-Criteria Decision Analysis）多目标决策分析
MCGDS（Multi-Criteria Group Decision Support）多标准团体决议支持
mechanistic approach 机械型工作设计法
medical and health care 医疗保健
medical insurance 医疗保险
medical/physical ability inspection/physical ability test 体检
medicare provisions 医护规定
membership group 实属群体
mental models of employment 就业心智模式
mental ability test 逻辑思维测试
mentoring function 指导功能
merit pay 绩效工资
merit raise 绩效加薪
meta-analytic studies 隐含分析研究
metrics-driven staffing model 标准驱动招聘模式
mid-career crisis sub stage 中期职业危机阶段
minimum wage 最低工资
mission installation allowance 出差津贴
mixed-standard scale method 多重标准尺度法
monetary incentives 货币激励
motivational approach 激励型工作设计法
motivational factor 激励因素
motivational pattern 激励方式

motivation-hygiene theory 激励保健论
MPS—motivating potential score 激励潜能分数
multidimensional criteria 多边标准
multi-rater assessment; or 360-degree feedback 多角度评价法或360度反馈法
muscular tension 肌肉紧张

N

negligence ['neglidʒəns] n. 疏忽
nepotism ['nepətizəm] n. 重用亲信
norm [nɔ:m] n. 标准；规范
normally ['nɔ:məli] adv. 正常地；通常地
notation [nəu'teiʃən] n. 符号
notion ['nəuʃən] n. 概念；观念
novelty ['nɔvəlti] n. 新颖
Nation Labor Relations Act 国家劳工关系法
National Association of Professional Employer Organizations (NAPEO) 美国职业雇主组织国家联合会
National Labor Board 美国国家劳工委员会
National Labor Relation Act 美国国家劳工关系法案
National Mediation Board 美国国家调解委员会
national union (国家)总工会
NationsBank 美国联机银行(位于得克萨斯州)
needs assessment 需求评估
negligent hiring 随意雇佣
net effect 净效应
network career path 网状职业途径
New York Sanitation Department 纽约卫生部
NGT—nominal group technique 群体决策法
noncontributory plan 非付费退休金计划

nondirective interview 非定向面试
nondiscrimination rule 非歧视性原则
nonexempt employee 非豁免的员工
non-traditional employment relationship 非传统性雇佣关系
nonunionized firm 非工会化公司
nonverbal communication 非言语沟通
no-pay study leave 无薪进修假期
normal retirement 正常退休
normative analysis 规范分析法

O

obligation [ˌɔbliˈgeiʃən] n. 义务；职责
observation [ˌɔbzəˈveiʃən] n. 观察
obsession [əbˈseʃən] n. 迷住；困扰
obsolete [ˈɔbsəliːt] adj. 荒废的；陈旧的
obstacle [ˈɔbstəkl] n. 障碍；妨害物
omit [əuˈmit] v. 省略；疏忽
on-the-job [ˈɔnðəˈdʒɔb] adj. 在职的
operations [ˌɔpəˈreiʃənz] n. 运营
order [ˈɔːdə] v. 排序
orientation [ˌɔ(ː)rienˈteiʃən] n. 方向；定位；介绍
oriented [ˈɔːrientid] adj. 以……为导向的
outlay [ˈautlei] n. 费用
outset [ˈautset] n. 开始；开端
outsource [ˈautˌsɔːs] v. 外部采购
overwhelm [ˈəuvəˈwelm] v. 过于大量地给予
oblimin rotation 贡献循环比较法
observation method 观察法
occupational injuries and disabilities 因工伤残
occupational choice 职业选择

occupational disease 职业病
occupational environment 职业环境
occupational guidance 职业指导;就业指导
occupational health & safety training 职业安全与卫生培训
occupational market condition 职业市场状况
occupational mobility 职业流动性
occupational outlook handbook 职业展望手册
offer letter 录用通知书
office hour 答疑时间
off-the-job training 脱产培训
Old-age; Survivors; and Disability Insurance(OASD)
　　老年人、遗属及残疾保险
OMS—occupational measurement system 职业测定系统
on the downside 从不利的方面来讲
on boarding training 入职培训
on-the-job training 在职培训
open-door policy 门户开放政策
opinion survey 意见调查
organization change and development 组织变革与发展
organization character 组织特征
organization design 组织设计
organization development appraisal 组织发展评价
organization development method 组织发展方法
organization environment 组织环境
organization goal 组织目标
organization renewal 组织革新
organization size 组织规模
organization structure 组织结构
organizational capital punishment 组织性死刑
organizational structure 组织机构

organizational variable 组织变量
organizational analysis 组织分析
organizational authority 组织职权
organizational career planning 组织职业规划
organizational citizenship behavior 组织公民行为
organizational commitment 组织认同感
organizational diagnosis 组织诊断
organizational function 组织职能
organizational level 组织层次
organizational merger 组织合并
organizational orientation 组织定位
organizational/job stress 组织/工作压力
organization-centered career planning 以企业为中心的职业计划
organized administration 组织管理
orientation objective 岗前培训目标
orientation period 岗前培训阶段
OSHA standard 美国职业安全与健康局/职业安全与健康法案标准
out of line 不一致
out placement 岗外安置
out-of-court settlement 庭外和解
overall training 全面培训
oversea assignment 海外工作
overtime hour 加班工时
overtime wage 加班工资
overtime work 加班

P

pace [peis] n. 一步;速度;步调
parallel ['pærəlel] n. 相似
participant [pɑː'tisipənt] n. 参与者

payroll ['peirəul] n. 薪水册
penalize ['pi:nəlaiz] v. 处罚
penalty ['penlti] n. 处罚
pending ['pendiŋ] adj. 未决的
pension ['penʃən] n. 养老金;退休金
perceive [pə'si:v] v. 察觉
perception [pə'sepʃən] n. 理解;感知
performance [pə'fɔ:məns] n. 绩效
periodically [,piəri'ɔdikəli] adv. 周期性地
personality [,pə:sə'næliti] n. 个性
perspective [pə'spektiv] n. 观点;看法
persuasive [pə'sweisiv] adj. 有说服力的
pertinent ['pə:tinənt] adj. 有关的
petition [pi'tiʃən] v. 请求;恳求
petroleum [pi'trəuliəm] n. 石油
pharmaceutical [,fɑ:mə'sju:tikəl] adj. 制药的
phase [feiz] n. 阶段
pitfall ['pitfɔ:l] n. 缺陷
pivotal ['pivətəl] v. 关键的
placement ['pleismənt] n. 工作安排
plateau ['plætəu] v. 趋于稳定;停滞
polygraph ['pɔligrɑ:f] n. 测谎仪
pool [pu:l] n. 资源的集合
portion ['pɔ:ʃən] n. 一部分
pose [pəuz] v. 引起;造成
posit ['pɔzit] v. 提出
potent ['pəutənt] adj. 有力的
potential [pə'tenʃ(ə)l] adj. 潜在的;可能的
practical ['præktikəl] adj. 实际的
practicality [,prækti'kæliti] n. 实用性

precede [pri(:)'si:d] v. 先于
precedent [pri'si:dənt] n. 先例
preclude [pri'klu:d] n. 排除
predicate ['predikit] v. 断言
predictive [pri'diktiv] adj. 预言性的
predisposition [pri:ˌdispə'ziʃən] n. 易患病的体质
prejudice ['predʒudis] n. 偏见;成见
preliminary [pri'liminəri] n. 初步的
premium ['primjəm] n. 额外费用;奖金
preponderance [pri'pɔndərəns] n. 优势
present [pri'zent] v. 提出
prior ['praiə] adj. 优先的
priority [prai'ɔriti] n. 优先考虑的事
proactive [ˌprəu'æktiv] adj. (心理)前摄的
probability [ˌprɔbə'biliti] n. 可能性
prohibit [prə'hibit] v. 禁止;阻止
projective [prə'dʒektiv] adj. 投射的
prominent ['prɔminənt] adj. 卓越的;显著的
proposition [ˌprɔpə'ziʃən] n. 命题
prorate [prəu'reit] v. 按比例分配
prosecute ['prɔsikju:t] v. 起诉
prospective [prəs'pektiv] adj. 预期的
prosper [sə'vaiv] v. 发展
provision [prə'viʒən] n. 规定;供应
psychomotor [ˌsaikəu'məutə] adj. 精神性运动的
pursue [pə'sju:] v. 继续;从事
paired comparison method 配对比较法
panel/group interview 小组面试
PA—performance analysis 绩效分析
Parkinson's law 帕金森定律

participant diary 现场工人日记
participative management 参与式管理
part-time job 兼职
PAS—performance appraisal system 绩效评估体系
pattern bargaining 模式谈判
patterned behavior description interview 模式化行为描述面试
pay calculation 工资结算
pay card 工资卡
pay check/employee paycheck 工资支票
pay compression 压缩工资
pay day 发薪日
pay equity 报酬公平
pay freeze 工资冻结
pay grade 工资等级
pay period 工资结算周期
pay range 工资幅度
pay rate 工资率
pay rate adjustment 工资率调整
pay secrecy 工资保密
pay slip/envelop 工资单
pay survey 薪酬调查
pay/salary rate standard 工资率标准
payroll system 工资管理系统
payroll tax 工资所得税
payroll/wage analysis 工资分析
payroll/wage form 工资形式
payroll/wage fund 工资基金
pension plan 退休金计划
pension/retirement benefit 退休福利
people-first value "以人为本"的价值观

perceived career development 事业发展感知
perceived organizational support 感知组织支持
perceptual-motor approach 知觉运动型工作设计法
performance appraisal 成绩评价
performance appraisal 绩效评估
performance appraisal interview 绩效评估面谈
performance appraisal objective 绩效评估目标
performance appraisal period 考评期
performance appraisal principle 绩效评估原则
performance feedback 绩效反馈
performance management system 绩效管理制度
performance standard 绩效标准
performance appraisal 绩效评价
performance-reward relationship 绩效与报酬关系
periodic salary adjustment 定期薪资调整
permanent physical or psychological damage 永久性身心伤害
permissive management 放任式管理
personal constructs of appraisal systems 人事评估体系
personal traits 个性特征
personal character 个人性格；个性
personal grievance 个人抱怨
personal information record 人事档案
personal leave 事假
personality test 个性测试
personality-job fit theory 性格与工作搭配理论
personnel selection 选拔
personnel test 人格测验品格测验
physical characteristics 身体特征
physiological need 生理需要
piece-rate system 计件工资制

pink slip 解雇通知
point method 因素计点法
Polygraph Act(Employee Polygraph Protection Act of 1988)
　《雇员测谎保护法案》
polygraph test 测谎测试
position analysis questionnaire 职位分析问卷法
position description 职位描述
position vacant 招聘职位
positional level 职位层次
positional title 职称
post wage system 岗位工资制
potential work-force quality 潜在的劳力质量
power distance 权力距离
predictive validity 预测效度
premium plan/incentive system/reward system 奖金制
pre-natal/maternity leave 产假
preretirement planning programs 提前退休计划
prescribed group 正式群体
primary jurisdiction 优先税收管辖权
primary welfare 基本福利
prior to 在前
privacy right 隐私权
prize contest 奖励竞争
proactive learning behavior 前摄学习行为
probationary term/probation period 试用期
problem-solving team 问题解决团队
procedural justice 过程正义
process benchmarking 流程标杆管理
professional meeting 就业供需洽谈会
professional certificate 职业资格证书

professional competence/capacity 专业能力
professional ethics 职业道德
professional examination 专业考试
professional liability insurance 职业责任保险
professional manager 职业经理人
profit-sharing plan 利润分享计划
programmed instruction 程序教学
projective techniques 投射技术
projective personality test 人格投射测试
promotion from within 内部提拔
protected group 受保护群体
psychic reward 精神奖励
psychoanalysis 心理分析
psychological climate 社会心理环境
psychological stress 心理压力
psychological characteristic/feature 心理特征
psychological contract 心理/精神契约
psychological factor 心理因素
psychological goal 心理目标
psychological phenomenon 心理现象
psychological test/psychometry 心理测验心理测试
psychomotor abilities test 运动神经能力测试
public administration 公共管理

Q

quantifiable [kɔnti'faiəbl] *adj.* 可以计量的
quantify ['kwɔntifai] *v.* 量化
quantitative ['kwɔntitətiv] *adj.* 数量的;定量的
questionnaire [ˌkwestiə'nɛə] *n.* 调查表;问卷
quality of work life 工作环境质量理论

quality circles 质量圈
quantity of applicant 侯选人数量
questionnaire method 问卷调查法
quit rate 离职率

R

rambling ['ræmbliŋ] adj. 不连贯的
random ['rændəm] adj. 随机的
rational ['ræʃənl] adj. 理性的;合理的
rationale [ˌræʃəˈnɑːli] n. 基本原理
reaction [ri(ː)ˈækʃən] n. 反应
recognition [ˌrekəgˈniʃən] n. 认可;赏识
recommend [rekəˈmend] v. 推荐
recruit [riˈkruːt] v. 招收;补充
recruiter [riˈkruːtə(r)] n. 招聘人员
recruitment [riˈkruːtmənt] n. 招募;招工
redress [riˈdres] n. 矫正;赔偿
refer [riˈfəː] v. 指点到消息来源处寻求帮助
refute [riˈfjuːt] v. 驳倒
regardless [riˈgɑːdlis] adj. 不管
regulation [regjuˈleiʃən] n. 法规
rejection [riˈdʒekʃən] n. 拒绝
reliability [riˌlaiəˈbiliti] n. 信度
reluctant [riˈlʌktənt] adj. 不顾的;勉强的
remedy ['remidi] v. 补救;矫正
repertory ['repətəri] n. 轮演;循环
replicate ['replikit] v. 复制
reproach [riˈprəutʃ] v. 责备
rescind [riˈsind] v. 废除
resentment [riˈzentmənt] n. 怨恨

resident ['rezidənt] n. 居民
resilience [ri'ziliəns] n. 有弹力;恢复力
respectively [ri'spektivli] adv. 分别地
respondent [ris'pɔndənt] n. 回答者
retain [ri'tein] v. 保留受雇状态
retention [ri'tenʃən] n. 保持力;张力
reveal [ri'viːl] v. 显示;揭示
revenue ['revinjuː] n. 收入;税收
revise [ri'vaiz] v. 修订
rewarding [ri'wɔːdiŋ] adj. 值得的
rotation [rəu'teiʃən] n. 旋转
race discrimination 种族歧视
random errors 随机失误
ranking method 排序法
rating certificate 等级证书
ratio analysis 比率分析法
realistic job preview 实际岗位演习
reality shock 现实冲击
recreation leave allowance 休假津贴
recreation/sabbatical leave 休假
recruitment ditch 招聘渠道
recruitment examination 招聘考试
recruitment method 招聘方法
recruitment optional program 招聘备择方案
recruitment task guide 招募工作指导
red-circled employee 红圈员工
reducing accident 减少事故
reducing burnout 减少衰竭
reengineering the corporation 企业再造
reference check 背景调查

reference letter 推荐信
reference check 个人证明材料检查
refusing applicant 拒绝求职者
regardless of 不管
regency effect 近因性错误
regression analysis 回归分析
regular earning/pay/wage 固定工资
regular incentive 常规奖励
reinforcement theory 强化理论
relative to 相对于
relevant covariates 相关的协方差
reliability evaluation 信度评估
repertory grid procedure 循环坐标法
replacement cost 重置成本
requirement identification 需求识别
requisite task attributes theory 必要任务属性理论
resume inventory 简历数据库
resumption from leave 销假
retirement age 退休年龄
retirement fund 退休基金
return of talent 人才回流
rewarding by merit/pay according to work 业绩报酬
right to rest and leisure 休息权
risk pay planning 风险工资计划
role ambiguity 角色模糊
role behavior 角色行为
role conflict 角色冲突
role playing 角色扮演
roles of HRM 人力资源管理角色
roll-down training 自上而下分级培训法

rush hours 上班高峰时间

S

sanitation [ˌsæniˈteiʃən] n. 卫生；卫生设施
scant [skænt] adj. 不足的
schedule [ˈskedʒjul] v. 制定计划
screening [ˈskriːniŋ] n. 筛选
segment [ˈsegmənt] n. 段；节；片断
segregate [ˈsegrigeit] v. 隔离
seminars [ˈseminɑː] n. 研究会
senior [ˈsiːnjə] adj. 资格较老的；高级的
seniority [siːniˈɔriti] n. 资历
sensitivity [ˌsensiˈtiviti] n. 敏锐；敏感
session [ˈseʃən] n. 会议；开庭
severity [siˈveriti] n. 严肃；严重
sheer [ʃiə] adj. 完全的
shift [ʃift] n. 移动；轮班；移位
shirk [ʃəːk] v. 逃避；推卸
simulate [ˈsimjuleit] v. 模拟
simultaneously [ˌsiməlˈteiniəsli] adv. 同时地
situational [ˌsitjuˈeiʃənəl] adj. 视情况而定的
slogan [ˈsləugən] n. 口号
slot [slɔt] n. 职位
soar [sɔː] v. 高飞；剧增
solicit [səˈlisit] v. 恳求
sophistication [səˌfistiˈkeiʃən] n. 复杂性
span [spæn] v. 横越
specially [ˈspeʃəli] adv. 特别地
specify [ˈspesifai] v. 明确说明
spectrum [ˈspektrəm] n. 光；光谱

spice [spais] n. 调味品
sponsor ['spɔnsə] v. 发起;主办
spontaneous [spɔn'teiniəs] adj. 自然产生的
stabilize ['steibilaiz] v. 稳定
stage [steidʒ] v. 安排和进行
stark [stɑːk] adj. 十足的
statistics [stə'tistiks] n. 统计学
statute ['stætjuːt] n. 法令;条例
stem [stem] v. 滋生
stigma ['stigmə] n. 污名
stipulate ['stipjuleit] v. 规定;保证
stockholder ['stɔkhəuldə(r)] n. 股东
strategic [strə'tiːdʒik] adj. 战略上的
structure ['strʌktʃə] v. 设计
subcontract [sʌb'kɔntrækt] n. 转包合同
subjectivity [ˌkʌbdʒek'tivəti] n. 主观性
subordinate [sə'bɔːdinit] n. 下属
subsequent ['sʌbsikwənt] adj. 后来的
subset ['sʌbset] n. 子集
substantial [səb'stænʃəl] adj. 实质的;充实的
substantially [səb'stænʃ(ə)li] adv. 充分地
sue [suː] v. 提出诉讼
sufficient [sə'fiʃənt] adj. 充分的;足够的
supervision [ˌsjuːpə'viʒən] n. 监督;管理
supervisory [ˌsjuːpə'vaizəri] adj. 管理的;监督的
supplement ['sʌplimənt] v. 补充
supposedly [sə'pəuzidli] adv. 按照推测
suppress [sə'pres] v. 抑制
survey [səː'vei] n. 测量;调查
survive [sə'vaiv] v. 生存

switch [switʃ] v. 转换
symposia [sim'pɔzimː] n. [sim'pɔziəm] 讨论会(symposium 的复数)
synthesize ['sinθisaiz] v. 合成
safety director 安全负责人
safety inspection 安全检验
safety measure 安全措施
safety program 安全方案
safety training 安全培训
salary administration 薪水管理
salary band/range 薪水范围
salary survey 薪资调查
sales force 销售人员
satisficing decision model 满意决策模型
scrap rates 人事费用
security guard 警卫
selection criteria 选拔准则
selection decision 选拔决策
self-actualization need 自我实现需要
self-assessment tool 自我评估工具
self-employed workers 自营工
self-funding insurance program 自筹保险计划
self-managed work team 自我管理工作团队
self-perception theory 自我知觉理论
self-serving bias 自我服务偏差
senior employee 高级职员
sensitivity training 人际敏感性训练
serialized/sequential interview 系列式面试
service industries 服务业
severance pay 告别费
sexual harassment 性骚扰

sexual discrimination 性别歧视
sexual harassment 性骚扰
shift differential 值班津贴
short-term contract 短期合同
silver handshake 银色握手
simulation exercise 模拟练习
single-loop learning 单环学习
situational interview 情景面试
situational leadership theory 情境领导理论
skill inventory 技能量表
skip-level interview 越级谈话
social cohesion 社会内聚力
social dominance orientation 社会支配取向
social norms 社会规范
social security 社会保障
Social Security Act 社会保障法
social security 社会保障
sociotechnical approach 社会技术方法
sound absorber 隔音材料
spacing of sessions 培训间隔安排
special purpose team 特殊目的团队
special training 特别训练
specialized course 专门课程
spot bonus 即时奖金
stabilization sub stage 稳定阶段
staff authority 参谋职权
standard labor cost 标准人工成本
standard wage rate 标准工资率
State divisions of employment security and labor 州立就业安全与劳动部
statutory holidays 法定假期

statutory right 法定权利
stock option 持股权
straight piece-rate system 直接计件工资制
strategic HRD 战略性人力资源开发
strategic HRM 战略性人力资源管理
strength/weakness balance sheet 强/弱平衡表
stress interview 压力面试
stress source 压力来源
strictness/leniency tendency 偏松或偏紧倾向
structure employment 结构性就业
structured interview 结构化面试
subject-matter experts（SMEs）主题专家
subordinate appraisal 下级考评
succession planning system 接班人规划系统
suggestion system 建议制度
superordinate appraisal 上级考评
supplement pay 补充报酬
supplemental unemployment benefit 补充性失业福利
survey feedback 调查反馈
survival rate 留任率
survivor benefits 遗属补偿金
sympathy strike 同情罢工
system structure 系统结构
systematic training model 分类训练模式
systemic thinking 系统性思考

T

tacit ['tæsit] adj. 默许的
tailor ['teilə] v. 适应；适合；调整
tardiness ['tɑːdinis] n. 缓慢

taxonomy [tækˈsɔnəmi] n. 分类法;分类学
tease [tiːz] v. 强求;找出
telecommute [ˌtelikəˈmjuːt] v. 远程办公
template [ˈtemplit] n. 模板
tenurability [ˌtenjərəˈbiliti] n. 可成为终身职位
tenure [ˈtenjuə] n. 终身职位;任期
term [təːm] n. 期限;条款
termination [ˌtəːmiˈneiʃən] n. 终止
thereunder [ðɛərˈʌndə] adv. 在那下面;依据
thoroughly [ˈθʌrəli] adv. 彻底地
threatening [ˈθretəniŋ] adj. 胁迫的;危险的
thrust [θrʌst] n. 本质;要点
tight [tait] adj. 供不应求的
tout [taut] v. 吹捧
trainee [treiˈniː] n. 练习生
transfer [trænsˈfəː] n. 调动
triad [ˈtraiəd] n. 三个/人一组
trigger [ˈtrigə] v. 引发;引起;触发
tryout [ˈtraiˌaut] n. 试验;试用;尝试
turbulent [ˈtəːbjulənt] adj. 剧烈的
turnover [ˈtəːnˌəuvə] n. 人事变动;营业额
tacit learning behavior 默学行为
TA—transactional analysis 人际关系心理分析(交互作用分析)
TAT—thematic apperception test 主题统觉测试
tax equalization plan 税负平衡计划
team building 团队建设
team spirit 协作精神
team/group incentive plan 团队激励计划
telecommuting job 远距离工作
termination at will 随意解雇

test reliability 测试信度

test validity 测试效度

the Age Discrimination in Employment Act 劳工法的年龄歧视

the base year 基年

the checklist method 表格核对法

the Civil Rights Act 民权法案

the critical-incident appraisal method 重大事件评价法

the Equal Employment Opportunity Commission (EEOC) 就业机会均等委员会

The Equal Pay Act 同酬法案

the essay appraisal method 文字叙述评价法

The Fair Labor Standards Act 合理劳动标准法案

The federal Department of Labor 联邦劳动部

the hot-stove rule 趁热打铁原则

The Immigration Reform and Control Act (IRCA) 移民改革和管制法

the occupational safety and health act 职业安全与健康法案

the overall legal framework 整体法律框架

the physical work environment 工作物理环境

the timing of appraisal 评价时耗

the work standards approach 工作标准法

the trade union law of the People's Republic of China 《中华人民共和国工会法》

time horizon 时间范围

time sensitive 时间敏感的

time management 时间管理

timework work 计时工作

TM—transcendental meditation 超自然冥想

to account for 说明

to adhere to 坚持

to arrive at 努力达到

to cling to 依附
to conform to 遵照
to depart from 离开
to detract from 降低
to fit into 适合
to get cross 传达
to grapple with 处理
to keep track of 跟踪
to make a difference 要紧
to make do with 设法应付
to make sense of 弄懂……的意思
to pay the difference 付差额金
to relate to 涉及
to resort to 求助
to serve as 充当
to shed light on 使某事清楚明白地显示出来
to skim off 提出精华
to spell out 详细解释；详细阐释
to think the highest of 对……的看法最高
trade union 工会
traditional career path 传统职业途径
training & development manager 培训经理
training administration 培训管理
training design 培训设计
training function 培训职能
training item 培训项目
training needs analysis 培训需求分析
training outcome 培训结果
training plan 培训计划
training specialist 培训专员

travel allowance 旅行津贴
traveling expenses standard 差旅费标准
trend analysis 趋势分析
trial-run employment 模拟就业
tricks of the trade 行业窍门

U

ultimate ['ʌltimit] adj. 最后的;最终的;根本的
unambiguous ['ʌnæm'bigjuəs] adj. 不含糊的;明确的
underestimation ['ʌndəˌresti'meiʃən] n. 低估
underlying ['ʌndə'laiiŋ] adj. 根本的;潜在的
underreport ['ʌndəri'pɔːt] v. 少报收入等;低估
undertake [ˌʌndə'teik] v. 采取
underutilize [ˌʌndə'juːtilaiz] v. 未充分使用
undue ['ʌn'djuː] adj. 不适当的
unethical ['ʌn'eθikəl] adj. 不道德的
univocal [ˌjuːni'vəukəl] adj. 意义明确的
update [ʌp'deit] v. 使现代化;更新
utility [juː'tiliti] n. 效用性
utilize [juː'tilaiz] v. 利用
unauthorized aliens 没有公民权的外国人
underlying characteristics 潜在特征
undue hardship 过度重负
unemployment compensation 失业补偿金
Unemployment Compensation Commission 失业补偿委员会
Unemployment insurance (UI) 失业保险
unemployment compensation 失业津贴
unemployment insurance 失业保险
unemployment rate 失业率
union authorization card 工会授权卡

union steward/delegate 工会代表
union-free policy 无工会政策
unit performance 单位绩效
unit labor cost 单位劳动成本
unitary structure U 型结构(一元结构)
unregistered employment 隐性就业
unsafe act 不安全行为
unsafe condition 不安全条件
unstructured interview 非结构化面试

V

vacancy ['veikənsi] n. 空缺
valid ['vælid] adj. 有效的;正确的
validate ['vælideit] v. 使有效
validation [,væli'deiʃən] n. 确认
validity [və'liditi] n. 效度
value ['vælju:] n. 价值标准
variance ['vɛəriəns] n. 不一致;变化
vary ['vɛəri] v. 变化
vehicle ['vi:ikl] n. 手段
ventilation [venti'leiʃən] n. 通风
verify ['verifai] v. 查证;核实
versus ['və:səs] prep. 与……相对
veteran ['vetərən] n. 退伍军人
via ['vaiə] prep. 通过;经由
virtually ['və:tjuəli] adv. 事实上;实质上
volatile ['vɔlətail] adj. 可变的;不稳定的
valid information 确切信息
value-based hiring 价值观为基础的雇佣
variable compensation 可变报酬

verbal reasoning 语言推理
vestibule training 新员工培训技工学校培训
videoconferencing 视频会议
violence in the workplace 工作场所暴力
virtual classroom 虚拟课堂
virtual organization 虚拟组织
virtual team 虚拟团队
voluntary pay cut 自愿减少工资方案
voluntary protection program 自愿保护项目
VPT—vocational preference test 职业性向测试

W

walk-in ['wɔːkˌin] n. 未经预约而来的人
warrant ['wɔrənt] v. 辩解;保证
weight [weit] n. 权数
withdraw [wiðˈdrɔː] v. 收回;撤消
working ['wəːkiŋ] adj. 运转的
wage accounting 工资核算
wage audit 工资审计
wage by seniority system/wage-by-age system 工龄工资制
wage control 工资控制
wage curve 工资曲线
wage deduction 工资扣除额
wage in cash 现金工资
wage in kind 实物工资
wage in sliding scale 浮动工资
wage index 工资指数
wage level 工资水平
wage plan 工资计划
wage policy 工资政策
wage rate per hour 计时工资

wage standard 工资标准
wage structure 工资结构
wage system 工资制度
wage-incentive plan 奖励工资制
WBS-work breakdown structure 工作分解结构
web-based training 网上培训
weighted checklist 权重核对表格法
welfare management 福利管理
welfare staff 福利工作人员
wellness program 平安计划
work documentation 工作证件
work load 工作量
work schedule 工作时间安排
work & life balance 工作生活平衡
work age 工龄
work attitude 工作态度
work behavior 工作行为
work demand 工作要求
work efficiency 工作效率
work out 合力促进
work pressure 工作压力
work sample 工作样本
work sampling technique 工作样本技术
work schedule 工作进度表
worker involvement 雇员参与
workplace learning 工作场所学习
work-related misconduct 失职
work-related injury leave 工伤假
work-sample test 工作样本测试
wrongful discharge 不当解雇

REFERENCES

[1] HOLLENBECK N, WRIGHT G. Human resource management: gaining a competitive advantage[M]. Marrickville: The Austen Press, 1994.
[2] BYARS L, RUE L. Human resource management [M]. New York: The McGraw-Hill Companies, Inc. , 2004.
[3] HANDY S L, MOKHTARIAN P L. The future of telecommuting[J]. Futures, 1996, 28: 227-240.
[4] HARTMAN R I, STONER C R, ARORA R. Developing successful organizational telecommuting arrangements: worker perceptions and managerial prescriptions[J]. SAM Advanced Management Journal,1992,57: 35-42.
[5] HILL E J, MILLER B C, WEINER S P, et al. Influences of the virtual office on aspects of work and work/life balance[J]. Personnel Psychology, 1998, 51: 667-683.
[6] KHAN M B, TUNG L L, TURBAN E. Telecommuting: comparing Singapore to southern California[J]. Human Systems Management, 1997, 16: 91-98.
[7] WALDMAN D, BOWEN D. The acceptability of 360-degree appraisals: a customer-supplier relationship perspective[J]. Human Resource Management, 1998, 37 : 117-129.
[8] WINTERTON J, WINTERTON R. Does management development add value? [J]. British Journal of Management, 1997, 8: 65-76.
[9] YAMNILL S, MCLEAN G. Factors affecting transfer of training in Thailand [J]. Human Resource Development Quarterly,2005, 16: 323-344.
[10] DEMBE A E. Preserving workers' compensation benefits in a managed health care environment [J]. Journal of Public Health Policy, 1998, 19 (2): 200-218.
[11] GHOSHAL S, BARTLETT C A. The individualized corporation: a

fundamentally new approach to management [M]. London: Heinemann, 1997.
[12] GRATTON L. Living strategy: putting people at the heart of corporate purpose [M]. London: Pearson, 2000.
[13] GUNZ H. Careers and corporate cultures [M]. Oxford: Basil Blackwell, 1989.
[14] GUNZ H, JALLAND M. Managerial careers and business strategies [J]. Academy of Management Review, 1996, 21(3):718-756.
[15] SPENCER L M, SPENCER S M. Competence at work: models for superior performance[M]. New York: John Wiley & Sons, Inc., 1993.
[16] MAURER T, MITCHELL D, BARBEITE F. Predictors of attitudes toward a 360-degree feedback system and involvement in post-feedback management development activity [J]. Journal of Occupational and Organizational Psychology, 2002, 75: 87-107.
[17] MIRABILE R J. Everything you wanted to know about competency modeling [J]. Training and Development, 1997, 51:73-77.
[18] NICHOLLS J. Achievement motivation: conceptions of ability, subjective experience, task choice, and performance[J]. Psychological Review, 1984, 91: 328-346.
[19] NICHOLLS J. Students as educational theorists [M]. Hillsdale: Lawrence Erlbaum Associates, 1992.
[20] NOE R, WILK S. Investigation of factors that influence employees' participation in development activities[J]. Journal of Applied Psychology, 1993, 78(2): 291-302.